COUNTY DOWN

A

TOPOGRAPHICAL DICTIONARY

OF THE PARISHES, VILLAGES AND TOWNS
OF COUNTY DOWN IN THE 1830s

ILLUSTRATED WITH
CONTEMPORARY MAPS AND ENGRAVINGS

BY SAMUEL LEWIS

PREFACE

BY BRIAN M. WALKER

BELFAST

PUBLISHED BY FRIAR'S BUSH PRESS

2003

THIS SELECTED EDITION
PUBLISHED 2003
BY FRIAR'S BUSH PRESS
160 BALLYLESSON ROAD
BELFAST, BT8 8JU
NORTHERN IRELAND

FIRST PUBLISHED 1837
BY S. LEWIS & CO.
87 ALDERSGATE STREET, LONDON

ISBN 0-946872-62-7

TEXT COPIED BY ITRONICS LTD, 9 FLEET STREET, DUBLIN 2

PRINTED BY DATAPLUS PRINT & DESIGN
13 HILL STREET, DUNMURRY, BT17 OAD

PREFACE

This volume brings together three important contemporary sources of information about life and society in County Down in the 1830s. The text is taken from the monumental two-volumed topographical dictionary of Ireland, published by Samuel Lewis in 1837. His work covered all of Ireland in alphabetical order in a grand total of 1,405 double columned pages. Maps of the main County Down towns have been photographed from the first edition Ordnance Survey maps for the county, which were published in 1835, and are integrated into the text. A considerable number of engravings, mostly from the 1830s, has also been included. In the case of all three components of this book-the topographical text, the maps and the engravings, the period of the 1830s witnessed new heights in the availability and worth of such sources. Brought together here in this particular form, the material presents a special view of the parishes, villages and towns of County Down in the period before the great changes of Victorian Ireland. It gives a compelling record of agriculture, industry, population, buildings and antiquities in the county over 160 years ago.

Samuel Lewis, publisher

Our knowledge about the life of Samuel Lewis is fairly limited. We do know, however, that during the 1830s and 1840s he ran a publishing business in London, first at 87 Aldersgate Street and secondly at 13 Finsbury Place South. He died in 1865. More is known about the outcome of his publishing efforts, in particular the very successful series of topographical dictionaries for which he was responsible. His 4 volumed topographical dictionary for England appeared in 1831 (7th edition 1849) to be followed a year later by a similar two volumed work for Wales (4th edition 1849). In 1837 he produced a two volumed dictionary for Ireland (2nd edition 1842), accompanied by an atlas of the counties of Ireland. Finally, he published a three volumed topographical dictionary for Scotland in 1846.[1]

Production of the Irish dictionary involved a vast entreprenurial enterprise.[2] Starting in early 1833 agents were dispatched to all parts of Ireland to gather information for the work and also to obtain advance subscribers. The dictionary was priced at two guineas per volume while the atlas was also available for two guineas. As was explained in the preface to the first volume, compared to England and Wales, there was less available for Ireland in the form of county histories and other such work, so it was important to gain extensive personal information. His principal sources of information were local landowners and clergy. When the dictionary appeared finally in 1837, the list of subscribers (including many of his informants) ran to a total of nearly 10,000 names, including large numbers in County Down.

The publication of the Irish dictionary led to considerable controversy, caused not by the content of the volumes but by objections from some of those listed as subscribers to being included on the list. A number of legal cases ensued over questions of liability for payment for the two books. There seems to have been relatively little debate over the accuracy of the contents. The 1842 revised edition made some corrections but also updated the figures in accordance with the 1841 census and replaced educational material with extra material on the railways. The entries reprinted here for County Down are from the first edition and so relate to the 1830s.

This dictionary by Lewis gives a unique coverage of life in Ireland, parish by parish and town by town. No-one before had produced such an extensive survey. At the same time as the appearance of these volumes by Lewis, an enterprise was underway to record Irish society and economy as part of the Ordnance Survey (O.S.), with the writing of memoirs to accompany the production of the first O.S. maps for Ireland. This project collapsed finally in 1840, however, after only the northern counties had been investigated, and just one volume was published for the parish of Templemore in County Londonderry. Only in the last decade of the 20th century have these memoirs been published.[3] These volumes by Lewis are very valuable for us today not just because he gathered important personal information at local level but also because he availed of much of the statistical and factual information which was now becoming available for Ireland, often through parliamentary papers and reports. In particular, he used the 1831 census report, new educational data and O.S. acreage figures.

At the same time, we must be aware of some of the perspectives and weaknesses of the material. A man of his time, Lewis approached his work from the standpoint of a society run by the gentry. The parishes are those of the Church of Ireland which was the established church and which, therefore, was given priority over other churches in these descriptions. We must appreciate that some of his accounts of Irish pre history and archaeology would be questioned by historians and archaeologists today. His information on these matters reflects the state of knowledge about them at the time, which changed considerably in the course of the 19th century, thanks to the work of people such as John O'Donovan. For example his references to 'druidical altars', and some of his accounts of the origins of the early people of Ireland would not now be accepted. Those interested in the composition of placenames should check Lewis's interpretation with modern works on the subject.[4] It should also be noted that Lewis gives distances in Irish miles (10 Irish miles equal a little over 12 British miles). Spellings of names have been left as found in the original text.

Maps and map makers
The year 1835 witnessed the publication of the first 6 inch O.S. maps for County Down. Run by officers of the Royal Engineers, and starting in the 1820s, a complete mapping survey of the whole country was carried out under the auspices of the Ordnance Survey of Ireland, based at Phoenix Park in Dublin.[5] This led to the appearance in 1833 of the first six inches to the mile maps for County Londonderry, to be followed by similar maps for all the Irish counties over the next nine years. This surveying project was a vast undertaking which involved considerable expenditure and manpower. The result was a very extensive cartographic record for Ireland, which had no equivalent in the world at the time. In 1810 James Williamson had produced a fine four section map for County Down, but this was now superceded by the O.S. production.

In this volume plans of 15 of the main towns in County Down have been copied from the original 6 inch O.S. maps for the county. For sake of greater clarity the town maps have been magnified by 40%. It must be remembered that while all the County Down O.S. maps were published in 1835, the actual surveying could have been done in the previous one or two years. We have also included a map of

County Down from Lewis's atlas. One of the advantages of this map is that it gives the location of the parishes, and while it does not show the parish boundaries, nonetheless, it can be helpful to give people some idea of which parish their area is located in. The maps in the atlas were based on drawings reduced from the Ordnance Survey and other surveys.

Artists and engravers

The period from the early 1820s to the early 1840s witnessed an upsurge in the appearance of topographical views of Ireland, partly due to technological advances, such as the advent of line engraving on steel in the early 1820s. The bulk of the illustrations in this book come from the 1830s, although some are as late as 1846. The publication of the weekly *Dublin Penny Journal*, 1832-35, with its many wood engravings, was an important new departure in the level of illustrated material available at a low cost. The journal carried topographical articles and illustrations on many parts of Ireland. Besides *The Dublin Penny Journal*, there now appeared a large number of illustrated books, covering special areas or all of Ireland. Well known artists, such as George Petrie (who worked for the Ordnance Survey for a time in the 1830s), were employed to provide drawings to be engraved for these works.

Of special interest in this activity is the work of a number of northern artists. Views by the Belfast born Andrew Nicholl (1804-86) appeared frequently, both in *The Dublin Penny Journal* and in various published tours and guides. John Molloy (1798-1877) was an art master in Belfast, who was responsible for illustrations of large private houses in the Belfast neighbourhood, which were engraved and published in 1832 in Belfast and London in a book entitled *Belfast scenery in thirty views*.[6] James Howard Burgess (c.1817-90) of Belfast was a skilled topographical artist who provided 25 views for S.C. Hall's *Ireland: its scenery, character, &c.* (London, 1846), and all the pictures in Marcus Ward's *Illustrations of the north of Ireland* (Belfast, c.1850).[7]

In recent times engravings such as these have often been used to illustrate texts, but usually there has been little attempt to name the artist and engraver involved or to accurately date the picture. In this volume, however, an effort has been made to identify both the artist and engraver responsible for a particular piece of work. This has not been possible in every case and where the full information has not been given this is because it is not available. The title of the book, and the date and place of publication, has been given with each print so that we can establish a date for the particular view.

Brian M. Walker   **Belfast, 2003**

References

[1] See Frederick Boase, (ed) *Modern English biography*, vol.2 (London, 1965) p.417.

[2] This enterprise is discussed well by Tim Cadogan in his introduction to *Lewis's Cork* (Cork, 1998).

[3] Angelique Day and Patrick McWilliams, *Ordnance survey memoirs of Ireland*, vols.1-40 (Belfast, 1990-98).

[4] See the Co. Down volumes in the series *Placenames of Northern Ireland*, general editor Gerald Stockman, series editor Nollaig Ó Muraíle. See also Patrick McKay, *A dictionary of Ulster placenames* (Belfast, 1999).

[5] See J.H. Andrews, *A paper landscape: the ordnance survey in 19th century Ireland* (Oxford, 1993; second edition, Dublin, 2002).

[6] See modern commentary by Hugh Dixon and Fred Heatley in *Belfast scenery in thirty views*, 1832 (reprint Belfast, 1983).

[7] See John Hewitt, *Art in Ulster* (Belfast, 1977). Biographical notes by Theo Snoody.

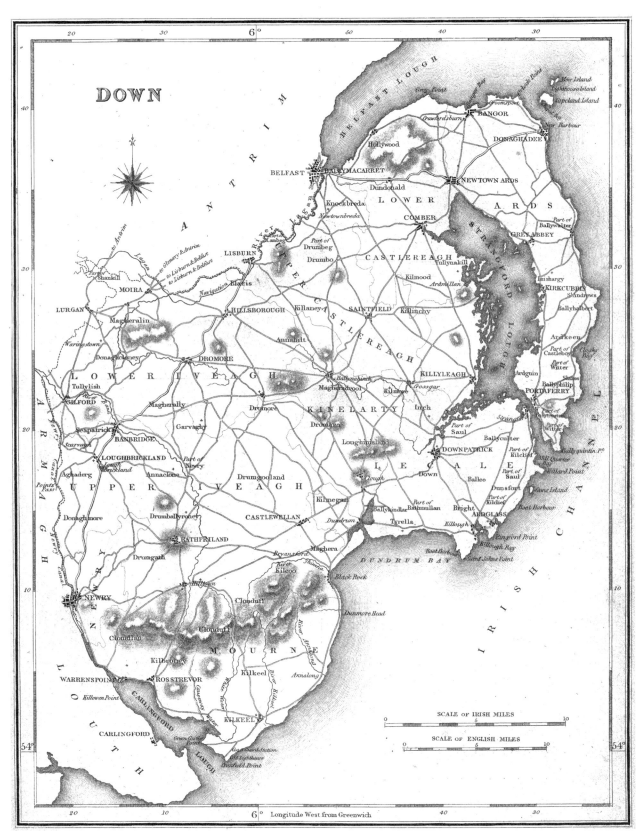

Down. Drawn by R. Creighton and engraved by I. Dower. From Lewis's Atlas, (London, 1837).

COUNTY DOWN

A

TOPOGRAPHICAL DICTIONARY

DOWN (County of), a maritime county of the province of ULSTER, bounded on the east and south by the Irish sea, on the north by the county of Antrim and Carrickfergus bay, and on the west by the county of Armagh. It extends from 54° 0′ to 54° 40′ (N. Lat.), and from 5° 18′ to 6° 20′ (W. Lon.); and comprises an area, according to the Ordnance survey, of 611,404 acres, of which, 502,677 are cultivated land, 108,569 are unprofitable bog and mountain, and 158 are under water. The population, in 1821, amounted to 325,410, and in 1831, to 352,012.

This county, together with a small part of that of Antrim, was anciently known by the name of Ulagh or Ullagh, in Latin Ulidia (said by some to be derived from a Norwegian of that name who flourished here long before the Christian era), which was finally extended to the whole province of Ulster. Ptolemy, the geographer, mentions the Voluntii or Uluntii as inhabiting this region; and the name, by some etymologists, is traced from them. At what period this tribe settled in Ireland is unknown: the name is not found in any other author who treats of the country, whence it may be inferred that the colony was soon incorporated with the natives, the principal families of whom were the O'Nials, the Mac Gennises, the Macartanes, the Slut-Kellys, and the Mac Gilmores. The county continued chiefly in the possession of the same families at the period of the settlement of the North of Ireland in the reign of King James, at the commencement of the seventeenth century, with the addition of the English families of Savage and White, the former of which settled in the peninsula of the Ardes, on the eastern side of Strangford Lough, and the latter in the barony of Dufferin, on the western side of the same gulf. It is not clearly ascertained at what precise period the county was made shire ground. The common opinion is that this arrangement, together with its division into baronies, occurred in the early part of the reign of Elizabeth. But from the ancient records of the country it appears that, previously to the 20th of Edw. II., here were two counties distinguished by the names of Down and Newtown. The barony of Ardes was also a separate

jurisdiction, having sheriffs of its own at the same date; and the barony of Lecale was considered to be within the English pale from its first subjugation by that people; its communication with the metropolis being maintained chiefly by sea, as the Irish were in possession of the mountain passes between it and Louth. That the consolidation of these separate jurisdictions into one county took place previously to the settlement of Ulster by Sir John Perrott, during his government, which commenced in 1584, is evident from this settlement comprehending seven counties only, omitting those of Down and Antrim because they had previously been subjected to the English law.

The first settlement of the English in this part of Ulster took place in 1177, when John de Courcy, one of the British adventurers who accompanied Strongbow, marched from Dublin with 22 men-at-arms and 300 soldiers, and arrived at Downpatrick in four days without meeting an enemy. But when there he was immediately besieged by Dunleve, the toparch of the country, aided by several of the neighbouring chieftains, at the head of 10,000 men. De Courcy, however did not suffer himself to be blockaded, but sallied out at the head of his little troop, and routed the besiegers. Another army of the Ulidians having been soon after defeated with much slaughter in a great battle, he became undisputed master of the part of the county in the vicinity of Downpatrick, which town he made his chief residence, and founded several religious establishments in its neighbourhood. In 1200, Roderic Mac Dunleve, toparch of the country, was treacherously killed by De Courcy's servants, who were banished for the act by his order; but in 1203 he himself was seized, while doing penance unarmed in the burial-ground of the cathedral of Down, by order of De Lacy, the chief governor of Ireland, and was sent prisoner to King John in England. The territory then came into the possession of the family of De Lacy, by an heiress of which, about the middle of the same century, it was conveyed in marriage to Walter de Burgo. In 1315, Edward Bruce having landed in the northern part of Ulster, to assert his claim to the throne of Ireland, this part of the province suffered severely in consequence of the military movements attending his progress southwards and his return. Some years after, William de Burgo, the representative of that powerful family, having been killed by his own servants at Carrickfergus, leaving an only daughter, the title and possessions were again transferred by marriage to Roger Mortimer, Earl of March, through whom they finally became vested in the kings of England.

It is partly in the diocese of Down, and partly in that of Dromore, with a small portion in that of Connor. For purposes of civil jurisdiction it is divided into the baronies of Ardes, Castlereagh, Dufferin, Iveagh Lower, Iveagh Upper, Kinelearty, Lecale, and Mourne, and the extra-episcopal lordship of Newry. It contains the borough, market, and assize town of Downpatrick; the greater part of the borough, market, and assize town, and sea-port of Newry; the ancient corporate, market, and post-towns of Bangor, Newtown-Ardes, Hillsborough, and Killyleagh; the sea-port, market, and post-towns of Portaferry and Donaghadee; the market and post-towns of Banbridge, Saintfield, Kirkcubbin, Rathfriland, Castlewellan, Ballinahinch, and Dromore; the sea-port and post-towns of Strangford, Warrenpoint, Rosstrevor, Ardglass, and Killough; the sea-port of Newcastle, which has a penny-post; the post-towns of Clough, Comber, Dromaragh, Hollywood, Moira, Loughbrickland, Kilkeel, and Gilford; and a part of the suburb of the town of Belfast, called Ballymacarret. Prior to the Union it sent fourteen members to the Irish parliament, namely, two for the county at large, and two for each of the boroughs of Newry, Downpatrick, Bangor, Hillsborough, Killyleagh, and Newtown-Ardes. It is at present represented by four members, namely, two for the county, and one for each of the boroughs of Newry and Downpatrick. The number of voters registered at the last general election was 3,729. The election for the county takes place at Downpatrick. Down is included in the north-east circuit: the assizes are held at Downpatrick, where are the county gaol and court-house: quarter sessions are held at NewtownArdes, Hillsborough, Downpatrick, and Newry: the number of persons charged with criminal offences and committed to prison, in 1835, was 468, and of civil bill commitments, 87. The local government is vested in a lord-lieutenant, 19 deputy lieutenants, and 120 other magistrates, besides whom there are the usual county officers, including two coroners. There are 30 constabulary police stations, having in the whole a force of 5 chief and 30 subordinate constables and 114 men, with 6 horses, the expense of whose maintenance is defrayed equally by Grand Jury presentments and by Government. There are a county infirmary and a fever hospital at Downpatrick, and dispensaries situated respectively at Banbridge, Kilkeel, Rathfriland, Castlewellan, Dromore, Warrenspoint, Donaghadee, Newry, Newtownbreda, Hollywood, Hillsborough, Ardglass, and Bangor, maintained equally by private subscriptions and Grand Jury presentments. The amount of Grand Jury presentments for 1835 was £43,103.7.0$^1/_4$, of which £5,257.6.2 was for the public roads of the county at large; £17,226.19.2 was for the public roads, being the baronial charge; £11,923.18.4 for public buildings and charities, officers' salaries, &c.; £3,429.1.5$^1/_2$ for police; and £5,266.1.10$^3/_4$ in repayment of a loan advanced by Government, In the military arrange. ments it is included in the northern district, and contains three barrack stations for infantry, namely, two at Newry and one at Downpatrick. On the coast there are nineteen coast-guard stations, under the command of two inspecting commanders, in the districts of Donaghadee and Newcastle, with a force of 15 chief officers and 127 men.

The county has a pleasing inequality of surface, and exhibits a variety beautiful landscapes. The mountainous district is in the south, comprehending all the barony of Mourne, the lordship of Newry, and a considerable portion of the barony of Iveagh: these mountains rise gradually to a great elevation, terminating in the towering peak of Slieve Donard; and to the north of this main assemblage is the detached group of Slieve Croob, the summit of which is only 964 feet high. There are several lakes, but none of much extent: the principal are Aghry or Agher, and Erne, in Lower Iveagh; Ballyroney, Loughbrickland, and Shark, in Upper Iveagh; Ballinahinch, in Kinelearty; and Ballydowgan, in Lecale. The county touches upon Lough Neagh in a very small portion of its north-western extremity, near the place where the Lagan canal discharges itself into the lake. Its eastern boundary, including also a portion of the northern and southern limits, comprehends a long line of coast, commencing at Belfast with the mouth of the Lagan, which separates this county from that of Antrim, and proceeding thence along the southern side of Carrickfergus bay, where the shore rises in a gentle acclivity, richly studded with villas, to the Castlereagh hills, which form the back ground. Off Orlock Point, at the southern extremity of the bay, are the Copeland islands, to the south of which is the town and harbour of Donaghadee, a station for the mail packets between Ireland and Scotland. On the coast of the Ardes are Ballyhalbert bay, Cloughy bay, and Quintin bay, with the islets called Burr or Burial Island, Green Island, and Bard Island. South of Quintin bay is the channel, about a mile wide, to Strangford Lough, called also Lough Cone. The lough itself is a deep gulf stretching ten miles into the land in a northern direction, to Newtown-Ardes, and having a south-western offset, by which vessels of small burden can come within a mile of Downpatrick. The interior is studded with numerous islands, of which Boate says there are 260: Harris counts 54 with names besides many smaller; a few are inhabited, but the others are mostly used for pasturage, and some are finely wooded. South of Strangford Lough are Gun's island, Ardglass harbour, and Killough bay Dundrum bay, to the south-west, forms an extended indentation on the coast, commencing at St. John's Point, south of Killough, and terminating at Cranfield Point, the southern extremity of the county, where the coast takes a northwestern direction by Greencastle, Rosstrevor, and Warrenpoint, to Newry, forming the northern side of the romantic and much frequented bay of Carlingford.

The extent and varied surface of the county necessarily occasion a great diversity of soil: indeed there exists every gradation from a light sandy loam to a strong clay; but the predominant soil is a loam, not of great depth but good in quality, though in most places intermixed with a considerable quantity of stones of every size. When clay is the substratum of this loam, it is retentive of water and more difficult to improve; but when thoroughly cultivated, its produce is considerable and of superior quality. As the subsoil approaches to a hungry gravel, the loam diminishes considerably in fertility. Clay is mostly confined to the eastern coast of the Ardes and the northern portion of Castlereagh, in which district the soil is strong and of good quality. Of sandy ground, the quantity is still less, being confined to a few stripes scattered along the shores, of which the most considerable is that on the bay of Dundrum: part of this land is cultivated, part used as grazing land or rabbit-warren, and a small portion consists of shifting sands, which have hitherto baffled all attempts at improvement. There is a small tract of

land south of the Lagan, between Moira and Lisburn, which is very pro. ductive, managed with less labour than any of the soils above mentioned, and earlier both in seed-time and harvest. Gravelly soils, or those intermixed with waterworn stones, are scattered over a great part of the county. Moory grounds are mostly confined to the skirts of the mountains; the bogs, though numerous, are now scarcely sufficient to afford a plentiful supply of fuel: in some parts they form the most lucrative portion of the property. The rich and deep loams on the sides of the larger rivers are also extremely valuable, as they produce luxuriant crops of grass annually without the assistance of manure.

The great attention paid to tillage has brought the land to a high state of agricultural improvement. The prevailing corn crop is oats, of which the favourite sorts are the Poland, Blantire, Lightfoot, and early Holland; wheat is sown in every part, and in Lecale is of excellent quality, and very good also in Castlereagh barony; barley is a favourite crop, mostly preceded by potatoes; rye is seldom sown, except on bog; much flax is cultivated; and turnips, mangel-wurzel, and other green crops are very general. Though, from the great unevenness of surface, considerable tracts of flat pasture land are very uncommon, yet on the sides of the rivers there are excellent and extensive meadows, annually enriched by the

View of Warrenpoint and Carlingford Lough. Drawn by T. Creswick and engraved by J. Hinchliffe. From S.C. Lewis, Ireland: its scenery, character, &c., *vol.3 (London, 1846).*

overflowing of the waters; and, in the valleys, the accumulation of the finer particles of mould washed down from the sides of the surrounding hills produces heavy crops of grass. Many of the finest and most productive meadows are those which lie on the skirts of turf bogs, at the junction of the peat and loam: the fertility of the compound soil is very great, the vegetation rapid, and the natural grasses of the best kind. Artificial grasses are general; clover in frequent cultivation, particularly the white. Draining is extensively and judiciously practised; and irrigation is successfully resorted to, especially upon turf bog, which, when reclaimed, is benefited by it in an extraordinary manner. In the management of the dairy, butter is the chief object: considerable quantities are sold fresh in the towns, but the greatest part is salted and sent to Belfast and Newry for exportation. Dung is principally applied as manure for raising potatoes, and great attention is paid by the farmers to collect it and to increase its quantity by additional substances, such as earth, bog soil, and clay. Lime, however, is the most general manure. At Ballinahinch, the most central part of the county, limestone of three kinds may be seen at a small distance from each other, the blue from Carlingford, the red from Castlespie, and the white from Moira, a distance of fourteen miles; the white is most esteemed. Limestone gravel is used in the neighbourhood of Moira, and found to be of powerful and lasting efficacy. Marling was introduced into Lecale about a century ago: the result of the first experiments was an immediate fourfold advance in the value of land, and the opening of a corn trade from Strangford; but the intemperate use of it brought it into discredit for some time, though it has latterly, under more judicious management, resumed its former character. Shell-sand is used to advantage on stiff clay lands; and sea-weed is frequently applied to land near the coast, but its efficacy is of short duration. Turf bog, both by itself and combined with clay, has been found useful. The system of burning and paring is practised only in the mountainous parts. In the neighbourhood of towns, coal-ashes and soot are employed: the ashes of bleach-greens, and soapers' waste, have been found to improve meadows and pastures considerably. The attention of the higher class of farmers has been for many years directed to the introduction of improved implements of husbandry, most of which have had their merits proved by fair trial: threshing machines are in general use. In no part of the country is the art of raising hedges better understood, although it has not yet been extended so universally as could be desired. In many parts the enclosure is formed of a ditch and a bank, from four to eight feet wide, and of the same depth, without any quicks; sometimes it is topped with furze, here called whins, In the mountainous parts the dry stone wall is common.

The cattle being generally procured more for the dairy than for feeding, special attention has not been paid to the improvement of the breed: hence there is a mixture of every kind. The most common and highly esteemed is a cross between the old native Irish stock and the old Leicester long-horned, which are considered the best milchers. But the anxiety of the principal resident landowners to improve every branch of agriculture having led them to select their stock of cattle at great expense, the most celebrated English breeds are imported, and the advantages are already widely diffusing themselves. The North Devon, Durham, Hereford, Leicester and Ayrshire breeds have been successively tried, and various crosses produced; that between the Durham and Leicester appears best adapted to the soil and climate, and on some estates there is a good cross between the Ayrshire and North Devon; but the long-horned is still the favourite breed of the small farmer. Great improvements have also been made in the breed of sheep, particularly around Hillsborough, Seaford, Downpatrick, Bangor, Cumber, Saintfield, and other places, where there are several fine flocks, mostly of the new Leicester breed. In other parts there is a good cross between the Leicester and old native sheep. The latter have undergone little or no change in the vicinity of the mountains; they are a small hardy race, with a long hairy fleece, black face and legs, some of them horned; they are prized for the delicacy and flavour of their mutton. The breed of pigs has of late been very much improved: the Berkshire and Hampshire mostly prevail; but the most profitable is a cross between the Dutch and Russian breeds, which grows to a good size, easily fattens, and weighs well; the greater number are fattened and slaughtered, and the carcases are conveyed either to Belfast or Newry for the supply of the provision merchants, where they are mostly cured for the English market. The breed of horses, in general, is very good. There are some remains of ancient woods near Downpatrick, Finnebrogue, Briansford, and Castlewellan; and the entire county is well wooded. The oak every where flourishes vigorously; in the parks and demesnes of the nobility and gentry there is a great quantity of full-grown timber, and extensive plantations are numerous in almost every part, particularly in the vale of the Lagan, from Belfast to Lisburn, and around Hollywood, and many of the hills have been successfully planted.

The Mourne mountains, extending from Dundrum bay to Carlingford bay, form a well-defined group, of which Slieve Donard is the summit, being, according to the Ordnance survey, 2,796 feet above the level of the sea, and visible, in clear weather, from the mountains near Dublin: granite is its prevailing constituent. To the north of these mountains, Slieve Croob, composed of sienite, and Slieve Anisky, of hornblende, both in Lower Iveagh, constitute an elevated tract dependent upon, though at some distance from, the main group. Hornblende and primitive greenstone are abundant on the skirts of the granitic district. Mica slate has been noticed only in one instance. Exterior chains of transition rocks advance far to the west and north of this primitive tract, extending westward across Monaghan into Cavan, and on the north-east to the southern cape of Belfast Lough, and the peninsula of Ardes. The primitive nucleus bears but a very small

View of Belfast from Knockbreda. Drawn by Andrew Nicholl and engraved by J. Smith. From The parliamentary gazetteer of Ireland, *vol.1 (London, 1846).*

proportion, in surface, to these exterior chains, which are principally occupied by grauwacke and grauwacke slate, In the Mourne Mountains and the adjoining districts an extensive formation of granite occurs, but without the varieties found in Wicklow, agreeing in character rather with the newer granite of the Wernerians: it constitutes nearly the whole mass of the Mourne mountains, whence it passes across Carlingford bay into the county of Louth. On the north-west of these mountains, where they slope gradually into the plain, the same rock reaches Rathfriland, a table land of inconsiderable elevation. Within the boundaries now assigned, the granite is spread over a surface of 324 square miles, comprehending the highest ground in the North of Ireland. Among the accidental ingredients of this formation are crystallised hornblende, chiefly abounding in the porphyritic variety, and small reddish garnets in the granular: both varieties occur mingled together on the top of Slieve Donard. Water-worn pebbles, of porphyritic sienite, occasionally containing red crystals of feldspar and iron pyrites, are very frequent at the base of the Mourne mountains, between Rosstrevor and Newcastle: they have probably been derived from the

disintegration of neighbouring masses of that rock, since, on the shore at Glassdrummin, a ledge of porphyritic sienite, evidently connected with the granitic mass of the adjoining mountain, projects into the sea. Greenstone slate rests against the acclivities of the Mourne mountains, but the strata never rise high, seldom exceeding 500 feet. Attempts have been made to quarry it for roofing, which it is thought would be successful if carried on with spirit. Feldspar porphyry occurs in the bed of the Finish, north-west of Slieve Croob, near Dromara, and in a decomposing state at Ballyroany, north-east of Rathfriland. Slieve Croob seems formed, on its north-east and south-east sides, of different varieties of sienite, some of them porphyritic and very beautiful: this rock crops out at intervals from Bakaderry to the top of Slieve Croob, occupying an elevation of about 900 feet. Grauwacke and grauwacke slate constitute a great part of the baronies of Ardes, Castlereagh, and the two Iveaghs: it is worked for roofing at Ballyalwood, in the Ardes; and a variety of better quality still remains undisturbed at Cairn Garva, south-west of Conbigg Hill. Lead and copper ores have been found in this formation at Conbigg Hill, between Newtown-Ardes and Bangor, where a mine is now profitably and extensively worked. Two small limestone districts occur, one near Downpatrick on the southwest, and the other near Comber on the northwest, of Strangford Lough. The old red sandstone has been observed on the sides of Strangford Lough, particularly at Scrabo, which rises 483 feet above the lough, and is capped with greenstone about 150 feet thick; the remaining 330 feet are principally sandstone, which may be observed in the white quarry in distinct beds of very variable thickness, alternating with grauwacke. This formation has been bored to the depth of 500 feet on the eastern side of Strangford Lough, in the fruitless search for coal, which depth, added to the ascertained height above ground, gives from 800 to 900 feet as its thickness. The greatest length of this sandstone district is not more than seven miles; it appears to rest on grauwacke. Coal, in three seams, is found on the shores of Strangford, and two thin seams are found under the lands of Wilnmount, on the banks of the Lagan; there are also indications of coal in two places near Moira. Chalk appears at Magheralin, near Moira, proceeding thence towards the White mountains near Lisburn, and forming a low table land. The quarries chiefly worked for freestone are those of Scrabo and Kilwarlin, near Moira, from the latter of which flags are raised of great size and of different colours, from a clear stone-colour to a brownish red. Slates are quarried on the Ardes shore, between Bangor and Ballywalter, and near Hillsborough, Anahilt, and Ballinahinch: though inferior to those imported from Wales in lightness and colour, they exceed them in hardness and durability. In the limestone quarries near Moira, the stone is found lying in horizontal strata intermixed with flints, in some places stratified, and in others in detached pieces of various forms and sizes: it is common to see three of these large flints, like rollers, a yard long and twelve inches each in diameter, standing perpendicularly over each other, and joined by a narrow neck of limestone, funnel-shaped, as if they had been poured when in a liquid state into a cavity made to receive them. Shells of various kinds are also found in this stone.

The staple manufacture is that of linens, which has prevailed since the time of Wm. III., when legislative measures were enacted to substitute it for the woollen manufacture. Its establishment here is owing greatly to the settlement of a colony of French refugees, whom the revocation of the edict of Nantes had driven from their native country, and more especially to the exertions of one of them, named Crommelin, who, after having travelled through a considerable part of Ireland, to ascertain the fitness of the country for the manufacture, settled in Lisburn, where he established the damask manufacture, which has thriven there ever since. The branches now carried on are fine linen, cambrics, sheetings, drills, damasks, and every other description of household linen. Much of the wrought article, particularly the finer fabrics, is sent to Belfast and Lurgan for sale; the principal markets within the county are Dromore (for finer linens), and Rathfriland, Kilkeel, Downpatrick, Castlewellan,

Ballinahinch, Banbridge, Newry, Dromore, and Kirkcubbin, for those of inferior quality. The cotton manufacture has latterly made great progress here; but as the linen weavers can work at a cotton loom, and as the cotton weavers are unqualified to work at linen, the change has not been in any great degree prejudicial to the general mass of workmen, who can apply themselves to one kind when the demand for the other decreases. The woollen manufacture is confined to a coarse cloth made entirely for domestic consumption, with the exception of blanketing, which was carried on with much spirit and to a great extent, particularly near Lisburn. The weaving of stockings is pretty generally diffused, but not for exportation. Tanning of leather is carried on to a large extent: at Newry there is a considerable establishment for making spades, scythes, and other agricultural implements and tools; and there are extensive glass-works at Newry and Ballimacarett. Kelp is made in considerable quantities along the coast and on Strangford lough, but its estimation in the foreign market has been much lowered by its adulteration during the process.

There is a considerable fishery at Bangor, for fat fish of all kinds, and for cod and oysters; also at Ardglass for herrings, and at Killough for haddock, cod, and other round fish; the small towns on the coast are also engaged in the fishery, particularly that of herrings, of which large shoals are taken every year in Strangford lough, but they are much inferior in size and flavour to those caught in the main sea. Smelts are taken near Portaferry; mullet, at the mouth of the Quoile river, near Downpatrick; sand eels, at Newcastle; shell fish, about the Copeland islands; and oysters, at Ringhaddy and Carlingford.

The principal rivers are the Bann and the Lagan, neither of which is navigable within the limits of the county: the former has its source in two neighbouring springs in that part of the mountains of Mourne called the Deer's Meadow, and quits this county for Armagh, which it enters near Portadown, where it communicates with the Newry canal. The Lagan has also two sources, one in Slieve Croob, and the other in Slieve-na-boly, which unite near Waringsford: near the Maze it becomes the boundary between the counties of Down and Antrim, in its course to Carrickfergus bay. There are also the Newry river and the Ballinahinch river, the former of which rises near Rathfriland, and falls into Carlingford bay; and the latter derives its source from four small lakes, and empties itself into the southwestern branch of Strangford lough. This county enjoys the benefit of two canals, viz., the Newry navigation, along its western border, connecting Carlingford bay with Lough Neagh; and the Lagan navigation which extends from the tideway at Belfast along the northern boundary of the county, and enters Lough Neagh near that portion of the shore included within its limits. It originated in an act passed in the 27th of Geo. II.: its total length is 20 miles; but, from being partly carried through the bed of the Lagan, its passage is so much impeded by floods as to detract much from the benefits anticipated from its formation.

There are two remarkable cairns; one on the summit of Slieve Croob, which is 80 yards round at the base and 50 on the top, and is the largest monument of the kind in the county: on this platform several smaller cairns are raised, of various heights and dimensions. The other is near the village of Anadorn, and is more curious, from containing within its circumference, which is about 60 yards, a large square smooth stone supported by several others, so as to form a low chamber, in which were found ashes and some human bones. A solitary pillar stone stands on the summit of a hill near Saint-field, having about six feet of its length above the ground. Among the more remarkable cromlechs is that near Drumbo, called the Giant's Ring, also one on Slieve-na-Griddal, in Lecale; there is another near Sliddery ford, and a third is in the parish of Drumgooland; others less remarkable may be seen near Rathfriland and Comber. There are two round towers: one stands about 24 feet south-west of the ruins of the church of Drumbo, and the other is close to the ruins of the old church of Maghera: a third, distinguished for the symmetry of its proportions, stood near the cathedral at Downpatrick, but it was taken down in 1790, to make room for rebuilding part of that edifice. Of the relics of antiquity entirely composed of earth, every variety is to be met with. Raths surrounded by a slight single ditch are numerous, and so situated as to be generally within view of each other. Of the more artificially constructed mounds, some, as at Saintfield, are formed of a single rampart and foss; others with more than one, as at Downpatrick, which is about 895 yards in circuit at the base, and surrounded by three ramparts: a third kind, as at Dromore, has a circumference of 600 feet, with a perpendicular height of 40 feet; the whole being surrounded by a rampart and battlement, with a trench that has two branches, embracing a square fort, 100 feet in diameter: and there are others very lofty at Donaghadee and Dundonald, with caverns or chambers running entirely round their interior. A thin plate of gold, shaped like a half moon, was dug out of a bog in Castlereagh; the metal is remarkably pure, and the workmanship good though simple. Another relic of the same metal, consisting of three thick gold wires intertwined through each other, and conjectured to have formed part of the branch of a golden candlestick, was found near Dromore. Near the same town have been found a canoe of oak, about 13 feet long, and various other relics; another canoe was found at Loughbrickland, and a third in the bog of Moneyreagh. An earthen lamp of curious form was dug up near Moira, the figures on which were more remarkable for their indecency than their elegance.

There are numerous remains of monastic edifices, of which the principal are at Downpatrick, those of Grey abbey on the shore of Strangford lough, and at Moville near Newtown-Ardes, Inch or Innis-Courcy near Downpatrick, Newry, Black abbey near Ballyhalbert, and Castlebuoy, or Johnstown in the Ardes. The first military work which presents itself in the southern extremity of the county is Greencastle, on the shore of Carlingford bay, said to have been built by the De Burgos, and afterwards commanded by an English constable, who also had charge of Carlingford castle: these were considered as outworks of the pale, and therefore intrusted to none but those of English birth. The castle of Narrow-water is of modern date, being built by the Duke of Ormonde after the Restoration. Dundrum castle is finely situated upon a rock overlooking the whole bay to which it gives name: it was built by De Courcy for the Knights Templars, but afterwards fell into the hands of the Magennis family. Ardglass, though but a small village, has the remains of considerable fortifications: the ruins of four castles are still visible. Not far from it is Kilclief castle, once the residence of the bishops of Down; between Killough and Downpatrick are the ruins of Bright and Skreen castles, the latter built on a Danish rath, as is that of Clough; in Strangford lough are Strangford castle, Audley's castle, and Walsh's castle; Portaferry castle was the ancient seat of the Savages; in the Ardes are also the castles of Quintin, Newcastle, and Kirkestown; the barony of Castlereagh is so called from a castle of the same name, built on a Danish fort, the residence of Con O'Neill; near Drumbo is Hill Hall, a square fort with flanking towers; Killileagh Castle is now the residence of Hamilton Rowan, Esq.; and at Rathfriland are the ruins of another castle of the Magennises. General Monk erected forts on the passes of Scarva, Poyntz, and Tuscan, which connect this county with Armagh, the ruins of which still exist. At Hillsborough is a small castle, which is still maiintained in its ancient state by the Marquess of Downshire, hereditary constable; and other castles in various parts have been taken down. The gentlemen's seats are numerous, and many of them are built in a very superior style of architecture; they are all noticed in their respective parishes.

Mineral springs, both chalybeate and sulphureous, abound, but the former are more numerous. Of these, the most remarkable are Ardmillan, on the borders of Strangford lough; Granshaw, in the Ardes; Dundonnell, three miles north-west of Newtown-Ardes; Magheralin, Dromore, Newry, Banbridge, and Tierkelly. Granshaw is the richest, being equal in efficacy to the strongest of the English spas. The principal sulphureous spa is near Ballinahinch: there is an alum spring near the town of Clough. The Struel springs, situated one mile south-east of Downpatrick, in a retired vale, are celebrated not only in the neighbourhood and throughout Ireland, but in many parts of the continent, for their healing qualities, arising not from their chymical but their miraculous properties: they are dedicated to St. Patrick, and are four in number, viz., the drinking well, the eye well, and two bathing wells, each enclosed with an ancient building of stone. The principal period for visiting them is at St. John's eve, on which occasion tlie water rises in the wells, supernaturally, according to the belief of those who visit them. Penances and other religious ceremonies, consisting chiefly of circuits made round the wells for a certain number of times, together with bathing, accompanied by specified forms of prayer, are said to have been efficacious in removing obstinate and chronic distempers. A priest formerly attended from Downpatrick, but this practice has been discontinued since the year 1804. Not far distant are the walls of a ruined chapel, standing north and south: the entrance was on the north, and the building was lighted by four windows in the western wall. St. Scorden's well, in the vicinity of Killough, is remarkable from the manner in which the water gushes out of a fissure in the perpendicular face of a rock, on an eminence close to the sea, in a stream which is never observed to diminish in the driest seasons.

Pearls have been found in the bed of the Bann river. Fossil remains of moose deer have been found at different places; and various kinds of trees are frequently discovered imbedded in the bogs. This county is remarkable as being the first place in Ireland in which frogs were seen: they appeared first near Moira, in a western and inland district, but the cause or manner of their introduction is wholly unknown. The Cornish chough and the king-fisher have been occasionally met with near Killough; the bittern is sometimes seen in the marshes on the sea-coast; the ousel and the eagle have been observed in the mountains of Mourne; and the cross-bill at Waringstown. Barnacles and widgeons frequent Strangford lough and Carrickfergus bay in immense numbers during winter; but they are extremely wary. A marten, as tall as a fox, but much longer, was killed several years since at Moira, and its skin preserved as a curiosity. Horse-racing is a favourite amusement with all classes, and is here sanctioned by royal authority; Jas. II. having granted a patent of incorporation to a society to be called the Royal Horsebreeders of the county of Down, which is still kept up by the resident gentry, and has produced a beneficial effect in improving the breed of race-horses. Downshire gives the title of Marquess to the family of Hill, the descendants of one of the military adventurers who came to Ireland in the reign of Elizabeth.

AGHADERG, or AGHADERRICK, a parish, partly in the barony of LOWER but chiefly in that of UPPER IVEAGH, county of DOWN, and province of ULSTER, on the road from Newry to Belfast; containing, with the towns of Loughbrickland and Scarvagh, 8981 inhabitants. This place formed part of the grant made by Queen Elizabeth, in 1585, to Sir Marmaduke Whitchurch, who built a castle on the shore of Loughbrickland, which was dismantled by Cromwell's army, and remained in ruins till 1812, when it was taken down and a dwelling-house erected on its site. In 1690 William III. encamped here with his army from the 14th to the 25th of June, on his march to the Boyne: vestiges of the camp may still be traced, and Dutch coins are frequently found in the neighbourhood. The parish, according to the Ordnance survey, comprises 13,919 statute acres, of which $119\frac{1}{4}$ are covered with water, and 11,772 are applotted under the tithe act; of waste and bog there is one acre to every twenty of arable land, and the pasture land is in the proportion of one to every

five acres in tillage. The land is extremely fertile, and under a highly improved system of tillage: the bog is very valuable, being estimated at 32 guineas per acre. Great quantities of clay-slate are raised here for mending the roads and for building purposes; and slate quarries have been formerly worked, but are now discontinued. The Newry Canal, in its progress to Lough Neagh, forms the western boundary of the parish and the county. There are two lakes; Loughbrickland, which forms the summit level of the canal, is skirted on its western shore by the road from Dublin to Belfast; Loughadian, near the western boundary of the parish, is rendered highly picturesque by the beautiful grounds and rich plantations of Union Lodge, the seat of W. Fivey, Esq. Among the other gentlemen's seats are Scarvagh House, the handsome residence of J. Lushington Reilly, Esq.; Loughbrickland-House, of N.C. Whyte, Esq.; Lisnagrade, of E.H. Trevor, Esq.; and Woodville House, of R. Boardman, Esq. The manufacture of linen is carried on to a considerable extent, many persons being employed at their own houses in weaving damask, diapers, drills, shirtings, and sheetings, for the Banbridge manufacturers. The living is a vicarage, in the diocese of Dromore, and in the patronage of the bishop; the rectory is united, by charter of the 7th of Jas. I., to the rectories of Seapatrick, Drumballyroney, and Tullylish, and part of those of Drumgooland and Magherally, together constituting the corps of the deanery of Dromore, in the patronage of the Crown. The tithes amount to £746.14.3, of which £497.16.2 is payable to the dean, and £248.18.1 to the vicar. The gross annual value of the deanery, as returned by the Commissioners on Ecclesiastical Revenues, is £1,483.19. The church is a large handsome edifice, in the early English style, erected in 1688, and a lofty square tower surmounted by an octagonal spire of hewn stone was added to it, for which the late Board of First Fruits, in 1821, granted a loan of £500. The glebe-house is a handsome residence; the Board, in 1801, gave £100 towards its erection, and also purchased a glebe of 24 acres for the vicar. The R.C. parish is co-extensive with that of the Established Church, and is the benefice of the Vicar-general; there are two chapels, one in Loughbrickland, a large and handsome edifice, and a smaller at Lisnagead. There are three places of worship for Presbyterians, one near the lake in connection with the Synod of Ulster, another at Glascar with the Seceding Synod, and a third at Scarvagh, all of the first class; one for Covenanters near Scarvagh, and one for Primitive Methodists at Loughbrickland. There are two public schools, in which are about 100 boys and 70 girls; and eleven private pay schools, in which are about 400 boys and 290 girls. Some remains of an ancient church exist in the townland of Drumsallagh; and about half a mile to the south-west of Loughbrickland are three upright stones, called 'the three sisters of Greenan,' apparently the remains of an ancient cromlech: they are situated on a gentle eminence, and near them is a fourth lying in a ditch. In 1826, a canoe formed out of a solid piece of oak was found in Meenan bog; and in a small earthwork near it were found several gold ornaments, earthen pots, and other relics of antiquity. At Drummillar is a vast cairn of loose stones, 60 feet high and 226 feet in circumference.-See LOUGHBRICKLAND and SCARVAGH.

ANACLOAN, or ANNAGHLONE, a parish, in the barony of UPPER IVEAGH, county of DOWN, and province of ULSTER, 3 miles (S.E. by E.) from Banbridge, on the river Bann, and on the road from Banbridge to Castlewellan, containing 3,426 inhabitants. It comprises, according to the Ordnance survey, 6,544³/₄ statute acres: the lands are fertile and in a high state of cultivation; there is no waste land, and only about 200 acres of bog, which is daily becoming more scarce and valuable. The living is a rectory, in the diocese of Dromore, and in the patronage of the Bishop: the tithes amount to £188.3.8. The church is a neat small edifice in good repair. The glebe-house was built by aid of a gift of £200 and a loan of £600 from the late Board of First Fruits, in 1818: the glebe comprises 204 acres. In the R.C. divisions the parish is the head of a union or district, comprising also that of Drumballyroney, and containing a chapel in each parish. There are places of worship for Presbyterians in connection with the Synod of Ulster and the Seceding Synod; the former of the third, and the latter of the second class. There are three schools, affording instruction to about 190 boys and 100 girls; also four private schools, in which are about 90 boys and 60 girls. Near the church is Tanvally fort, one of the largest and most perfect in this part of the country, and within sight of it are many others of smaller dimensions.

ANADORN, a village, in the parish of LOUGHAM ISLAND, barony of KINELEARTY, county of DOWN, and province of ULSTER, 3 miles (N.) from Clough; containing 93 inhabitants. This place, with an extensive surrounding district, formerly belonged to the ancient and powerful family of the McCartans, who had a castle here, situated on an eminence, or mound, now called Castlehill; but McCartan having joined in the rebellion of the Earl of Tyrone, his estates became forfeited to the crown. The village is situated on the road from Ballynahinch and Hillsborough to Downpatrick: it appears to have been much neglected, but it has been recently purchased by Col. Forde, who has already commenced a series of improvements. Fairs are held on May 14th and Nov. 8th.

ANAHILT, a parish, partly in the barony of KINELEARTY, but chiefly in that of LOWER IVEAGH, county of DOWN, and province of ULSTER, 3 miles (E.S.E.) from Hillsborough; containing 3,755 inhabitants. This parish is intersected by numerous roads, of which the principal are those leading respectively from Hillsborough and Dromore, and from Lisburn to Downpatrick, and from Belfast and Lisburn to Rathfriland. It comprises, according to the Ordnance survey, 6,777¹/₄ statute acres, of which 6,069 are in Lower Iveagh, and 708¹/₂ in Kinelearty, and is principally arable and pasture land, but mostly under tillage: 6,202 acres are applotted under the tithe act. The lands are in a state of excellent cultivation:

under-draining is well understood and extensively practised. In the townland of Cluntogh there is a fine slate quarry. The inhabitants combine with agricultural pursuits the weaving of linen and cotton for the manufacturers of the neighbouring towns, and the women and girls are employed in spinning. A penny post has been lately established from Hillsborough. The principal seats are Larch field, the handsome mansion and extensive demesne of W. Mussenden, Esq., and Lough Aghery, the residence of James Magill, Esq. The living is a rectory and vicarage, in the diocese of Dromore, and in the patronage of the Bishop: the tithes amount to £367.5.4. The church was built in 1741, at the sole expense of the Rev. T. Smith, then rector of the parish; and the tower was added to it by the Marquess of Downshire, in 1768. The glebe-house was built, in 1793, by the Rev. J. Doubourdieu, then rector, at an expense of £845.16.2: the glebe comprises 60 acres, contiguous to the church. In the R.C. divisions the parish forms part of the union or district of Magheradroll, also called Dunmore. There is a place of worship near Hillsborough for Presbyterians in connection with the Synod of Ulster, also one for those in connection with the Seceding Synod, at Lough Aghery, both of the first class. A free school of about 150 boys and 100 girls was founded in 1796, by Thos. Jamieson, Esq., who bequeathed £1,000 for its support; it is further endowed 'with four acres of land given by the Marquess of Downshire, who also contributed towards defraying the expense of building the school-houses. Near Larchfield are two schools, supported by W. Mussenden, Esq., and Mrs. Forde, in which about 80 boys and 70 girls are educated and partly clothed; and there are also three private schools, in which are about 120 boys and 70 girls. Robert Sharland, Esq., a native of Barnstaple, Devon, who died on the 6th of May, 1833, bequeathed from £2,000 to £3,000 in trust to the clergy of the parish and the proprietor of one or two townlands, for the erection of ten almshouses for ten aged men and ten aged women, and a house for the housekeeper, to each of whom he assigned £5 per ann.: the buildings were about to be commenced in the spring of 1835. The burial-ground about the church occupies the site of an ancient fort, which is the innermost of four enclosures, the whole occupying about 9 acres, and sloping to the east in a regular glacis. There are also numerous forts on the hill, all within view of each other, and several relics of antiquity have been discovered here.

ANDREW'S (ST.), a parish, in the barony of ARDES, county of DOWN, and province of ULSTER, comprising the post-town of Kirkcubbin, and containing, with the parishes of Ballywalter or Whitechurch, Ballyhalbert, and Innishargy, 7,618 inhabitants. This parish, together with those which are now united with it, formed part of the possessions of a Benedictine monastery founded as a cell to the abbey of St. Mary, at Lonley, in Normandy, by John de Courcey, who died in 1210; and though designated, in the charter of foundation, the abbey of St. Andrew de Stokes, is more generally known by the appellation of the Black Abbey. It was seized into the king's hands as an alien priory in 1395, and was granted to the Archbishop of Armagh, who annexed it to his see; and after the dissolution it fell into the hands of the O'Neils. On the rebellion of O'Neil it escheated to the crown, and was granted to Sir James Hamilton, who assigned it to Sir Hugh Montgomery, Lord of the Ardes; but in 1639 it was finally awarded to the Archbishop of Armagh. The parishes of Ballywalter or Whitechurch, Ballyhalbert, and Innishargy are all included under the general name of St. Andrew's, and comprise, according to the Ordnance survey, 12,907 statute acres, of which 4,012 are in St. Andrew's (including Ballyhalbert) and its islands. The land is fertile and in a high state of cultivation; but the fences are in bad condition, and in many places the system of draining is very inefficient. A large quantity of bog has been lately reclaimed by the Rev. Hugh Montgomery, which is now under cultivation and produces good crops. There are several gentlemen's seats, of which the principal are Spring Vale, the residence of G. Matthews, Esq.; Echlinville, of J. Echlin, Esq.; Glastry, of F. Savage, Esq.; and the Roddens, of J. Blackiston, Esq., all handsome and spacious mansions ornamented with thriving plantations. The post-town of Kirkcubbin is situated on the shore of Strangford Lough, on the west, and is separately described; and off the coast, on the east, are two islets, called respectively Green Island and Bur or Burrial, the former connected with the shore by a strand which is dry at low water; and the latter is remarkable as being the most eastern point of land in Ireland. There are some yawls and fishing smacks belonging to these islands; and about a mile to the north of Green Island is John's port, a small harbour for fishing boats, sheltered by a rock, called the Plough. On this coast is also a creek called Cloughy bay, having a bottom of clean sand; it has several fishing boats and wherries, and a coast-guard station has been established there, which is one of the twelve forming the district of Donaghadee. At the commencement of the last century, the churches of these parishes were in ruins; and, in the 2nd of Anne, an act was obtained for uniting the parishes and erecting a church in the centre of the union. The living is denominated the vicarage of St. Andrew's, or the union of Ballywalter, in the diocese of Down, and in the patronage of the Lord-Primate: the tithes amount to £1,200, of which, £800 is payable to the Primate, as rector, and £400 to the vicar. The church, a spacious structure, was erected in the year 1704. The glebe-house, a handsome residence close to the town of Kirkcubbin, and about 2¹/₄ miles from the church, was built about 50 years since, and has been greatly improved by the Rev. F. Lascelles, the present incumbent, at an expense of nearly £400: the glebe comprises about 30 acres, valued at £77.18 per annum. In the R.C. divisions this union forms part of the district of Upper Ardes, also called Portaferry. There are three places of worship for Presbyterians in connection with the Synod of Ulster, situated respectively at Ballywalter, Kirkcubbin, and Glastry, all of the second class;

one at Ballyhamlin in connection with the Remonstrant Synod, and one for Independents. There are six schools, two of which are supported by Lord Dufferin and J. Echlin, Esq., respectively, and two are infants' schools, supported by Miss Keown. In these schools are about 550 children of both sexes; and there are also four private schools, in which are about 100 boys and 80 girls. The sum of £50 per ann., payable out of the estate of Ballyatwood, was bequeathed by the Countess of Clanbrassil for clothing the poor on that estate. At Cloughy are the extensive ruins of a commandery of the Knights of St. John of Jerusalem, founded in 1189, by Hugh de Lacie, and called Castlebuoy; not far from which are the ruins of Slane church. Kirkstown castle, a heavy pile of building, erected in the reign of Jas. I., is in tolerable repair, and the tower in excellent preservation. – See KIRKCUBBIN.

ARDGLASS, a sea-port, post-town, and parish, in the barony of LECALE, county of DOWN, and province of ULSTER, 5¹/₂ miles (S.E. by E.) from Downpatrick, and 80³/₄ miles (N.N.E.) from Dublin; containing 2,300 inhabitants, of which number, 1,162 are in the town. This place derives its name, signifying in the Irish language 'the High Green,' from a lofty green hill of conical form, called the Ward, and situated to the west of the town: from the remains of several castles it appears to have been formerly a place of some importance. Jordan's Castle is memorable for the gallant and protracted defence that it made during the insurrection of the Earl of Tyrone, in the reign of Elizabeth, and derived its present name from its loyal and intrepid proprietor, Simon Jordan, who for three years sustained the continued assaults of the besiegers, till he was at length relieved by the Lord-Deputy Mountjoy, who sailed with a fleet from Dublin and landed here on the 17th of June, 1611; and after relieving the garrison, pursued the insurgents to Dunsford, where a battle took place, in which they were nearly annihilated; and Jordan was rewarded for his services by a concordatum from the Queen. The port of Ardglass appears to have been in a flourishing condition from a very early period; a trading company from London settled here in the reign of Hen. IV., and in the reign of Hen. VI. it had an extensive foreign trade and was superior to any other port in the province of Ulster. At that time the town had received a charter of incorporation, was governed by a mayor, and had a port-admiral and revenue officers. Hen. VIII. granted the customs of the port, then worth £5,000 per annum, to Gerald Fitzgerald, Earl of Kildare, in whose family they remained till 1637, when, with certain privileges enjoyed by the port of Carrickfergus, they were purchased by the crown, and the whole was transferred to Newry and Belfast, from which time the trade of Ardglass began to decline and the town ultimately became only a residence for fishermen. It was formerly the property of a branch of the Leinster family, of whom the last resident, Lord Lecale, sold the manor to W. Ogilvie, Esq., who had married the Dowager Duchess of Leinster, and under whose auspices the town recovered its former importance; at his decease it

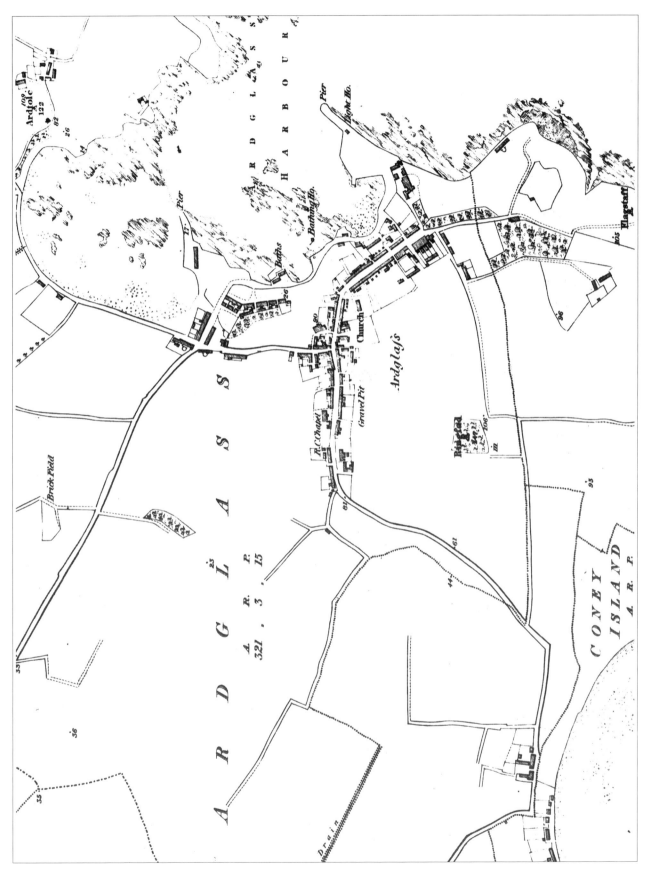

Ardglass. Part of 6 inch O.S. map of Co. Down, sheet 45, published 1835 (reproduced at 140%).

descended to his heir, Major Aubrey W. Beauclerc, its present proprietor.

The town is pleasantly and advantageously situated on the eastern coast, and on the side of a hill overlooking the sea, and is well known to mariners by two conspicuous hills, one on the west, called the Ward of Ardglass, and the other on the east, called the Ward of Ardtole. Mr. Ogilvie, on its coming into his possession in the year 1812, built entire streets, a church and school-house, and an elegant hotel; he also constructed hot, cold, and vapour baths; built and furnished lodging-houses for the accommodation of visiters, and rendered it one of the most fashionable watering-places in the North of Ireland. The town in its present state consists of one long street, nearly of semicircular form, from which several smaller streets branch off: in front of the inner bay is a range of excellent houses, called the Crescent; and there are many good houses in front of the harbour, adjoining which is a long range of building in the castellated style, called the New Works, although they are so old that nothing is known either of the time or the purpose of their erection. They form together a line of fortifications, 250 feet in length from east to west, and 24 feet in breadth, close to the shore; the walls are three feet in thickness and strengthened with three towers, one in the centre and one at each extremity. These buildings were originally divided into thirty-six apartments, eighteen on the ground floor and eighteen above, with a staircase in the centre; each of the lower apartments had a small arched door and a large square window, which renders it probable that they had been shops occupied by merchants at some very early period, possibly by the company of traders that settled here in the reign of Hen. IV. About the year 1789, Lord Chas. Fitzgerald, son of the Duke of Leinster, who was then proprietor, caused that portion of the building between the central and the western tower to be enlarged in the rear, and raised to the height of three stories in the castellated style; and from that time it has been called Ardglass Castle, and has been the residence of the proprietor of the estate. It was formerly called Horn Castle, either from a great quantity of horns found on the spot, or from a high pillar which stood on its summit previously to its being roofed; and near it is another castle, called Cow'd Castle, signifying the want of horns, from a word in the Scottish dialect, of which many phrases are still in use in the province. In a direct line with Ardglass Castle, and due west of it, are Cow'd Castle above noticed, and Margaret's Castle, both square ancient structures having the lower stories arched with stone; and on the north-west side of the town, on a considerable elevation, are two other castles, about 20 feet distant from each other, the larger of which is called King's Castle and the smaller the Tower; they have been partly rebuilt and connected with a handsome pile of building in the castellated style. Jordan's castle, previously noticed, is an elegant building, 70 feet high, standing in the centre of the town, and having at the entrance a well of excellent water. The surrounding scenery is beautiful,

and the air salubrious; the green banks of Ardtole and Ringfad, on the north and south sides of the bay, overhang the sea, where ships of the largest burden can approach within an oar's length of the bold and precipitous rocks that line the coast. From the Ward of Ardglass is a delightful prospect extending from 30 to 40 miles over a fertile country: on the south-west, beyond Killough and the beautiful bay of Dundrum, are seen the lofty mountains of Mourne rising in sublime grandeur; on the east, the Isle of Man, and on the north-east, the Ayrshire mountains of Scotland, in distant perspective, appearing to rise from the ocean, and embracing with their extended arch more than one half of the horizon. During the fishing season the view of the sea from this place is rendered peculiarly striking and animated by the daily arrival and departure of vessels, and the numerous shoals of mackarel, pollock, and other fish visible on the surface of the water for miles. There are no manufactures; the labouring classes being wholly employed in the fisheries off the north-east coast, of which this place is the common centre. During the season there are frequently in the harbour, at one time, from 300 to 400 vessels from Donaghadee, Carlingford, Skerries, Dublin, Arklow, and the Isle of Man, but principally from Penzance, on the coast of Cornwall. The boats come regularly into the harbour to dispose of their fish, which is quickly purchased by carriers, who take it into the interior of the country, and by merchants who cure it; but chiefly by masters of sloops and small craft, who wait in the harbour for the arrival of the fishing boats, and proceed directly to Dublin or Liverpool to dispose of the herrings fresh. These sloops usually perform two trips in the week, and the masters frequently make from £20 to £50 by each cargo. The harbour is admirably adapted for trade and steam navigation; and, since the erection of the new pier, is sufficient to accommodate steamers of any tonnage, and there is sufficient depth of water for vessels of 500 tons burden, which can enter at any state of the tide. There is an inner harbour, where a quay and pier have been erected for the accommodation of the fishing vessels; it is called Kimmersport, and is capable of accommodating a great number of fishing-boats, exclusively of other vessels of 100 tons burden; but the sea recedes from it at low water. On the quay are capacious stores for corn, in which an extensive trade is carried on. Adjoining the outer harbour a pier was completed, in 1814, at an expense of £14,000. The new pier was constructed in 1834, at an expense of £25,000, by Mr. Ogilvie, under the superintendence of Sir John Rennie: it extends 300 feet from the extremity of the old pier into deep water, and is 20 feet broad; it is built of large blocks of stone from the Isle of Man, hewn and dressed, forming a breakwater, and affording a beautiful promenade embracing fine views of the Isle and Calf of Man. A handsome lighthouse is now being erected on the pier, which is connected with the land by a very capacious wharf covering nearly an acre of ground, with a basin of semicircular form, beyond which are the quays for the colliers. The harbour is situated in lat. 54° 15′ 20″ (N.), and lon. 5° 35′ 20″ (W.); and the trade of the port is rapidly increasing. There is a patent for a market and four fairs. A constabulary police force, and a coast-guard station, forming one of the seven that constitute the district of Newcastle, have been established here. A manorial court is held for debts and pleas to the amount of £100.

By an order in council, dated Oct. 19th, 1834, the townlands of Jordan's Crew and Kildare's Crew, formerly belonging to the parish of Ballee, and the townland of Ross, formerly in the parish of Kilclief, were permanently united to this parish, which now comprises 1,137 statute acres, according to the Ordnance survey. The lands, which are all arable, are very fertile and in a profitable state of cultivation; there is not a rood of waste land or bog. At a short distance from the town, and near the shore, are extensive quarries of good rubble stone, from which were raised the materials used in the construction of the numerous buildings lately erected in the parish, and partly in the building of the pier, for the easier conveyance of which a rail-road, a quarter of a mile in length, was laid down. The living was formerly a perpetual curacy, and the rectory formed part of the union of Ballyphilip and corps of the chancellorship of Down, which union was lately dissolved on the recommendation of the Ecclesiastical Commissioners, and Ardglass is now an independent rectory and benefice, in the diocese of Down, and in the patronage of the Bishop; the tithes amount to £130. The church was built on the site of an ancient edifice, the late Board of First Fruits having granted £800 as a gift and £400 as a loan, in 1813 it is a handsome edifice, with a tower and spire 90 feet high. In digging the foundation, an oblong stone, broader at the top than at the bottom, was found near the place of the ancient altar, and is still in the churchyard: it has at the top a dove sculptured in relief; in the centre the crucifixion; and on each side a shield of arms. Underneath are some lines in curiously raised letters of the old English character, from which, though rendered almost unintelligible by intricate literal combinations, it appears to have been dedicated to the memory of Mrs. Jane O'Birne, in 1573. The Ecclesiastical Commissioners have lately granted £130 for the repair of this church. The glebe-house was built in 1815, a quarter of a mile from the church, at an expense of £500, of which £450 was a gift and £50 a loan from the late Board of First Fruits. The glebe contains three plantation acres. In the R.C. divisions this parish is united with Dunsford, by which latter name the union is generally known. Each has a chapel; that of Ardglass is a very neat edifice, built in 1829 on a spacious site given by Mr. Ogilvie. There is a school under the Trustees of Erasmus Smith's Charity, in which are about 90 boys and 80 girls; also four private schools, in which are about 60 boys and 50 girls, and a dispensary.

About half a mile to the north-east of the town, on a hill in the townland of Ardtole, are the ruins of an ancient place of worship, called the old church of Ardtole, of which the eastern gable, with a large arched opening, and the two side walls, more than three feet in thickness, are remaining, and are of strong but very rude masonry. In Ardtole creek, on the north-east side of the bay, is a natural cavern with a large entrance, which gradually contracts into a narrow fissure in the rock, scarcely admitting one person to creep through it; the elevation is very great, from which circumstance the townland probably derived its name Ardtole, signifying 'high hole:' some persons have penetrated a considerable way into this cavern, but no one has explored it fully. Ardglass formerly gave the title of Earl to the family of Cromwell, and subsequently that of Viscount to the Barringtons.

ARDGUIN, or ARDQUIN, a parish, in the barony of ARDES, county of DOWN, and province of ULSTER, on Lough Strangford, and on the road from Portaferry to Belfast; containing, with part of the post-town of Portaferry, 994 inhabitants. There appears to have been a monastery at this place, founded at a very early period: according to Harris' History of Down it was the priory of Eynes, which, on the authority of a patent roll among the public records, was seized by the crown during the war between England and France, and was granted, in 1411, by Hen. IV. to Thomas Cherele. It afterwards became the chief residence of the bishops of Down, of whom the last that resided here was Dr. Echlin, who was consecrated to the see in 1614. According to the Ordnance survey the parish comprises 3,043 statute acres, of which 80 are under water. The soil, though in some parts interspersed with rocks which rise above the surface, is in general fertile; the lands are in a good state of cultivation; there is neither waste nor bog. Clay-slate is raised for building, and for mending the roads. Portaferry House, the splendid mansion of Col. A. Nugent, is situated in a richly planted demesne, with an extensive park ornamented with stately timber. Here are several mills for flour and oatmeal, and for dressing flax; the situation of the parish on Strangford Lough affords great facility of conveyance by water. A manorial court is held for the recovery of debts not exceeding five marks, with jurisdiction over the whole of the parish. The living is a rectory, in the diocese of Down, held by the bishop, who appoints a curate, for whose stipend he has set apart certain lands belonging to the see. No church appears to have existed here from a period long prior to the Reformation till the year 1829, when the present edifice was erected by Dr. Mant, the present bishop; it is a neat small building with a square tower, and occupies a picturesque situation on an eminence between Lough Strangford and Lough Cowie, which latter is a fresh-water lake of considerable extent. There is neither glebe nor glebe-house; the lands appear to have been granted as mensal lands to the see, and consequently to have been tithe-free; but their exemption is at present a subject of dispute, and the tithes are returned under the composition act as amounting to £289.19.7$\frac{1}{2}$, payable to the bishop. In the R.C. divisions the parish forms part of the union or district of Upper Ardes. There is a Sunday school; also a pay school, in which are about

42 boys and 32 girls. There are considerable remains of the monastery and episcopal palace, which shew that the buildings were originally of very great extent. – See PORTAFERRY.

ARDKEEN, a parish, in the barony of ARDES, county of DOWN, and province of ULSTER, 3 miles (N. by E.) from Portaferry; containing 2176 inhabitants. This place derives its name, originally Ard-Coyne, from its situation on the shores of a lake, which was formerly called Lough Coyne. It was one of the most important strong holds of the ancient Irish, who made it a place of refuge from the violence and rapacity of the Danes, and had a large and well-fortified camp protected on three sides by the sea, with extensive pastures in the rear for their cattle. On this point of land, jutting into the lough and forming a fertile peninsula nearly surrounded by every tide, Raymond Savage, one of the followers of De Courcy, erected a strong castle in 1196, which became the chief residence of that family, whose descendants throughout the whole of the insurrection remained firmly attached to the English monarchs. In 1567, Shane O'Nial, who had overrun and destroyed the neighbouring country on every side, besieged this castle, but was so vigorously repulsed that he retreated with great loss and never penetrated farther southward into the Ardes. The parish comprises, according to the Ordnance survey, 4,800$^1/_2$ statute acres, of which 169 are islands, and 114 are covered with water. The living was formerly a perpetual curacy, in the diocese of Down, and the rectory formed part of the union of Inch and the corps of the prebend of St. Andrew's in the cathedral of Down; but the Ecclesiastical Commissioners having recommended the dissolution of the union on the next avoidance of the prebend, Ardkeen and the northern part of Witter were constituted a distinct rectory, in the patronage of the Bishop, in 1834, by consent of the prebendary, and the perpetual curate was made rector: the tithes amount to £464.18.9. The church is situated on the peninsula and at the extreme western boundary of the parish; it is a small ancient edifice, and contains several monuments to the family of Savage, its original founders. The glebe-house was built at an expense of £500, of which £450 was a gift and £50 a loan from the late Board of First Fruits, in 1816: the glebe comprises 12$^1/_2$ Cunningham acres, valued at £1 per acre and subject to a rent of £4 per annum. In the R.C. divisions this parish is included within the unions or districts of Upper and Lower Ardes: the chapel at Lisbawn is connected with that of Ballygelgat, in the parish of Witter. A school of 76 boys and 84 girls is supported by Col. and Lady H. Forde, who contribute £50 per annum; there are also a Sunday school and a private school. The only remains of the castle are the foundations; the fosses are tolerably perfect, and some of the gardens and orchards may be traced.

BALLEE, or BALLY, a parish, in the barony of LECALE, county of DOWN, and province of ULSTER, 3 miles (S.E. by E.) from Downpatrick, on the road to Ardglass; containing 2,598 inhabitants. It formerly comprised, according to the Ordnance survey, 6,427$^3/_4$ statute acres, of which 6,282 acres were applotted under the tithe act; but the townlands of Jordan's Crew and Kildare's Crew have been severed from it under the Church Temporalities Act, and united to the parish of Ardglass, and Ballystokes has been annexed to Saul, with their tithes and cure of souls; the tithes of Ballyhosit have been also appropriated to the incumbent of Ardglass, but the cure of souls remains to the rector of Ballee. It is wholly under cultivation; the land is very good, and there is neither waste land nor bog. Ballyhosit House, the residence of T. Gracy, Esq., is a large and handsome edifice; Ballee House is in the occupation of R. Stitt, Esq.; the glebe-house is commodious and well built, and there are many other good houses, principally occupied by wealthy farmers. Until lately it formed part of the corps of the deanery of Down, but the union was dissolved under the provisions of the Church Temporalities Act, which came into operation on the 1st of Nov., 1834, and after the preferment of the late dean, when a new arrangement was effected by act of council. The living is now an independent rectory, in the diocese of Down, and in the gift of the Crown. The entire tithes of the parish amounted to £598.14.3, of which, under the new arrangements, £340.13 is payable to the rector of Ballee, subject to a deduction of £25.3 appropriated to the economy fund of the cathedral; and of the remainder, £146 is payable to the dean, £97 to the rector of Ardglass, and £14 to the rector of Saul. The church is a large plain edifice without a tower, built on the foundations of a former structure in 1749. The glebe house was built at an expense of £500, of which £450 was a gift and £50 a loan from the late Board of First Fruits, in 1816; and there is a glebe of seven acres. In the R.C. divisions it is the head of a union or district, which also comprises the parish of Ballyculter, and contains three chapels, situated respectively at Ballycrottle, in Ballee, and at Strangford and Cargagh, in Ballyculter. There is a large meeting-house for Presbyterians in connection with the Remonstrant Synod, of the second class. The parochial school, in which 40 boys and 28 girls are taught, is supported conjointly by the rector and Hugh Johnson, Esq., of London, and there are two others. There are also four private schools, in which are 113 boys and 90 girls. J. Dunn, an eccentric itinerant dealer, by will in 1798, gave £100 in trust to A. Gracy, Esq., who purchased with it a chief-rent at Ballymote, in the parish of Downpatrick, which is divided annually between the Presbyterian poor of Down and Ballee. R. Glenny left £100, the interest to be equally divided among the poor Catholics, Protestants, and Presbyterians of the parish, but it is not now available; and Mrs. Kelly, of Loughkeland, by will in 1805, gave £100 in trust to Mr. Gracy, with which he purchased a house in Downpatrick, now let on lease at an annual rent of £10, which is distributed among the poor at Christmas. Near the mountain of Slieve-na-Gridel, which, according to the Ordnance survey, rises 414 feet above the level of the sea, is a remarkable druidical altar, the table stone of which is 11 feet long and 9 broad; and on the townland of Ballyalton is an ancient burial-ground, in which are some curiously inscribed stones. A splendid golden torques, richly ornamented and set with gems, was found near the glebe in 1834.

BALLINAHINCH, a market and post-town, in the parish of MAGHERADROLL, barony of KINELEARTY, county of DOWN, and province of Ulster, 8 miles (E.) from Dromore, and 74^1/$_2$ (N. by E.) from Dublin; containing 970 inhabitants. This town was founded by Sir George Rawdon, Bart., after the insurrection of 1641, as appears by the patent of Chas. II. granting the manor of Kinelearty to the Rawdon family, which, after reciting that Sir George had built a town and two mills, and had repaired the church, and that a large space had been appropriated for holding markets and fairs, created that manor, with a demesne of 1,000 acres and courts leet and baron, and granted the privilege of a market to be held on Thursday, and two fairs annually. During the disturbances of 1798, the main body of the insurgents, after being repulsed near Saintfield, took post here on Windmill-hill and on some high ground in the demesne of the Earl of Moira, a descendant of Sir G. Rawdon. On the 12th of June, Gen. Nugent marched against them from Belfast with the Monaghan regiment of militia, part of the 22nd dragoons, and some yeomanry infantry and cavalry; and was joined near this place by Lieut. – Col. Stewart with his party from Downpatrick, making in all about 1,500 men. The insurgents were soon driven from their post on the Windmill-hill, and the king's troops set fire to the town. Both parties spent the night in preparations for a general action, which took place at an early hour on the following morning, and was maintained about three hours with artillery, but with little effect. At length the Monaghan regiment of militia, posted with two field-pieces at Lord Moira's gate, was attacked with such determined fury by the pikemen of the insurgents that it fell back in confusion on the Hillsborough cavalry, which retreated in disorder; but these troops having rallied, while the Argyleshire fencibles entering the demesne, were making their attack on another side, the insurgents retired to a kind of fortification on the top of the hill, which for some time they defended with great courage, but at length gave way and dispersed in all directions; the main body fled to the mountains of Slieve Croob, where they soon surrendered or retired to their several homes, and thus was the insurrection terminated in this quarter. The town is situated on the road from Dromore to Saintfield, and consists of a square and four streets, comprising, in 1831, 171 houses, many of which are well built. The market is on Thursday, and is well supplied; and fairs are held on the first Thursday in January, Feb. 12th, March 3rd, April 5th, May 19th, July 10th, Aug. 18th, Oct. 6th, and Nov. 17th. A linen-hall was built by the Earl of Moira, but it has fallen into ruins. Here is a station of the constabulary police. A court for the manor of Kinelearty was formerly held, in which debts to the amount of £10 were recoverable, but it has fallen into disuse. There is a large court-house in the square, built by

Lord Moira in 1795, but now in a dilapidated state. The same nobleman also built a church in 1772, which having fallen into decay was taken down in 1829, and a new edifice was erected on its site, towards which £850 was granted by the late Board of First Fruits; the tower and spire of the old building remain on the west side of the present church. Opposite to it is a spacious R.C. chapel; and there are three places of worship for Presbyterians, one in connection with the Synod of Ulster, and the others in connection with the Seceding Synod. A school for girls is supported by voluntary contributions. In a picturesque and fertile valley, two miles south of the town, is a powerful sulphureous chalybeate spring, which is much resorted to during summer, and has been highly efficacious in scrophulous disorders: there are two wells, one for drinking and the other for bathing, but sufficient accommodation is not provided for the numbers that repair to the spot. – See MAGHERADROLL.

BALLYCULTER, a parish, in the barony of LECALE, county of DOWN, and province of ULSTER; containing, with the post-town of Strangford, 2,221 inhabitants. It is situated on Lough Strangford, and comprises, according to the Ordnance survey, (including islands and detached portions) 5,177^1/$_2$ statute acres, of which 1,753 are applotted under the tithe act; about four-fifths are arable and pasture, and the remainder, excepting about 70 acres of woodland and 40 of water, is wasteland and bog. The soil is very fertile, and the land is in a state of excellent cultivation; a considerable quantity of corn is sent to Liverpool and Glasgow. At Tallyratty are some lead mines, which were worked in 1827, and found very productive; the ore is considered to be of superior quality, but they are not now worked. Castle Ward, the splendid seat of Lord Bangor; Strangford House, the residence of the hon. Harriet Ward; and Strangford Lodge, that of J. Blackwood, Esq., are situated in the parish. The village is neatly built, and is one of the most pleasant in the county. A manor court is held at Strangford every three weeks by the seneschal of the lord of the manor, in whom are vested very extensive privileges; its jurisdiction extends over the parish and the river of Strangford. The living is a rectory, in the diocese of Down, and was formerly annexed to the deanery of Down, from which it was separated in 1834, and made a distinct rectory, in the patronage of the Crown; the tithes amount to £387.15.7. The church, a spacious and handsome structure, was erected in 1723, and a tower and spire were added to it in 1770: the Ecclesiastical Commissioners have lately granted £295 for its repair. There is a chapel at Strangford, the private property of Lord De Roos, of which the rector is chaplain. The glebe-house was built by aid of a gift of £450 and a loan of £50 from the late Board of First Fruits, in 1817: there is a glebe at Strangford, comprising 6a.2r.37p. Lord Bangor is about to build a glebe-house in or near the village for the residence of the rector. In the R.C. divisions the parish forms part of the union or district of Ballee; there arc two chapels, one at Strangford and the other at Cargagh; and there are two places of worship for

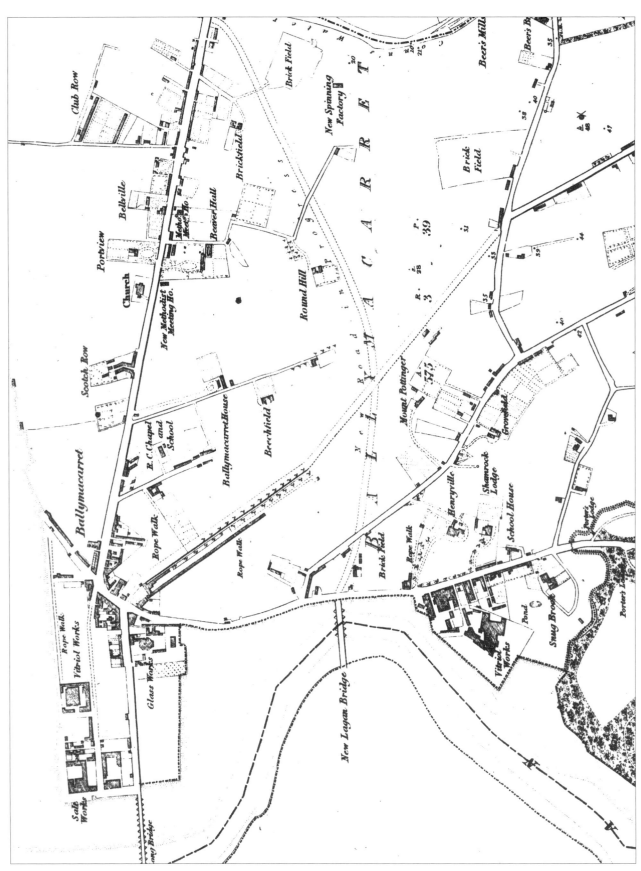

Ballymacarret. Part of 6 inch O.S. map of Co. Down, sheet 4, published 1835 (reproduced at 140%).

16

Wesleyan Methodists. In the village is a handsome school-house, with residences for a master and mistress, built in 1824, and supported by an annual donation of £50 from Lord Bangor, and a small donation from the rector. An infants' school is supported entirely by the Hon. Harriet Ward. These schools afford instruction to about 94 boys and 84 girls; and there are also two pay schools, in which are about 82 boys and 48 girls, and four Sunday schools. Near the church are four handsome alms-houses, built in 1832 at the expense of Lady Sophia Ward, who endowed them with £40 per annum, payable out of the estate of Lord Bangor for ever; the management is vested in three trustees, of whom the rector for the time being is one. Within the parish are three castles erected by De Courcy and his followers after the conquest of Ulster; one is situated close to the quay at Strangford, one on the creek below Castle Ward, and the third is Audley Castle on a rock opposite to Portaferry.

BALLYHALBERT, a parish, in the barony of ARDES, county of DOWN, and province of ULSTER, 3 miles (N.E.) from Kirkcubbin: the population is returned with the union of St. Andrew's. It comprises, according to the Ordnance survey (including islands), 4,012 statute acres. The village, which in 1831 contained 322 inhabitants, is situated on the eastern coast, and on the road from Portaferry to Donaghadee: it contains about 70 houses, and is a coast-guard station, forming one of the twelve which constitute the district of Donaghadee. Off the coast is Burr Island, the most eastern point of land in Ireland. The parish is in the diocese of Down, and is one of the three of which the vicarages were consolidated by the 2nd of Queen Anne into the union of Ballywalter, or vicarage of St. Andrew's; the rectory is appropriate to the Lord. Primate. The tithes amount to £388.2.6, of which £258.15 is payable to the appropriator, and £129.7.6 to the incumbent. On the next avoidance of the benefice of St. Andrew's, this parish will become a separate living, in the patronage of the Lord-Primate. There are some remains of the old church near the village. In the R.C. divisions it forms part of the union or district of Lower Ardes or Ballygelget. There is a place of worship for Presbyterians in connection with the Synod of Ulster; also a school.

BALLYKINDLAR, a parish, in the barony of LECALE, county of DOWN, and province of ULSTER, 3 miles (N.E.) from Clough; the population is returned with the parish of Tyrella. This parish derives its name, signifying the 'Town of the Candlestick,' from the appropriation of its tithes to furnish lights for the cathedral of Christchurch, Dublin. It is situated on the bay of Dundrum, on the eastern coast, and on the road from Newry to Ardglass, and comprises, according to the Ordnance survey, 2,038$^1/_2$ statute acres, the property of the Marquess of Downshire. A considerable portion of the surface consists of sand hills, and the land is in general very indifferent. There was formerly an extensive tract of bog, which was drained in 1819, and is now wholly under cultivation. It is a rectory, in the diocese of Down, entirely appropriate to

the economy funds of the cathedral of Christchurch, Dublin the tithes amount to £54.5.64$^1/_2$. There has been neither church nor incumbent in the parish since the Reformation. On the shore of the inner bay of Dundrum, or Clough bay, are some ruins of the ancient parish church. In the R.C. divisions it is the head of a union or district, also called Tyrella, comprising the parishes of Ballykindlar and Tyrella, and part of Loughin-island, and containing chapels at Ballykindlar and Dromaroad. Near the former is a school-house.

BALLYMACARRETT, a town and parish, forming part of the suburbs of BELFAST, in the barony of UPPER CASTLEREAGH, county of DOWN, and province of ULSTER; containing 5168 inhabitants. This place, previously to 1825, was simply a townland in the parish of Knockbreda, or Bredagh, and in the history of the county, published in 1744, is described as containing only two buildings, Mount Pottinger and a mill. It is now become a populous and flourishing town, occupying a site formerly covered by every tide, but which has been reclaimed by an extensive embankment stretching from Conswater westward to the river Lagan, opposite to the quays of Belfast, and thence on the shore of that river to Ormeau, the splendid residence of the Marquess of Donegal. The town, which in 1831 contained 257 houses, forms an appendage to Belfast, from which it is separated only by the river Lagan, which here separates the counties of Down and Antrim, and over which is a stone bridge of 21 arches: it is irregularly built, but has been greatly improved by the formation of several new streets; and a handsome bridge of five arches, about 400 yards above the long bridge, and opening a more direct communication with the southern part of Belfast, has been lately erected under an act obtained in 1831, at an expense of £6,000, raised in transferable shares of £25 each. The first manufacture established here was that of glass; and since the first glass-house was built, in 1776, two other extensive establishments have been erected, though at present only one is in operation. A pottery upon a very large scale was soon afterwards established; and previously to the removal of the duty on salt, there were two extensive works for the manufacture of that article from rock salt brought from England, for exportation, which are now discontinued. The Lagan foundry, for the manufacture of steam-engines and other machinery on the most improved principles, affords employment to 140 persons: and in 1832 the first patent machine for making paper ever introduced into Ireland was made at these works. A very extensive rope-yard and sail-cloth manufactory, affording employment to 130 persons, are carried on; and two large vitriol works, of which one, established in 1799, was the second erected in the kingdom, are in full operation for supplying the bleachers, dyers, and calico printers in the neighbourhood. There are also extensive starch-manufactories, and meal and flour-mills driven by steam and water; and two large mills for spinning linen yarn were erected in 1834, and employ more than 300 persons. The manufacture of calico and muslin is carried on upon a very extensive scale, affording employment to several hundred persons. Here is a constabulary police station. This place was erected into a parish by an act of the 12th of Geo. III., and comprises 575 statute acres, which are exempt from tithes; about 28¹/₂ acres are under water, and the remainder are arable and pasture. The living is a perpetual curacy, in the diocese of Down, and in the patronage of the Rector of Knockbreda: it is endowed with the tithes of Ballynafeigh, an adjoining townland, amounting to £50, which is augmented from Primate Boulter's fund. The church, a neat building, was erected in 1826 by aid of a grant of £800 from the late Board of First Fruits and by subscription. In the R.C. divisions the parish forms part of the union or district of Belfast, in the diocese of Connor; the chapel was built in 1829. There are places of worship for Presbyterians in connection with the Synod of Ulster and the Seceding Synod, and for Covenanters and Wesleyan Methodists. There are five schools in which about 298 boys and 182 girls are instructed; also three pay schools, in which are about 90 boys and 50 girls.

BALLYPHILIP, a parish, in the barony of ARDES, county of DOWN, and province of ULSTER; containing, with the post-town of Portaferry, 3,090 inhabitants. This parish is situated between Strangford Lough and the eastern coast, and comprises, according to the Ordnance survey, 2,430 statute acres, of which 1839 are applotted under the tithe act. The land is fertile, and, with the exception of about 30 acres of bog, called Ballygaroegan Moss, which supplies the inhabitants with fuel, is in a good state of cultivation. Within its limits is Carney or Kerney Point, off which are two dangerous shoals, called Carney Pladdy and Butter Pladdy. The living is a rectory, in the diocese of Down, with the vicarage of Ballytrustin and the rectories of Slanes and Ardglass united by charter in the 7th of Jas. I., which four parishes constitute the union of Ballyphilip and the corps of the chancellorship of Down, in the patronage of the Bishop the tithes amount to £208.16.9; and the gross income, including tithe and glebe, is £490.10 per annum. The church, situated in the town of Portaferry, is a neat modern edifice, erected in 1787, and has been lately repaired by a grant of £343 from the Ecclesiastical Commissioners. The glebe-house was built in 1818, at an expense of £1,090, of which £825 was a loan from the late Board of First Fruits, and £265 was added by the present incumbent, and is chargeable on his successors. The glebe comprises 15 Cunningham acres, valued at £45 per annum. It was recommended by the Commissioners of Ecclesiastical Inquiry, in 1831, that the parish of Ardglass, being seven miles distant, and in which a perpetual curacy of small value has been erected, should be severed from the union, and an equivalent given to the chancellor. In the R.C. divisions the parish forms part of the unions or districts of Lower and Upper Ardes, which latter is united to part of Ardkeen, Witter, Ballytrustin, Slanes, and Ardguin; there are two chapels, one near Portaferry, a spacious and handsome edifice, and the other at Witter, three miles distant. There are

places of worship at Portaferry for Presbyterians in connection with the Synod of Ulster, of the second class, and for Wesleyan Methodists. A parochial school of 70 boys and 70 girls, at Portaferry, is aided by an annual donation of £30 late currency from Andrew Nugent, Esq., who built the school-house, and by a smaller from the rector; there are also seven pay schools in the parish, in which are about 60 boys and 60 girls. A bequest of £3 per annum to the poor, by one of the Bangor family, is charged on the Castle-Ward estate. An ancient church, which, according to tradition, belonged to a wealthy abbey, formerly occupied the site of the present glebe-house, near which human bones, tombs, and extensive foundations are frequently dug up. Bankmore, a large and perfect rath, and a smaller fort at Ballytrustin, are within the parish. The late Marquess of Londonderry received the rudiments of his education in the glebe-house, under Dr. Sturrock, then chancellor of Down, and incumbent of this parish. – See PORTAFERRY.

BALLYTRUSTIN, a parish, in the barony of ARDES, county of DOWN, and province of ULSTER, 1 mile (S.E.) from Portaferry; containing 735 inhabitants. This parish, which is not noticed in the Down survey, is situated on the eastern coast; it comprises, according to the Ordnance survey, including detached portions, 1,681³/₄ statute acres. The soil is fertile, and the lands are all in an excellent state of cultivation, producing abundant crops. It is a vicarage, in the diocese of Down, and is part of the union of Ballyphilip and corps of the chancellorship of Down; the rectory is impropriate in John Echlin, Esq. The tithes amount to £190.4.2¹/₂ of which £117.14.5. is payable to the impropriator, and £72.9.9¹/₂ to the vicar. There are some remains of the ancient church, and the churchyard is the chief burial-place of the R.C. parishioners. In the R.C. divisions it forms part of each of the unions or districts of Lower and Upper Ardes. At Kerney is a school of 100 boys and 80 girls, aided by subscription and an annual donation of £8 from Dr. Blacker, on whose estate the school-house was erected by a grant of £100 from the Lord-Lieutenant's fund. At Ballyfounder is a very large rath, nearly perfect.

BALLYWALTER, or WHITECHURCH, a parish, in the barony of ARDES, county of DOWN, and province of ULSTER, 4 miles (N.E.) from Kirkcubbin: the population is returned with the union of St. Andrew's. This parish is situated on the eastern coast, and with a detached portion comprises, according to the Ordnance survey, 3,379 statute acres. The village, which in 1831 contained 664 inhabitants, is situated in lat. 54° 32′ 20″ (N.), and lon. 5° 28′ (W.), and is a coast-guard station, forming one of the twelve that constitute the district of Donaghadee. It is a vicarage, in the diocese of Down, and is part of the union of Ballywalter or St. Andrew's; the rectory is appropriate to the Lord-Primate. The tithes amount to £339.18.1, of which £226.12.1 is payable to the Lord-Primate, and £113.6 to the incumbent. On the next avoidance of the benefice of St. Andrew's, this parish will become a separate living, in the patronage of the Lord-Primate. In the R.C. divisions it forms part of the union or district of Lower Ardes. There are two places of worship for Presbyterians in connection with the Synod of Ulster. Some ruins of the old church yet exist.

BANBRIDGE, a market and post-town, in the parish of SEAPATRICK, barony of UPPER IVEAGH, county of DOWN, and province of ULSTER, 10 miles (N.N.E.) from Newry, and 60 miles (N.) from Dublin; containing 2,469 inhabitants, but since the last census the population has much increased. This flourishing town was anciently called Ballyvally, and acquired its present name from the erection of a bridge over the Bann in 1712, on the formation of a new line of road from Dublin to Belfast. The old road passed a little to the north of it, and crossed the Bann at Huntley Glen by a ford, through which the army of Wm. III.passed on the 11th of June, 1690, on its march to the Boyne. It is situated on both sides of the river, and in 1831 contained 446 houses, many of which are handsome and well built; the larger portion is on the western side, on an eminence sloping to the river, and communicating with the smaller by the bridge, which is a handsome structure of hewn granite: the streets are wide, and the entire town wears an aspect of neatness and comfort surpassed by few places in this part of the country. In the centre of the principal street to the west of the river formerly stood the market-house, a large and inconvenient building, which was taken down in 1832 to make way for a series of improvements. Prior to that period the street was very steep and difficult of access; but an excavation, 200 yards long and 15 feet deep, has been made along its centre, crossed by a handsome viaduct of one elliptic arch of hewn granite, under which the mail coaches and other vehicles pass. The street being very wide, a carriage road was left on each side of the excavation, running parallel with it and on a level with the ground floors of the houses, shops, and public buildings: these side roads are protected throughout their entire length by a stone wall rising from the bottom of the excavation to the height of three feet above their level. The excavation interrupts the communication between the houses on the opposite sides of the street; but the viaduct being placed at the intersection of the streets obviates that inconvenience. This great undertaking was completed in 1834, at an expense, including the erection of the viaduct and the formation of its approaches, of £19,000.

The town is comparatively of modern origin, and has risen with uncommon rapidity to an eminent degree of commercial importance as the head of the principal district of the linen manufacture. Even when almost every port was closed against the introduction of Irish linens, and the trade was nearly lost to the country, those of Banbridge found a ready market; and when the energies of the linen merchant on the old system were nearly paralysed by foreign competition, the merchants of this place created a new trade, by commencing as manufacturers on an extensive scale, and opening an intercourse with America and other parts. The numerous falls

on the river and the uniform supply of water appear to have attracted the attention of the manufacturers soon after bleaching became a separate branch of the trade; and shortly after the application of machinery to this department, several mills were erected on its banks, mostly on a small scale, as the process at that time was very tedious and every web of considerable value. Although a formidable barrier to enterprise resulted from the unsettled state of the country, and the system of selling only through the factors in Dublin restricted the operations of the trade and regulated the prices, the linen merchants of this district seem to have gradually prospered, as, in 1772, there were no less than 26 bleach-greens on the Bann river. At that time, however, the trade was principally carried on at Gilford, and the webs were mostly marked as 'Gilford linens,' and, after the introduction of linen seals, were nearly all sealed there. The Dromore merchants also transacted an important business; the liner fabrics had even acquired the name of 'Dromores,' and a great quantity of the higher numbers is still woven in and around that town, but principally for the Banbridge manufacturers. At present comparatively very little business is done at either of those places, the entire trade of this part of the country having concentrated itself in the vicinity of Banbridge, which has thus become one of the most important inland manufacturing towns in Ireland. Linen of every description is manufactured and bleached in the neighbourhood: at Brookfield, Huntly Glen, Seapatrick, Millmount, Ballydown, and Ashfield are manufacturers on a large scale, for whom more than 66,000 webs are annually finished, comprising linens of various quality, sheeting, diapers, damasks, drills, cambrics, &c., by a vast number of weavers, who work in their own dwellings and are dispersed over the surrounding parishes. There are very extensive bleach-greens at Ballievey, Ballydown, Clibborn Vale, Millmount, Milltown, Springvale, Mill-Park, Hazelbank, Banford, and Mountpleasant, where 185,710 webs were bleached and finished in 1834, being nearly equal to the entire quantity bleached in this county at the end of the last century. At Seapatrick is an extensive establishment for weaving union cloths by machinery, in which are employed 100 power-looms impelled by a water-wheel 15 feet in diameter and 22 feet broad on the face. There are also very large thread manufactories for home consumption and exportation at Huntley Glen, Milltown, and Banbridge; a mill for spinning linen yarn at Coose, and adjoining it, chemical works for the supply of the bleachers. These different establishments provide employment for more than 2,000 persons connected with this branch of the linen trade alone. Branches of the Provincial Bank of Ireland and of the Northern and Belfast banking companies have been established here. The situation of the town on the great north road to Belfast, and in the centre of a fertile and highly cultivated district watered by the Bann, is very advantageous to its interests. It is within three miles of the Newry and Lough Neagh canal, to which a branch may be formed at little expense; this improvement appears

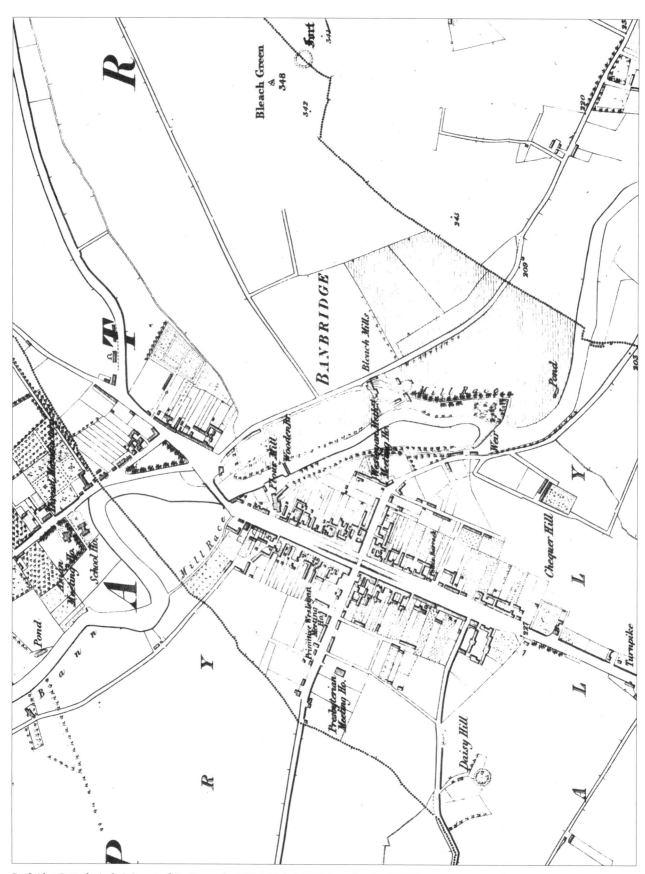

Banbridge. Part of 6 inch O.S. map of Co. Down, sheet 27, published 1835 (reproduced at 140%).

to have been at one period contemplated, from an excavation which is still traceable from Millmount down the valley on the south side of the Bann. Within an extent of four miles there are six good stone bridges over the Bann, besides several of wood: in 1690 there was not one bridge over this river throughout its entire course of 36 miles, from the mountains of Mourne to Lough Neagh. The Marquess of Downshire is proprietor of the town and a large tract of land in its vicinity. The principal seats in the neighbourhood are Ballievey House, the residence of G. Crawford, Esq.; Ballyvalley, of the Rev. J. Davis; Millmount, of R. Hayes, Esq.; Brookfield, of Brice Smyth, Esq.; Huntley Glen, of Hugh Dunbar, Esq.; the glebe-house, of the Rev. D. Dickinson; Edenderry, of W.A. Stewart, Esq.; Seapatrick House, of F. W. Hayes, Esq.; Lenaderg Cottage, of T. Weir, Esq.; and Banview, of G. Little, Esq. There are also several large and handsome houses in the town, the residences of wealthy merchants and professional gentlemen; and the farm-houses in the vicinity are built in a superior style of convenience and comfort. The market is on Monday, and is abundantly supplied with all kinds of provisions, and with pedlery and other commodities: the sale of yarn and brown linens, formerly very extensive, has declined since the new system of spinning and manufacturing was established, but considerable quantities of both are still disposed of. The market-house, situated in the centre of the town, close to the viaduct is a large and handsome edifice surmounted by a dome, and was built by the Marquess of Downshire in 1834, at an expense of £2,000: a brown linen hall was also erected by him in 1817, and a market-place for meal and grain in 1815. Fairs are held on the first Monday in every month; and fairs for horses, cattle, sheep, pigs, and manufactured goods are held on Jan. 12th, first Saturday in March, June 9th, August 26th, and Nov. 16th; the last is a very noted fair for horses. Petty sessions are held once a fortnight, and here is a chief station of the constabulary police.

The parochial church, situated in this town, is a handsome cruciform edifice, with a tower surmounted by a spire, recently built at an expense of about £3,000, which was chiefly raised by subscriptions among the more wealthy parishioners. Near it is a large and handsome meeting-house, recently completed for Presbyterians in connection with the Remonstrant Synod, and of the first class, in lieu of an old one erected in 1720: and there are also one for Presbyterians in connection with the Synod of Ulster, of the third class, and, at a short distance from the town, one for Seceders; besides a place of worship each for Wesleyan and Primitive Methodists. A school, in which about 60 boys and 50 girls are taught, is endowed with £50 per ann. and 1½ acre of land: the school premises, including residences for the master and mistress, were built by subscription, towards which the Marquess of Downshire contributed £90. Here is also a dispensary. Within half a mile from the town, on the Dromore road, a sulphureous chalybeate spring has been lately discovered, the water of which having been analysed is found to equal that of Aix la Chapelle, and is efficacious in scorbutic complaints. This is the birth-place of the late Baron McClelland, third baron of the Exchequer; and near the town was born Dr. Dickson, Bishop of Down and Connor. – See SEAPATRICK.

BANGOR, a sea-port, incorporated market and post-town, and a parish, partly in the barony of LOWER CASTLEREAGH, but chiefly in that of ARDES, county of DOWN, and province of ULSTER, 11½ miles (N.E. by E.) from Belfast, 21 miles (N.) from Downpatrick, and 91½ miles (N. by E.) from Dublin; containing 9,355 inhabitants, of which number, 2,741 are in the town. The origin and early history of this ancient town are involved in some obscurity, and have been variously described by different writers. The most authentic records concur in stating that, about the year 555, St. Comgall founded here an abbey of Regular Canons, which may have led to the formation of a town, if one did not exist previously, and over which he presided fifty years, and died and was enshrined in it. Some time subsequently to the foundation of the abbey, a school was established here under the personal direction of St. Carthagus, which in progress of time became one of the most eminent seminaries in Europe, and was resorted to by numbers of young persons of distinction from various parts and, according to some writers, when Alfred founded or restored the university of Oxford, he sent to the great school at Bangor for professors. In 613 the town was destroyed by fire, and in 674 the abbey was burnt. In the beginning of the ninth century they suffered severely from the predatory incursions of the Danes, in one of which, about the year 818, these merciless marauders massacred the abbot and about 900 monks. In 1125 it was rebuilt by Malachy O'Morgair, then abbot with the addition of an oratory of stone, said by St. Bernard to have been the first building of stone and lime in Ireland; and from which this place, anciently called the 'Vale of Angels,' derived the name of Beanchoir, now Bangor, signifying the 'White Church,' or 'Fair Choir.' Malachy was soon afterwards appointed to the see of Connor, and held with it the abbacy of Bangor till his preferment to the archbishoprick of Armagh. The abbey continued to flourish and was endowed

Bangor Castle. Drawn by J.H. Burgess and engraved by Evans. From S.C. Lewis, Ireland: its scenery, character, &c., *vol.3 (London, 1846).*

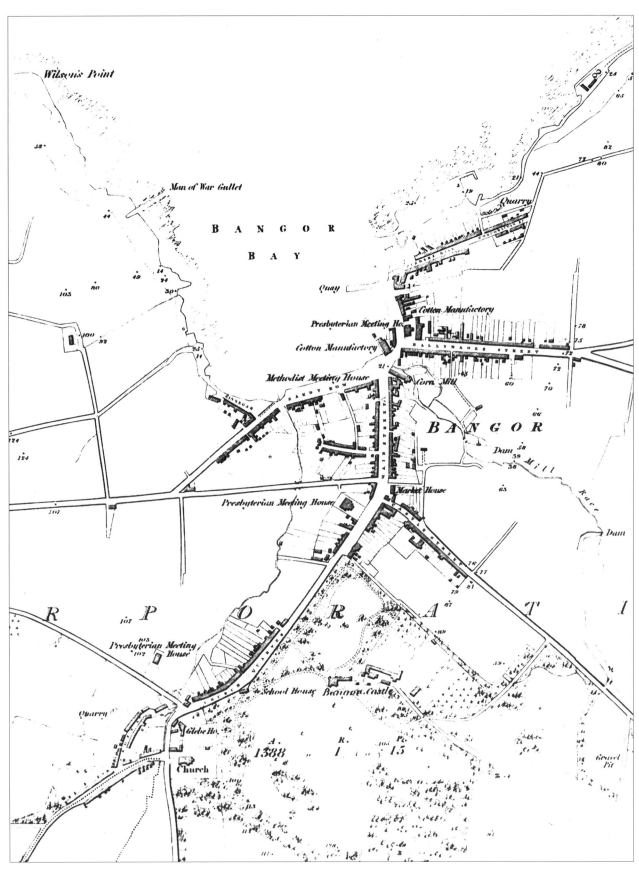

Bangor. Part of 6 inch O.S. map of Co. Down, sheet 2, published 1835 (reproduced at 140%).

with extensive possessions, which after the conquest were considerably augmented by the kings of England: amongst its lands was a townland in the Isle of Man, called Clenanoy, which the abbot held on the singular condition of attending the king of that island at certain times. In 1469, the buildings having fallen into decay through the abbot's neglect, Pope Paul II. transferred the possession of the abbey from the Regular Canons to the Franciscans, who continued to hold it till the dissolution. After that period, a great part of its lands was either granted to or seized by the O'Nials, who kept possession till the rebellion of Con O'Nial in the reign of Elizabeth, when it was forfeited to the Crown. Jas. I., on his accession to the throne, found the northern part of Ireland in a deplorable condition, and almost depopulated; and in the third year of his reign, resolving to plant English and Scottish colonies in Ulster, granted the site of the abbey, with all its former possessions in this county, to Sir James Hamilton, afterwards created Viscount Claneboye, who brought over a large number of Scots from Dunlop in Ayrshire, accompanied by their own minister, Robert Blair, who, although a Presbyterian, was presented to the church living of Bangor, and ordained in 1623 according to the Presbyterian form, the Bishop of Down officiating as a presbyter: he was afterwards appointed Scottish chaplain to Chas. I. From him were descended Robert Blair, of Athelstoneford, author of a poem called 'The Grave;' and the celebrated Hugh Blair, D.D., of Edinburgh, the former his grandson and the latter his great-grandson. From Sir J. Hamilton are descended, either lineally or collaterally, the families of Bangor, Dufferin, Killileigh, and some others of principal note in Ulster. In 1689, the advanced army of Wm. III. arrived here in seventy sail of transports under the command of Duke Schomberg, and disembarked at Groomsport, a fishing village about a mile from the town, where they encamped for the night; being well received and finding plenty of provisions, the transports, which had been furnished with supplies, sailed back to Chester for a reinforcement of troops.

The town is advantageously situated on the south side of Belfast Lough or Carrickfergus bay, and on the direct sea coast road from Belfast to Donaghadee; in 1831 it contained 563 houses, most of which are indifferently built, and is much frequented for sea-bathing during the summer. The streets are neither paved nor lighted, but are kept very clean; and the inhabitants are but indifferently supplied with water. There is a public library; and an Historical Society has been recently formed in connection with it. The cotton manufacture is carried on to a considerable extent in the town and neighbourhood, and affords employment to a great number of the inhabitants of both sexes in the weaving, sewing, and ornamental branches. It was first established here in the finer branches between the years 1783 and 1786, by the late George Hannay, who, if not the first, was at least one of the first persons who introduced that department of the manufacture into the North of Ireland. Two spinning factories were

subsequently erected under the patronage of the late Rt. Hon. Col. R. Ward, who constantly resided here and took an active interest in the improvement of the town; one was built by two gentlemen from Scotland in 1800: who conducted it till 1813, when it was purchased by a company, who kept the concern in full work till 1826, when it became the property of one of the partners, who now retains it: the other, in which Col. Ward held a share, and of which, on the dissolution of the partnership by the death of Mr. Hannay, he became sole proprietor, was built in 1804. The number of persons of both sexes constantly employed in these two factories varies from 260 to 280: those engaged in the weaving and sewing branches of the trade being dispersed over the parish, as well as resident in and immediately around the town, cannot so easily be enumerated. Many operatives from Belfast find employment; and agents have been commissioned by the Glasgow merchants to get goods manufactured here, from the superior manner in which the weaving and sewing are executed. The linen trade is also carried on to a limited extent, chiefly for home consumption. The trade of the port is inconsiderable: black cattle, horses, grain, and flax are exported: the only imports are coal and timber. The bay is well sheltered, and affords good anchorage in deep water for vessels detained by an unfavourable wind; and the harbour is capable of great improvement, although attempts made at the expense of individuals have failed. A small pier was built about the year 1760, by means of a parliamentary grant of £500 to the corporation for promoting and carrying on the inland navigation of Ireland. The market is on Tuesday, but is not well attended: the market-house was built of late years by the lords of the manor. Fairs for black cattle, horses, and pedlery are held on Jan. 12th, May 1st, Aug. 1st, and Nov. 22nd. The only toll or custom which appears to have been ever paid was that of the 'tongues' of cattle slaughtered in the market, which was claimed by the provost, but has been relinquished. The mail coach runs daily to and fromBelfast. A constabulary police force, and an establishment of the coast-guard in connection with the Donaghadee district, are stationed here.

The inhabitants were incorporated by charter of the 10th of Jas. I. (1613), under the style of 'The Provost, Free Burgesses, and Commonalty of the Borough of Bangor:' the corporation under the charter consists of a provost, 12 other free burgesses, and an unlimited number of freemen, with two serjeants-at-mace, but of whom only one town-serjeant is now appointed. The provost is elected from and by the free burgesses annually on the Feast of St. John (June 24th), and is sworn into office at Michaelmas; and the free burgesses are appointed during good behaviour, as vacancies occur, by a majority of the provost and remaining free burgesses: there is no separate class of freemen distinct from the free burgesses. The borough returned two members to the Irish -parliament until the Union, when the £15,000 granted in compensation for the abolition of its franchise was awarded in moieties to Henry Thomas, Earl of Carrick, and the trustees of the estate of

Nicholas, Viscount Bangor: the right of election was confined to the provost and free burgesses, and the provost was the returning officer. The charter constituted the provost clerk of the market and judge of a borough court of record, to be held every Saturday, with jurisdiction in personal actions to the amount of five marks; but it does not appear that this court has ever been held. Petty sessions are held once a fortnight, and a manorial court every third Thursday before the seneschal, with jurisdiction to the amount of £20, late currency: the proceedings are by attachment or civil bill. A court leet is held by the seneschal once a year, at which constables for the several townlands in the manor are appointed. The manor is held in moieties by Viscount Bangor and a member of the same family, Mr. Ward, a minor, who is the representative of the Earl of Carrick, a former proprietor. The property of the corporation consists of several plots of ground lying in various directions around the town, and containing altogether 59a. 1r. and 18p., now occupied in very small lots and at low rents by 43 tenants, and producing a gross rental of £52.13.2 per annum, which is generally applied to public and useful objects. The limits of the borough include the town and a small surrounding district, locally termed 'the corporation,' the exact boundaries of which are uncertain.

The parish is bounded on the north by the bay of Belfast, on the east by the Northern channel, on the south by the parishes of Donaghadee and Newtownardes, and on the west by that of Hollywood. It contains the Copeland islands, including which it comprises, according to the Ordnance survey, 17,027 statute acres, of which 12,597$\frac{1}{4}$ are in the barony of Ardes; the greater part is good arable and pasture land, mostly in excellent cultivation, especially the extensive estate of Portavo, and there are several others in the parish little inferior to it in point of husbandry; the farm-buildings are neat and comfortable, and the peasantry are of moral and very industrious habits. The first Parochial Ploughing Society in Ireland was established here in 1816, by the exertions and under the patronage of J. Rose Clealand, Esq., from which may be dated the origin of the North-east Farming Society and the commencement of agricultural improvement in the North of Ireland. Bangor moss is now nearly exhausted, and is gradually being brought into cultivation; but there is a large extent of bog called Cotton, and in the townland of Ballow is a small bog, in which were found the skeletons of several elks, the head of one of which, with the antlers, measuring nine feet from tip to tip, is preserved in the Royal Institution at Belfast. Several streams on which are corn and flax-mills intersect the parish, and there are three windmills for corn. The neighbouring bays produce a variety of fish; oysters of large size are taken in abundance. The surrounding scenery is pleasingly diversified, and enriched in some parts with stately timber, chiefly fir and oak; and in the vicinity of the several gentlemen's seats are thriving plantations of beech, sycamore, ash and poplar, of comparatively modern growth. The principal seats are Ballyleidy, that of Lord Dufferin, a handsome and spacious mansion pleasantly situated in a rich and extensive demesne; Bangor Castle, late the seat of the Rt. Hon. Col. Ward, surrounded with extensive grounds tastefully laid out; Crawfordsburn, of W. Sharman Crawford, Esq., M.P., pleasantly situated on the shore; Portavo, of D. Kerr, Esq., in a well-planted and richly cultivated demesne; and Ballow, of W. Steele Nicholson, Esq., and Rath-Gael House, of J. Rose Cleland, Esq., both embellished with thriving plantations. Slate is found in several pans, but has been only procured in one quarry, which has not been worked sufficiently deep to produce a quality capable of resisting the action of the atmosphere. There are also mines of coal, especially on the estate of Lord Dufferin, whose father opened and worked them on a small scale, since which time they have been abandoned; and a lead mine was worked here to some extent about thirty years since, in which copper ore and manganese were also found.

The living is an impropriate curacy, in the diocese of Down, and in the alternate patronage of Viscount Bangor and – Ward, Esq., in whom the rectory is impropriate. The parish is tithe-free, except two townlands, the property of Lord Dufferin, which pay tithe amounting to £52.6.9; the curacy is endowed with a money payment of £55.7.8 per ann. by the impropriators. The church was built near the site of the old abbey, in 1623, and a very neat tower and spire were subsequently added to it by a bequest of the late A. Moore, Esq., of Tyrone. In attempting to enlarge it, in 1832, the foundation was so much disturbed by injudicious excavations that it was found necessary to take it down, with the exception of the tower; and a spacious and handsome structure, in the later style of English architecture, was erected in the following year, at an expense of £935, which was defrayed by the parishioners, aided by subscriptions to a considerable amount from some of the landed proprietors. There is a very good glebe-house, with a glebe of 12 Cunningham acres. In the R.C. divisions this parish forms part of the union or district of Newtownardes; but there is no chapel within its limits. There are two meeting-houses for Presbyterians, the first was built originally about the year 1650, by a congregation which began the erection of a new and beautiful building in 1831, and the other was built in 1829 by a new congregation: they are both in connection with the Synod of Ulster, and one is of the first and the other of the third class. The Primitive and Wesleyan Methodists have also each a place of worship. A school for girls and an infants' school are supported by the executors of the late Col. Ward; an infants' school is also supported by Mrs. Trench; at Ballyleidy is a school for girls, founded and supported by Lady Dufferin; a school for boys and girls at Crawfordsburn built in 1832, by the late Lord Dufferin, is supported with a bequest by the late Mr. John McGowan and other contributors; and there are two national schools at Crawfordsburn and Conlig, besides six other schools in the parish, aided by subscriptions. In these schools are about 460 boys and 340 girls, many of the latter of whom are clothed in each under the benevolent patronage of Lady Dufferin; and there are also eight private pay schools, in which are about 120 boys and 50 girls, and eleven Sunday schools. The first Sunday school in Ireland was formed at Rath-Gael in 1788, by J.R. Cleland, Esq. Here is a dispensary; a mendicity society is supported by subscription, and there are a friendly society and a savings' bank. Adjoining the town is a property called 'Charity Lands,' let for £42.11.1 per annum, which is applied towards the support of some of the above institutions and other charitable purposes. Of the ancient abbey there is only a small fragment remaining in part of the garden wall of the glebe-house. Near the quay is an old building supposed to have been used as a custom-house, the tower of which has been converted into dwelling-houses. Vestiges of 25 raths and forts may he traced in the parish; the largest was Rath Gael, or 'fort of the strangers,' which extended over more than two acres and was encompassed by a double vallum; part of it is now occupied by the plantations and house of that name. Druidical relics have been frequently found in various parts of the parish. Christian O'Conarchy, the first abbot of Mellifont, was born at or near this place; he was consecrated Bishop of Lismore about the year 1150, and was constituted the pope's legate in Ireland; he died in 1186. William Hamilton, a very ingenious poet, was also born here in 1704; his works were printed in 12mo. at Edinburgh, in 1760, eight years after his death. Bangor gives the titles of Viscount and Baron to the family of Ward, to whom the town and a considerable portion of the parish belong.

BRIGHT, a parish, in the barony of LECALE, county of DOWN, and province of ULSTER, 3 miles (S. by E.) from Downpatrick; containing 2,030 inhabitants. This parish is situated on the road from Downpatrick to Killough, and comprises, according to the Ordnance survey, 5,544¼ statute acres, of which 5,503 are applotted under the tithe act. The land, with a trifling exception, is all in an excellent state of cultivation, and there is neither waste land nor bog. Oakley, the handsome residence of J. Birney, Esq., is situated in a fertile demesne of 168 acres, tastefully disposed and embellished with some of the finest timber in the county. The parish was formerly one of the six which constituted the union and the corps of the deanery of Down, from which it was separated by act of council in 1834, when, with the townland of Carradressy, which formerly belonged to Kilclief but was annexed to Bright by the same act, it was constituted a separate and distinct parish. The living is a rectory, in the diocese of Down, and in the patronage of the Crown: the tithes amount to £583.18.9. The church, a small edifice in the Grecian style, erected in 1745, is situated on the summit of an eminence, and is an excellent landmark for mariners: it contains an elegant monument to the memory of Lord Lecale. There is neither glebe-house nor glebe. In the R.C. divisions it is the head of a union or district, comprising also the parish of Rathmullen, and containing three chapels, situated respectively at Conierstown in Bright, and at Killough and

Rossglass in Rathmullen. Here is a school of about 80 boys and 50 girls, for which a school-house in the churchyard was built by subscription; also a pay school, in which are about 20 boys and 20 girls. Near the church are the ruins of Bright castle; and about a mile and a quarter to the west are those of Castle Screen, built within the area of a Danish rath, near which are the remains of the ancient abbey of Erynagh, founded by Magnell Makenlefe, King of Ulster, Sept. 8th, 1126 or 1127. This abbey was garrisoned against De Courcy in 1177, who, for that reason, levelled it with the ground and transferred its possessions to the abbey of Inch, which he subsequently founded in the Isle of Inis Courcy, on the ruins of a pagan temple. A circle of upright stones and other Druidical remains are still existing near the spot.

BRYANSFORD, a village, in the parish of KILCOO, barony of UPPER IVEAGH, county of DOWN, and province of LSTER, 2½ miles (S.) from Castlewellan containing 185 inhabitants. This village, which is situated on the road from Newry to Newcastle, contains about 30 houses neatly built, chiefly in the Elizabethan style, the gardens in front of which give it a comfortable and rural appearance, and the surrounding scenery is agreeably diversified. Tollymore Park, the seat of the Earl of Roden, is a beautiful residence situated in extensive grounds embellished with some of the finest larch trees in the country; it is approached by three noble entrances, called respectively the barbican, the central, and the hilltown; the central entrance from the village is through a very lofty archway, and in the lodge is kept a book for entering the names of visiters; the grounds are always open to the public. There is a good inn and posting-house, with every accommodation for families. The parish church of Kilcoo, a spacious edifice with a lofty embattled tower, is situated in the village; and at a short distance to the north of it is a R.C. chapel, belonging to the union of Bryansford or Lower Kilcoo; it is a neat edifice in the later English style, erected in 1831 at an expense of £900, on a site given by the Earl of Roden. A school for boys, built in 1826, is supported by the same nobleman; and

Bryansford House. From The Dublin Penny Journal, *vol.2, 1834.*

adjoining it is a circulating library also maintained by the Earl and gratuitously open to all the people of the village: there is a female school, built in 1822 and supported wholly by the Countess of Roden. – See KILCOO.

CASTLEBUOY, or ST. JOHNSTOWN, an extra-parochial liberty, in the barony of ARDES, county of DOWN, and province of ULSTER, 3 miles (N.E.) from Portaferry; containing 744 inhabitants. This place is situated on Cloghy bay, and, according to the Ordnance survey, comprises 1,358¼ statute acres. A commandery or preceptory of St. John the Baptist of Jerusalem, dependent on the priory of Kilmainham, was founded here by Hugh de Lacy, in 1189, which continued till the commencement of the fifteenth century; the building is now in ruins, and the family of Echlin possesses several townlands in freehold which have always enjoyed exemption from tithe and church cess, and also a manor which belonged to the commandery, the court of which is now held once in three weeks. The manor is called Cloghy, and the court has jurisdiction over the liberty of Castlebuoy, the parishes of Slanes and Ballytrustin, and part of Witter, and any sum not exceeding £5 is recoverable in it, either by attachment or civil bill process. The lofty tower of the castle and ruins of the church are situated in one of the most secluded and fertile

vales in the Ardes. On a chain of rock in the channel, three miles east from the shore, is the South Rock or Kilwarlin lighthouse. There is a private school, in which are about 70 boys and 60 girls.

CASTLEWELLAN, a market and post town, in that part of the parish of KILMEGAN which is in the barony of UPPER IVEAGH, county of DOWN, and province of ULSTER, 9 miles (W.S.W.) from Downpatrick, and 64¾ (N. by E.) from Dublin; containing 729 inhabitants. This place is situated on the mail coach road from Newry to Downpatrick, on the side of a small lake, and though partly surrounded by mountains, occupies rather a conspicuous site. The town is well built, and consists principally of an upper and lower square connected by a street, containing 122 houses, most of which are neat structures. There are barracks for two companies of infantry, a detachment from the military depot at Newry, usually stationed here. The bleaching of linen, which is the principal trade of the place, was first introduced here by Mr. Moffat, in 1749, since which time it has greatly increased, and several large bleach-greens have been established. Those of Messrs. Murland are capable of bleaching and finishing 20,000 pieces annually, and those of Mr. Steel, 8,000; a large propor tion of the linen is sent to the American and West India markets, the

Narrow Water. Drawn by R.O'C Newenham and engraved by J.D. Harding. From R.O'C Newenham, Picturesque views of the antiquities of Ireland, *vol.1, (London, 1830).*

remainder to England and Scotland. There is an extensive mill for spinning linen-yarn, erected in 1829, and the first for fine yarns ever established in Ireland; it is worked by steam and water power, and lighted with gas made on the premises; another is in course of erection on a very large scale, to be propelled by a water wheel 50 feet in diameter and 10 feet on the face. In these several establishments more than 500 persons are constantly employed. The manufacture of linen is also extensively carried on by Mr. J. Murland and Mr. Steel, the former employing 450 and the latter 300 persons. There are also some large corn-mills, and mills for dressing flax. The market is on Monday, and is amply supplied with provisions and pedlery, and large quantities of brown linen and linen-yarn are brought for sale every market day. Fairs are held on the first of February, May, June, and September, the 13th of November, and the Tuesday before Christmas. The market-house, situated in the centre of the upper square, is a neat building, with a belfry and clock, surmounted by a spire. A constabulary police force is stationed here; a manorial court, having jurisdiction over nine towalands in this parish and that of Drumgooland, is held every three weeks, in which debts to the amount of £10 are recoverable; and petty sessions are also held in the market-house every alternate Tuesday. Divine service, according to the rites of the Church of England, is performed every Sunday in the market-house. There are also in the town a R.C. chapel and places of worship for Presbyterians and Wesleyan Methodists. A school-house was built and endowed by J. Murland, Esq., for the gratuitous instruction of children of both sexes; and a school is supported by Earl Annesley. At the foot of Slieve-na-lat, and on the border of the lake, is an elegant cottage, built by Earl Annesley, and ornamented with gardens and pleasure grounds tastefully laid out, in which is a temple, commanding a fine view of the surrounding scenery. Earl Annesley enjoys the inferior title of Baron of Castlewellan, in the peerage of Ireland. – See KILMEGAN.

CLONALLON, a parish, in the barony of UPPER IVEAGH, county of DOWN, and province of ULSTER, 6 miles (S.S.E.) from Newry; containing, with the town and district parish of Warrenspoint, 8,630 inhabitants. This parish is situated on the bay of Carlingford, by which it is bounded on the south and west, and on the road from Newry to Rosstrevor, and comprises, according to the Ordnance survey, 11,658^1/$_4$ statute acres, of which about 200 acres are woodland, 150 bog, 200 mountain (including about 100 acres of bog on the summit), and 173^1/$_2$ under water; of the remainder, nearly two-thirds are arable and one-third pasture. A very extensive and lucrative oyster fishery is carried on, employing a great number of boats, and herrings are occasionally taken in large quantities. The gentlemen's seats are Narrow Water House, the residence of R. Hall, Esq., a splendid mansion of hewn granite quarried upon the estate, and built in the Elizabethan style; Drumaul Lodge, that of James Robinson, Esq.; and Clonallon House, that of the Rev. J. Davis. The living is a rectory and vicarage, in

the diocese of Dromore, united by charter of the 7th of Jas. I. to the rectory of Drumgath, together constituting the union of Clonallon and the corps of the chancellorship of Dromore, in the patronage of the Bishop: the tithes amount to £450, and the gross annual value of the benefice, tithe, and glebe included, is £961.10. The parish church is a very ancient edifice in good repair, and a church has been recently erected at Warrenspoint, which has been made a district curacy. The glebe-house is situated on a glebe of 190 acres of profitable land, valued at £339.10 per annum. The Ecclesiastical Commissioners have recommended the dissolution of the union on the miext avoidance, leaving Clonallon alone as the corps of the chancellorship. The R.C. parish is co-extensive with that of the Established Church; there are three chapels, situated respectively at Mayo, Burn, and Warrenspoint. There are a handsome new meeting-house for Presbyterians in connection with the Synod of Ulster, one for those in connection with the Remonstrant Synod, and one each for Wesleyan and Primitive Methodists. The parochial school is aided by the rector; and at Mayo is a national school, in which together are about 140 boys and 80 girls; and there is an infants' school of 30 boys and 40 girls. Here are the ruins of a square castle. Close to the ferry of Narrow Water, Hugh de Lacy, Earl of Ulster and lord-deputy of Ireland, built a castle in 1212, which remained entire till 1641; but the present remains are more probably those of a castle erected by the Duke of Ormonde in 1663. Not far distant was a small spot surrounded by the sea, called Nuns' Island, on which were formerly considerable ruins; but the embankment now in progress for defending the channel has obliterated every vestige of them; they were probably the ruins of a religious establishment, which gave name to the island, or perhaps those of the castle of De Lacy.

CLONDUFF, or CLANDUFF, a parish, in the barony of UPPER IVEAGH, county of DOWN, and province of ULSTER, 2^3/$_4$ miles (S.) from Rathfriland; containing, with the village of Hilltown, 7,916 inhabitants. This parish is situated on the river Bann, and on one of the roads leading from Newry to Downpatrick; and comprises, according to the Ordnance survey, 21,241^3/$_4$ statute acres, of which 889 are mountain, with a portion of bog, and the remainder good arable and pasture land, the former producing excellent crops. Eagle mountain, at the southern extremity of the parish, is 1084 feet above the level of the sea. The gentlemen's seats are King's Hill, the residence of W. Barron, Esq.; Cabra, the property of A. McMullan, Esq., recently erected on the site of the ancient residence of the Mac Gennis family; and Hilltown Parsonage, the residence of the Rev J.A. Beers. About a mile from the village of Hilltown, and on the river Bann, is a bleach-green, the first or uppermost on that river, which in its course becomes a most important stream to bleachers and manufacturers of linen. The parish anciently formed part of the possessions of the abbey of Bangor, and by an inquisition in 1605 was found to comprise 22 townlands, now increased to 25, which, with the exception of four within the bishop's court at Dromore, are within the jurisdiction of the manorial court of Rathfriland. The living is a vicarage, in the diocese of Dromore, and in the patronage of the Bishop; the rectory, with the exception of the tithes of four townlands, which belong to the vicar, is impropriate in the Earl of Clanwilliam. The tithes amount to £364.1.7, of which £164.4.3 is payable to the impropriator, and the remainder to the incumbent. The glebe-house is a handsome residence at Hilltown: the glebe comprises 21 acres of very good land. The church is also at Hilltown, which see. The R.C. parish is co-extensive with that of the Established Church; there are two chapels, one at Cabra, and one in the village of hilltown, where is also a place of worship for Presbyterians in connection with the Synod of Ulster, of the third class. Besides the parochial school at Hilltown, there are schools at Tamrye, Drumnascamph, Ballycashone, and Ballynagrapog, and a national school near Hilltown; and there are two pay schools, in which are about 100 children. About a mile to the east of Hilltown are the ruins of the old parish church, in a large and very ancient burial-ground, in which were interred, in 1809, John and Felix O'Neill, supposed to have been the last male descendants of the once powerful sept of Tir-Oen. A very handsome antique chalice, now in the possession of A. Murphy, Esq., of Rathfriland, and also a quern, in the possession of the Rev. J.A. Beers, were dug up in the churchyard in 1832.

CLOUGH, a post-town, in the parish of LOUGHIN-ISLAND, barony of KINELEARTY, county of DOWN, and province of ULSTER, 5 miles (S.W.) from Downpatrick, on the road to Newry, and 68³/₄ miles (N. by E.) from Dublin; containing 309 inhabitants. Here is a constabulary police station, and fairs are held on May 27th, July 5th, Oct. 21st, Nov. 22nd, and Dec. 23rd. In the vicinity are Seaforde House, the splendid mansion of M. Forde Esq.; Mount Panther, the beautiful seat of J. Reed Allen, Esq.; and Ardilea, that of the Rev. W. Annesley. Here is a large Presbyterian meeting-house in connection with the Synod of Ulster, but it has been closed several years. – See LOUGHIN-ISLAND.

COMBER, or CUMBER, a post-town and parish, partly in the barony of UPPER, but chiefly in that of LOWER CASTLEREAGH, county of DOWN, and province of ULSTER, 14 miles (N. by W.) from Downpatrick, and 91 (N. by E.) from Dublin; containing 8,276 inhabitants, of which number, 1,377 are in the town. St. Patrick founded an abbey here, of which nothing is now known. Brien Catha Dun, from whom the O'Nials of Clandeboy descended, and who fell by the sword of Sir John de Courcey, about 1201, also founded an abbey to the honour of the Blessed Virgin, and supplied it with monks of the Cistertian order from the abbey of Albalanda, in Carmarthenshire. John O'Mullegan was the last abbot, and voluntarily resigned the abbacy in 1543. The site and lands were granted, in the 3rd of Jas. I., to Sir James Hamilton, afterwards Lord Clandeboy, whose successors used the greater part of the materials in erecting a mansion near

the town, called Mount Alexander, which is now a heap of ruins, and the parish church occupies the site of the abbey. This place derives its name from the river on which it is situated, and which flows into Strangford Lough, on the east side of the parish. The town, which is tolerably well built, forms three streets and a large square, on the road from Belfast to Down-patrick. Messrs. Andrews and Sons have an extensive bleach-green here, where 20,000 pieces of linen are finished annually, principally for the London market; they have also large flour-mills and corn stores. There are two distilleries; one of them, which is the property of Messrs Millar & Co., is among the oldest in the North of Ireland, having been erected in 1765. The tide from Strangford Lough flows to within half a mile of the town, and at a trifling expense might be made very beneficial to it. Great advantages would also result from the erection of a pier near Comber water foot; vessels of 200 tons might then come in with every tide. Coal is at present brought up in small lighters, but the principal fuel is peat; there is a very extensive bog, called Moneyreagh, or the Royal Bog, from which great quantities are sent to Belfast and other places. Fairs are held on Jan. 5th, the second Monday in April, June 19th, and Oct. 28th, principally for farming horses and cattle. Here is a constabulary police station. A manorial court is held here every third Thursday, for the manor of Comber, or Mount Alexander, which has jurisdiction in debts not exceeding £2 over 30 townlands in the parish of Comber, Barnemagarry, in the parish of Kilmud, and Ballycloghan, in that of Saintfield. There is also a court for the recovery of debts not exceeding £20 late currency.

The parish, which includes the ancient parish of Ballyricard, comprises, according to the Ordnance survey, 17,420 statute acres, of which 16,134 are in Lower Castlereagh; about 20 are common, 117 water, and 150 or 200 bog; the remainder is arable and pasture land, of which three-fourths are under tillage. Agriculture is in a very improved state, and the soil is very productive. There are some good quarries of freestone, equal in fineness and durability to the Portland stone; and coal has been found in three places, but no mines have been opened. There are several gentlemen's seats, the principal of which are Ballybeen, the residence of J. Birch, Esq.; Ballyalloly, at present unoccupied; Killynether House, the residence of T. McLeroth, Esq.; and Maxwell Court, of J. Cairns, Esq. The living is an impropriate curacy, in the diocese of Down, and in the patronage of the Marquess of Londonderry, in whom the rectory is impropriate. The parish is tithe-free, with the exception of the townlands of Ballyanwood, Ballycreely, and Ballyhenry, the tithes of which are paid to the Marquess of Londonderry, who pays the curate's stipend. A glebe-house was built in 1738, towards the erection of which the late Board of First Fruits gave £100: the glebe consists of eleven acres. The church is a small ancient building, in the later style of English architecture, and contains some neat marble monuments, particularly those to the memory of the Rev. Robert Mortimer, Capt. Chetwynd, Lieut. Unet,

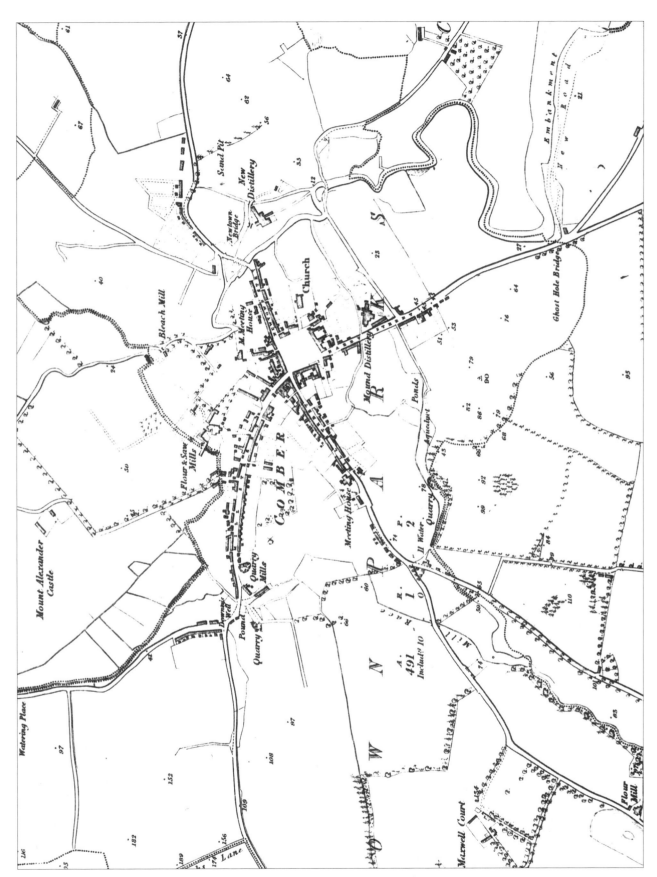

Comber. Part of 6 inch O.S. map of Co. Down, sheet 10, published 1835 (reproduced at 140%).

29

and Ensign Sparks, of the York fencible infantry, who fell in the battle of Saintfield, during the disturbances of 1798, and of the Rev. Messrs. Birch, father and son, the former of whom died in 1827, the latter in 1830, whose monument was erected by the subscriptions of 520 of their parishioners. Some fragments of the abbey are incorporated in its walls. There are a meeting-house at Comber for Presbyterians in connection with the Synod of Ulster, of the first class; another at Moneyreagh, connected with the Remonstrant Synod, of the same class; and a third at Gransha, connected with the Seceding Synod, of the second class: there is also a place of worship for Wesleyaa Methodists. The parochial school, in which about 100 boys and 70 girls are taught, was built in 1813, at the joint expense of the Marchioness of Lon-donderry and the trustees of Erasmus Smith's charity; the building is kept in repair by the Marchioness, who, in 1832, erected a house for the master. There are also national schools at Ballymaglaff, Tullygiven, and Ballystockart More than 300 children are educated in these schools, besides which, 740 are taught in 12 private schools. A house of industry was founded in 1824, by the Marquess of Londonderry, who subscribes £25 annually towards its support: it affords an asylum for 12 of the aged poor, and also distributes meal, potatoes, &c., to 60 families at their own dwellings. There is a large druidical altar in Ballygraphan, the table stone of which, now lying on the ground, measures 19 feet by 6 and is 4 feet thick: the five upright stones are in an adjoining hedge-row. Numerous forts and raths are scattered over the parish.

COPELAND ISLANDS, a cluster of three islands, situated at the south entrance of Belfast Lough, and in that part of the parish of BANGOR 'which is in the barony of ARDES, county of DOWN, and province of ULSTER, called respectively Copeland, Lighthouse and Mew islands. They derived their common name from the family of the Copelands, who settled here in the time of John de Courcey, in the 12th century, and of whose descendants, some are still to be found in the tract called Ballycopeland, on the mainland. Copeland island, the largest of the three, called also Big island and Neddrum, is 2 miles (N.N.E.) from Donaghadee, and about one mile from the mainland; it comprises about 200 acres, and contains 15 houses; near a small inlet, called Chapel bay, are the ruins of a church, with a burial-ground. About halfway between this island and the mainland is a rock, called the Deputy, on which a buoy is placed; and at the west end of the island is the Katikern rock, always above water, from which run two ledges about a cable's length, and on which a stone beacon has been erected. There is good anchorage on the west side of the island, and in Chapel bay on the south of Katikern, in from two to three fathoms of water, in all winds but those from the south-east. Lighthouse, or, as it is also called, Cross island, is about 1 mile (N.E.) from Copeland island, and is one furlong in length and about half a furlong in breadth, comprising about 24 acres. The Lighthouse from which it takes its name is a square tower, 70 feet high to the lantern,

which displays a light to the south-east, to guide vessels from the north and south rocks, which are $3^1/_2$ leagues distant, and to the north-west, to guard them from the Hulin or Maiden rocks lying between the mouths of Larne and Glenarm. The lighthouse is situated in lat. 54° 41' 15" (N.), and lon. 5° 31' (W.), and the light is plainly seen at Portpatnick and the Mull of Galway, in Scotland, from the latter of which it is 10 leagues distant. Mew island is a quarter of a furlong (E.) from Lighthouse island, and comprises about 10 acres of rocky pasture; it lies very low, and is extremely dangerous to mariners; in the sound between it and Copeland island is a flat rock with only three feet of water on it, called the Pladdens; and a rapid tide sets through the sound. Off this island the Enterprise, of Liverpool, a homeward-bound vessel from the coast of Guinea, was totally wrecked in 1801; she is said to have had on board £40,000 in dollars, which, with all her cargo, lay buried in the sea, till 1833, when Mr. Bell, by means of a diving apparatus, succeeded in recovering about 25,000 of the dollars, five brass guns, and other valuable property.

CROSSGAR, a village, in that part of the parish of KILMORE which is in the barony of UPPER CASTLEREAGH, county of DOWN, and province of ULSTER, 5 miles (N.) from Downpatrick, on the road to Belfast; containing 474 inhabitants and about 125 houses, mostly very small. It is noted only for its fairs, which are held on the second Wednesday in every month, and are well attended, particularly for the sale of horned cattle and pigs. It has a penny post to Downpatrick, and in the vicinity is Crossgar House, the residence of Hamilton, Esq., also that of the late E.S. Ruthven, Esq., and the handsome house and demesne of Redemon. – See KILMORE.

DONAGHADEE, a sea-port, and post-town, and a parish, in the barony of ARDES, county of DOWN, and province of ULSTER, $14^1/_4$ miles (N.E. by E.) from Belfast, and $94^1/_2$ (N.N.E.) from Dublin; containing 7,627 inhabitants, of which number, 2,986 are in the town. It is situated on the coast in lat. 54° 38' 20" and lon. 5° 31' 50", and is one of the three principal stations for post-office packets. It anciently belonged to the monastery of Black Abbey, in the county of Down. The town comprises several streets, which are wide and well kept, and contains 671 houses. From being the point of communication between Ireland and Scotland, as it is only 22 miles distant from Portpatrick, it has been a packet station from a very early period. The voyage across the channel is generally made by steam vessels in about three hours. Its natural harbour is small, but has lately been greatly improved by the erection of two large stone piers carried out on ledges of rock to a depth of sixteen feet at low water, and enclosing a space of about 200 yards each way outside the original harbour. A great part of the interior has been excavated to the same depth as the entrance; the original estimate for the improvement of this harbour, which commenced in 1821, was £145,453, of which up to Jan. 5th, 1834, £143,704,5.8 had been expended. When finished, vessels drawing 16 feet

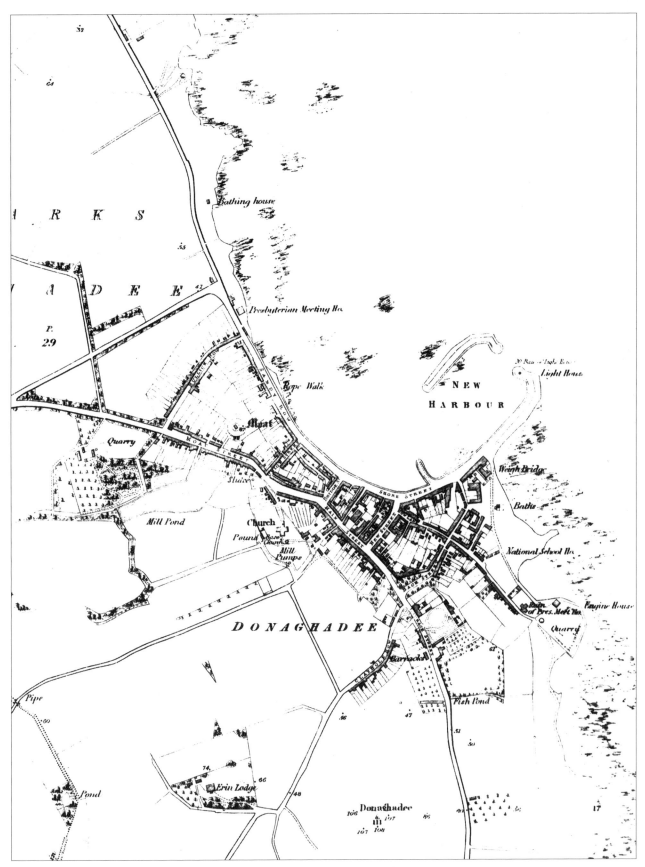

Donaghadee. Part of O.S. map of Co. Down, sheet 3, published 1835 (reproduced at 140%).

of water may safely enter it at any period of the tide. The stone of which the piers, lighthouse, &c., are built, is the Anglesey marble. The lighthouse, at the extremity of the south pier, is a stationary red light. Donaghadee is a creek to the port of Belfast, and has a harbour master and one custom-house officer. Its principal imports are coal and timber, and its principal exports, live cattle and pigs. Nearly all the poor females are employed in embroidering muslin, chiefly for the Glasgow manufacturers: above £20,000 per ann. is paid as wages for this work, which was introduced in 1805. There are many wind and water mills, several of which are employed in dressing flax, There is no regular market; fairs are held on June 13th, Aug. 16th, Oct. 10th, and on the second Saturday in December. It is a constabulary police station, and the head of a coast-guard district, under the control of a resident inspecting commander, which comprises the twelve stations of Hollywood, Bangor, Crawfordsburn, Orlock hill, Groomsport, Donaghadee, Millisle, Ballywalter, Ballyhalbert, Cloghy, Taragh, and Strangford.

The parish comprises, according to the Ordnance survey, 9,593 statute acres, which, with the exception of 32$\frac{1}{2}$ of water and about 1,000 of bog, marsh, and wasteland, are all arable: the land is in general well cultivated, producing very good crops. A considerable tract of bog, and part of Gransha moss, in this parish, are valuable as fuel, but are fast diminishing by cultivation. Slate of inferior value is obtained, and at a considerable depth is abundant and of excellent quality. Clay-slate is sometimes used for repairing the roads. A court of record is held by the seneschal of the manor, which has jurisdiction by attachment to the extent of £20, and by civil bill to the extent of 40s, over this parish, the district of Black Abbey, and the townland of Killyvalgen, in the parish of Ballywalter. It is held in the court-house once in three weeks, where also a court-leet is held annually in May, for the election of officers for the town and manor; and petty sessions are held every Wednesday. In the town are the handsome residences of D. Delacherois, Esq., its proprietor, and of S. Delacherois, Esq., Capt. Leslie, R.N., Mrs. G. Leslie, Mrs. Vaughan, and others; and near it are Carrodore Castle, the seat of N.D. Crommelin, Esq.; Ballywilliam Cottage, of Lady Charlotte Jocelyn; and the glebe-house, of the Rev. J. Hill. The living is a vicarage, in the diocese of Down, and in the patronage of the Lord Primate; at its institution it was endowed with all the alterages, and one-third of the tithes of corn and hay, and one-half of the townland of Mulletullenaghragh, as a glebe: the rectory is appropriate to the see of Armagh. The tithes amount to £720, of which £480 is paid to the lessee of the appropriator, and £240 to the vicar, The glebe-house was built in 1816; the glebe comprises 13 acres, The church is a large, ancient, cruciform structure, for the repair of which the Ecclesiastical Commissioners have recently granted £200. A lofty tower was built at its western end, in 1833, at the expense of D. Delacherois, Esq., aided by £50 bequeathed for that purpose by the late S. Delacherois,

Esq. In the R.C. divisions the parish is in the union or district of Newtown-Ardes. There are two Presbyterian meeting-houses in the town, one of which is in connection with the Synod of Ulster, also one at Mill-isle of the third class. At Ballycopeland is one in connection with the Seceding Synod, of the second class, and one in the same connection at Carrodore, of the third class, The Primitive Methodists also have a meeting-house in the town. The parochial school was founded by Lady Mount-Alexander, for the education of 30 boys; there are two schools under the National Board at Carrodore, one of which is aided by an annual donation from Mrs. Crommelin; a school of 70 girls is supported by subscription, and there are three others in the town: there are also an infants' school and 10 private schools in the parish. A dispensary and infirmary are supported in the customary manner. Lady Mount-Alexander, by will dated 1769, bequeathed a perpetual annuity of £120 payable out of her estates in this parish to charitable purposes. Dr. Sempil bequeathed £20 per ann., and S. Delacherois, Esq., gave £100, the interest of which, with the former bequest, is annually distributed among the poor by the vicar. Close to the harbour is a rath, seventy feet high with a large platform on its summit commanding a fine view of the channel and surrounding country. A castellated powder magazine has been erected on its top which is approached by winding roads cut round the sides. Many smaller raths are scattered over the parish.

DONAGHCLONEY, a parish, in the barony of LOWER IVEAGH, county of DOWN, and province of ULSTER, 2$\frac{1}{2}$ miles (S. by E.) from Lurgan, on the road to Banbridge; containing 5,657 inhabitants. It comprises, according to the Ordnance survey, 6,698 statute acres, of which 6,384 are very fertile and principally under tillage: there is also a considerable tract of valuable bog. Waringstown House, the residence of the Rev. Holt Waring, is a spacious and handsome mansion, erected in 1667 by William Waring, Esq., and situated in an extensive and richly planted demesne embellished with stately timber. During the war of 1688, a party of the Irish adherents of Jas. II. took possession of this house, which they garrisoned and retained till the arrival of Duke Schomberg, in the following year, when they were driven out by that general, who slept here for two nights. There are several other seats, of which the principal are the Demesne, the residence of J. Brown, Esq.; Tullycarn, of H. Magill, Esq.; and Donaghcloney, of J. Brown, Esq.; and also several residences of merchants and manufacturers. The manufacture of linens, lawns, cambrics, diapers, sheetings, and other articles is carried on to a great extent. The weaving of diapers, on its introduction into Ireland, was first established in this parish by the spirited exertions of Samuel Waring, Esq., who brought over a colony from England, and with his own hands made the first spinning wheel and reel on improved principles, from drawings which he had procured while travelling in Holland, and similar wheels are now universally used throughout Ireland. There is a very extensive bleach-green at Donaghcloney, in which 8,000 pieces are annually finished; and there is scarcely a house in the parish that is not, in some way, connected with this manufacture. The living is a rectory and vicarage, in the diocese of Dromore, formerly united by charter of Jas. I. to the rectories of Segoe and Moyntaghs, and part of the rectories of Magherally and Tullylish, together constituting the union of Donaghcloney and the corps of the archdeaconry of Dromore: but on the resignation of the Hon. and Rev. Pierce Meade, in 1832, the union was dissolved; Segoe alone became the corps of the archdeaconry, and this parish was constituted a separate and distinct benefice, in the patronage of the Bishop. The tithes amount to £261.6: there is neither glebe-house nor glebe. The church, situated in the neat village of Waringstown, near the mansion, is a very respectable edifice with a curious oak roof and has been lately much enlarged at the joint expense of the Ecclesiastical Commissioners and the proprietor of the estate: it was originally built at the expense of Win. Waring, Esq., who presented it to the parish, about the year 1680. Divine service is also performed in four school-houses in the parish, every Sunday evening and 'every alternate Thursday. In the R.C. divisions the parish forms part of the union or district of Tullylish. There is a place of worship for Presbyterians in connection with the Seceding Synod, of the first class. The parochial school is aided by an annual donation from the rector, and there are four other schools; in these together about 200 boys and 140 girls receive instruction: there are also five pay schools, in which are about 130 boys and 60 girls. The extensive cemetery of the parish is situated on the shore of the river Lagan; but there is not a vestige of the ancient church. A large bell was found in the bed of the river, and is now in the tower of Waringstown church; engraved upon it, in rude characters, is the inscription, 'I belong to Donaghcloney.' – See WARINGSTOWN.

DONAGHMORE, a parish, in the barony of UPPER IVEAGH, county of DOWN, and province of ULSTER, 5¼ miles (N. by E.) from Newry; containing 4,463 inhabitants. It is situated on the great road from Dublin to Belfast, and comprises, according to the Ordnance survey, 8,396¼ statute acres; there are 110 acres of wood land, 499 of bog, 16 of waste, and 48 of water; the rest is arable and pasture land, generally good and in a high state of cultivation. Many of the inhabitants are employed in the weaving of linen for the merchants of Banbridge. Fairs are held on the first Friday in every month for cattle, sheep, and pigs, at Sheepbridge, which consists of only two houses, on the Newry road. Drummantine, the seat of the late Arthur Innis, Esq.; Beech Hill, of E. Curteis, Esq.; and the glebe-house, of the Rev. M.J. Mee, are the principal residences in the parish. The living is a vicarage, in the diocese of Dromore, and in the patronage of the Lord-Primate, to whom the rectory is appropriate: the tithes amount to £451, of which £251 is payable to the Lord-Primate, and £200 to the incumbent. The glebe-house, which is large and handsome, was erected in 1786, on a good glebe of 36 Irish acres, comprehending the

townland of Tullagh, or Tullynacross, The church was built at the sole expense of Primate Boulter, in 1741: it is a small handsome edifice in good repair, with a lofty tower ornamented with buttresses, pinnacles, and finials, which was erected, in 1828, by voluntary contributions. The R.C. parish is co-extensive with that of the Established Church: a handsome chapel is now being built at Barr, and there is a small one at Ballyblaw. A meeting-house for Presbyterians, in connection with the Synod of Ulster, stands on the borders of this parish and that of Newry; and at the Rock is a large meeting-house for Seceders. There is a parochial school on the glebe, built in 1818, and principally supported by the vicar, who gives the master one acre of land rent-free; also a school at Derrycraw, built and supported by Trevor Corry, Esq.; and there are five private schools. In the churchyard is a remarkable old cross; beneath it is the entrance to an artificial cave, which extends a considerable distance, the sides being formed of loose stones, covered over with large flat, stones: near the centre is a cross or transept, forming two distinct chambers; the cave is about 3 feet wide, 5 feet high, and 62 feet long, and, at the cross, nearly 30 feet broad. The Dowagh, or Danes' Cast, passes through the western extremity of the parish, and in some places forms the boundary between it and Drumbanagher, and between the counties of Armagh and Down.

DOWNPATRICK, an unincorporated borough, market, and post-town, and parish, in the barony of LECALE, county of DOWN, (of which it is the chief town), and province of ULSTER, 18 miles (S.E. by S.) from Belfast, and 74 (N.) from Dublin; containing 9,203 inhabitants, of which number, 4,784 are in the town.

This place, which was anciently the residence of the native kings of Ullagh or Ulidia, was originally named Aras-Celtair and Rath-Keltair, one signifying the house and the other the castle or fortification of Celtair, the son of Duach; by Ptolemy it was called Dunum. Its present name is derived from its situation on a hill, and from its having been the chosen residence of St. Patrick, who, on his arrival here in 432, founded in its vicinity the abbey of Saul, and, shortly after, an abbey of regular canons near the ancient Doon or fort, the site of which was granted to him by Dichu, son of Trichem, lord of the country, whom he had converted to the Christian faith. St. Patrick presided over these religious establishments till his death in 493, and was interred in the abbey here, in which also the remains of St. Bridget and St. Columbkill, the two other tutelar saints of Ireland, were subsequently deposited. The town was constantly exposed to the ravages of the Danes, by whom it was plundered and burnt six or seven times between the years 940 and 1111; and on all these occasions the cathedral was pillaged by them. In 1177, John de Courcy took possession of the town, then the residence of Mac Dunleve, Prince of Ullagh, who, unprepared for defence against an invasion so unexpected, fled precipitately. De Courcy fortified himself here, and maintained his position against all the efforts of Mac Dunleve, aided by the native chieftains, for its recovery. In 1183, he displaced the canons and substituted a society of Benedictine monks from the abbey of St. Werburgh at Chester. Both he and Bishop Malachy III., endowed the abbey with large revenues; and in 1186 they sent an embassy to Pope Urban III. to obtain a bull for translating into shrines the sacred reliques of the three saints above named, which was performed with great solemnity by the pope's nuncio in the same year. De Courcy having espoused the claims of Prince Arthur, Duke of Brittany, assumed, in common with other English barons who had obtained extensive settlements in Ireland, an independent state, and renounced his allegiance to King John, who summoned him to appear and do homage. His mandate being treated with contempt, the provoked monarch, in 1203, invested De Lacy and his brother Walter with a commission to enter Ulster and reduce the revolted baron. De Lacy advanced with his troops to Down, where an engagement took place in which he was signally defeated and obliged to retreat with considerable loss of men. De Courcy, however, was ultimately obliged to acknowledge his submission and consent to do homage . A romantic description of the issue of this contest is related by several writers, according to whom De Courcy, after the termination of the battle, challenged De Lacy to single combat, which the latter declined on the plea that his commission, as the King's representative, forbade him to enter the lists against a rebellious subject, and subsequently proclaimed a reward for De Courcy's apprehension, which proving ineffectual, he then prevailed upon his servants by bribes and pro. mises to betray their master. This act of perfidy was carried into execution whilst De Courcy was performing his devotions unarmed in the burial-ground of the cathedral: the assailants rushed upon him and slew some of his retinue; De Courcy seized a large wooden cross, with which, being a man of great prowess, he killed thirteen of them, but was overpowered by the rest and bound and led captive to De Lacy, who delivered him a prisoner to the king. In 1205, Hugh de Lacy was made Earl of Ulster, and for a while fixed his residence at the castle erected here by De Courcy. In 1245, part of the abbey was thrown down and the walls of the cathedral much damaged by an earthquake. A desperate battle was fought in the streets of this town, in 1259, between Stephen de Longespee and the chief of the O'Neils, in which the latter and 352 of his men were slain. Edward Bruce, in his invasion of Ulster, in 1315, having marched hither, plundered and destroyed the abbey, and burnt part of the town: he again plundered the town three years afterwards, and on that occasion caused himself to be proclaimed King of Ireland at the cross near the cathedral. To subdue the opposition raised by the wealthy abbots of this district, under Primate Cromer, against the spiritual supremacy of Hen. VIII., Lord Grey, then lord-deputy, marched with a powerful army into Lecale, took Dundrum and seven other castles, and in May 1538, having defaced the monuments of

the three patron saints and perpetrated other acts of sacrilege, set fire to the cathedral and the town; three years afterwards, this act was made one of the charges on which he was impeached and beheaded. On the surrender of the abbey in 1539, its possessions, with those of the other religious establishments in the town, were granted to Gerald, eleventh Earl of Kildare. In 1552, the town was plundered and partially destroyed by Con O'Neil, Earl of Tyrone; and two years afterwards it was assaulted by his son Shane, who destroyed its gates and ramparts. During the war of 1641, the Protestants of the surrounding district having fled hither for protection, the town was attacked by the Irish under the command of Col. Bryan O'Neil, who burnt a magnificent castle erected by Lord Okeham, and committed a great slaughter of the townsmen; many that escaped were afterwards massacred at Killyleagh.

The town is built upon a group of little hills, on the south shore of the western branch of Lough Cone or Strangford Lough, and consists of four principal streets rising with a steep ascent from the market-place in the centre, and intersected by several smaller streets and lanes: on the eastern side the hills rise abruptly behind it, commanding views of a fertile and well-cultivated tract abounding with richly diversified and picturesque scenery. It is divided according to ancient usage into three districts, called respectively the English, Irish, and Scottish quarters, and contains about 900 houses, most of which are well built: the streets are well paved, and were first lighted with oil in 1830; and the inhabitants are amply supplied with water. An ancient ferry across the western arm of Strangford lough connected this town with the neighbourhood to the north until a bridge was erected about one mile from the town, with a tower gate-house upon it, which was destroyed and the bridge itself greatly damaged in 1641. A public library and news-room was erected by subscription in 1825; and races are held in July alternately with Hillsborough, under charter of Jas. II., on an excellent course one mile south of the town. The members of the Down Hunt hold their annual meetings in a handsome building in English-street, called the County Rooms, which is also used for county meetings, &c. The barracks are an extensive and convenient range of buildings, formerly the old gaol, in which a detachment of two companies from the garrison at Belfast is placed. The only article of maufacture is that of linen, principally yard wide, for the West Indies and the English market, and drills for Scotland, in which about 700 weavers, are employed. There are two ale breweries in the town. On the banks of the Quoile, one mile distant, are excellent quays, where vessels of 100 tons burden come in from Strangford lough: the principal imports are iron, coal, salt, timber, bark, and general merchandise: the exports are wheat, barley, oats, cattle, pigs, potatoes, and kelp. Formerly the tide flowed up close to the town, but in 1745 an embankment was constructed across the Quoile water, one mile distant, by the Rt. Hon. Edward Southwell, lord of the manor, which

Cathedral of the Holy Trinity, Downpatrick. Drawn by R.O'C. Newenham and engraved by J.D. Harding. From R.O'C Newenham, Picturesque views of the antiquities of Ireland, *vol.1, (London, 1830).*

restrained it to that point, and about 500 acres of land were recovered: this embankment was swept away by a storm, and a second was formed by Lord de Clifford, with floodgates, &c., but after much rain a considerable portion of meadow land in the neighbourhood of the town is yet inundated. The market is on Saturday; it is large and well supplied with provisions of all kinds, and with pedlery. Brown linen webs were formerly sold on the market day in the linen hall, but the sale has of late much declined. The market-house is an old low building, containing some good upper rooms, in which the petty sessions are held and the public business of the town is transacted. Fairs are held annually on the second Thursday in January, March 17th, May 19th, June 22nd, Oct. 29th, and Nov. 19th. This is a chief constabulary police station, with a force consisting of one officer, one constable, and seven men.

Downpatrick had a corporation at an early period, the existence of which is recognised in 1403, when letters of protection were granted to it by Hen. IV., under the title of the 'Mayor, Bailiffs, and Commonalty of the city of Down, in Ulster.' The borough returned two members to the Irish parliament so early as 1585: this privilege was exercised till the union, since which they have returned one member to

the Imperial parliament. The right of election was vested in the pot-wallopers, but under an act of the 35th of Geo. III. it was limited to the resident occupiers of houses of the annual value of £5 and upwards, who have registered twelve months before the election: the number of qualifying tenements under the old law was estimated at about 650. The act of the 2nd of Wm. IV., cap. 88, caused no alteration in the franchise or in the limits of the borough, which is co-extensive with the demesne of Down, containing 1,486 statute acres: the number of voters registered, in 1835, was 525. The senesehal appointed by the lord of the manor is the returning officer. The manor, which is the property of David Ker, Esq., is very ancient, its existence being noticed in a record dated 1403. A patent of it was granted to Lord Cromwell by Jas. I., in 1617, whereby sundry monasteries, lands, and tenements, including the demesne of Down, were erected into the manor of Downpatrick – the manorial court, in which the process is either by attachmeat or civil bill, is held by the senesehal every third Tuesday, and has jurisdiction to the amount of £10 over 67 townlands in the parishes of Downpatrick, Saul, Ballee, Bright, Ballyculter, and Inch. The seneschal holds a court leet for the manor in spring and at Michaelmas. Petty sessions are held every Thursday: the assizes for the county are held

35

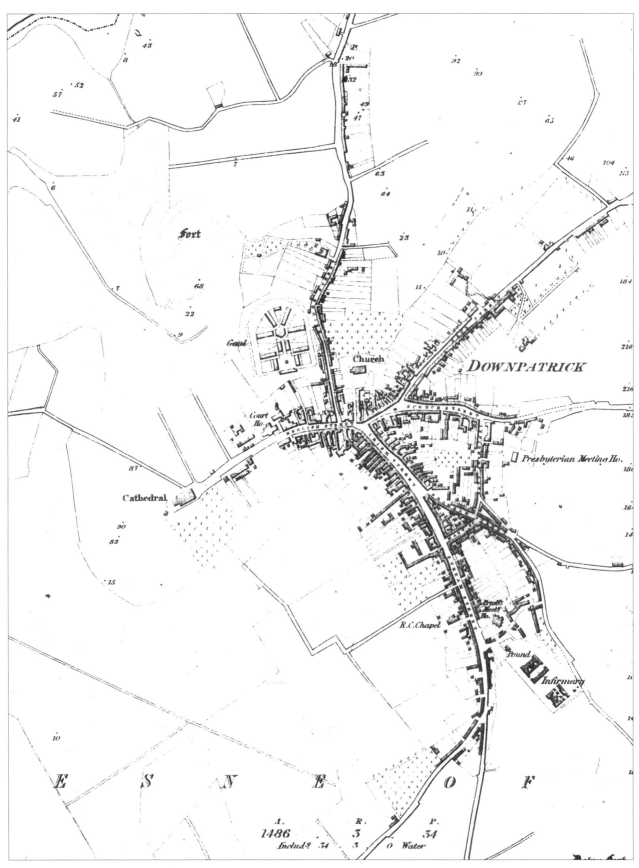

Downpatrick. Part of O.S. map of Co. Down, sheet 38, published 1835 (reproduced at 140%).

alternately here and at Newry; and the county quarter sessions for the division of Downpatrick are held here in March and October. The county hall, or court-house, which was considerably enlarged and improved in 1834, occupies an elevated site in English-street; it is a large and handsome edifice, consisting of a centre and two wings, approached by a fine flight of stone steps; the centre is appropriated to the criminal court, the eastern wing to the civil court, and in the western are preserved the county records, &c.; it also contains a suite of assembly-rooms. The county gaol is a very commodious building, erected in 1830 at an expense of £60,000, and occupying an area of one acre and a half: the internal arrangements and management are calculated to carry into the best effect the improved system of prison discipline, and have been recommended as a model for similar establishments by the inspector-general of prisons.

The SEE of DOWN is supposed to have originated in the abbey founded here by St. Patrick, but St. Carlan is said to have been the first bishop. Its early prelates are called Bishops of Dundalethglass, but it is probable that this see was generally included in the  diocese of Connor, prior to the episcopacy of Malachy O'Morgair, who became bishop in 1137, and separated it from Connor; his immediate successors are called bishops of Ulster by some historians. John Cely was the last bishop who, in modern times, held the bishoprick of Down separate from that of Connor: he was deprived of it for his crimes and excesses in 1441. Archbishop Prene recommended William Bassett, a Benedictine monk, to the Pope, as a successor to Cely, but the pope added this see to that of Connor, and they have remained united to the present time. John, the first bishop of Down and Connor, was not, however, allowed to enjoy his united bishopricks in peace; for Thomas Pollard claimed to be Bishop of Down, and is supposed to have been supported by the archbishop, but lost his cause in 1449. John was fined shortly before his death for not appearing upon summons in Parliament. Bishop Tiberius, who is stated to have very much beautified the cathedral, was succeeded, about 1526, by Robert Blyth, abbot of Thorney, in Cambridgeshire, who held these bishopricks in commendam, and resided in England. The last bishop before the Reformation was Eugene Magenis, who was advanced to these sees by Pope Paul III.; and although John Merriman, chaplain to Queen Elizabeth, was consecrated bishop in 1568, the pope appointed Miler Magragh to the united see: he, however, never had possession of the temporalties, and subsequently becoming a Protestant was made Archbishop of Cashel. John Tod, who had been educated at Rome, but had renounced popery, was nominated bishop by Jas. I., in 1604, and held the see of Dromore in commendam: he was tried before the High Commission

Court, which deprived him of the bishopricks, and afterwards poisoned himself in London. From 1660 to 1667 these sees were held by the celebrated Jeremy Taylor, who had also the administration of the see of Dromore, and was a privy counsellor and Vice Chancellor of the University of Dublin. Bishop Hutchinson, whose episcopacy commenced in 1720, had the church catechism translated into Irish, and printed in English and Irish, primarily for the use of the inhabitants of Rathlin, and hence it is called the Rathlin Catechism. Under the Church Temporalities Act, when either the bishoprick of Down and Connor, or of Dromore, becomes vacant, Dromore is to be added to Down and Connor, and the surviving bishop is to take the title of Bishop of Down, Connor, and Dromore, and the temporalities of the see of Dromore are to be vested in the Ecclesiastical Commissioners. The diocese is one of the ten that constitute the ecclesiastical province of Armagh: it comprehends part of the county of Antrim, and the greater part of Down, extending 52 British miles in length by about 28 in breadth, and comprises an estimated area of 201,950 acres, of which, 800 are in Antrim and 201,150 in Down. The gross annual revenue of the see of Down, on an average of three years ending Dec. 31st, 1831, amounted to £2,830.16.8$\frac{1}{2}$; and there are 6,411 acres of profitable land belonging to the diocese. The entire revenue of the united sees of Down and Connor averages £5,896 per annum, and the see lands comprise 30,244 statute acres. The chapter consists of a dean, archdeacon, precentor, and treasurer, and the two prebendaries of St. Andrew's and Dunsford. The abbey founded by St. Patrick appears to have been the first cathedral of this see; it was several times plundered and burnt by the Danes. It was repaired by Malachy O'Morgair, in 1137, and by Malachy III., aided by John de Courcy, in 1176, and was burnt in 1315 by Lord Edward Bruce. Having been repaired or rebuilt, it was again burnt, in 1538, by Lord Leonard de Grey. In 1609, Jas. I. changed the name of the cathedral from St. Patrick's to the Holy Trinity, which was its original designation; and on account of its being in a ruinous condition, Chas. II., in 1663, erected the church of Lisburn into a cathedral and bishop's see for the diocese of Down and Connor. It continued in ruins till the year 1790, when it was restored by a grant of £1,000 from Government and liberal subscriptions from the nobility and gentry of the county; and in the same year a rent-charge of £300 late currency on the tithes of the ancient union was appropriated by act of parliament for its repairs and for the support of an organist, three vicars choral, and six choristers. It is situated on an eminence to the west of the town, and is a stately embattled edifice chiefly of unhewn stone, supported externally by buttresses, and comprising a nave, choir, and aisles, with a lofty square tower at the west end, embattled and pinnacled, and smaller square towers at each corner of the east gable, in one of which is a spiral stone staircase leading to the roof. The aisles are separatcd from the nave by lofty elegant arches resting on massive piers, from the corbels of which spring ribs supporting the roof, which is richly groined and ornamented at the intersections with clusters of foliage. The lofty windows of the aisles are divided by a single mullion; the nave is lighted by a long range of clerestory windows, and the choir by a handsome east window divided by mullions into twelve compartments, which appears to be the only window remaining of the splendid edifice erected in 1412, and destroyed by Lord de Grey. Over the east window are three elegant niches with ogee pointed arches, contain ing on pedestals the remains of the mutilated effigies of St. Patrick, St. Bridget, and St. Columbkill. The choir is handsomely fitted up with stalls for the dignitaries. The cathedral was opened for the performance of divine service, after its restoration in 1817: the tower was completed in 1829, at an expense of £1,900. It contains a monument to the memory of Edward Cromwell, Baron Okeham, who was proprietor of nearly all Lecale, and who died and was buried here in 1607; and another to his grandson Oliver, Earl of Ardglass, who was interred in 1668. The cathedral service is not performed, the building being used rather as a second parish church. The consistorial court of the united diocese is at Lisburn: it consists of a vicar-general, two surrogates, a registrar, deputy-registrar, and several proctors. The registrars are keepers of the records of the united diocese, which consist of the documents relating to the see lands, benefices, inductions, and wills, the earliest of which is dated 1650. The number of parishes in the diocese is 43, which are comprehended in 37 benefices, of which 6 are in the patronage of the Crown, 2 in that of the Lord-Primate, 12 in that of the Bishop, 1 in the gift of the Provost and Fellows of Trinity College, Dublin, 13 in lay patronage, and the remainder are perpetual curacies, in the gift of the incumbents of the parishes out of which they have been formed. The number of churches is 40, and there are 2 other episcopal places of worship, and 25 glebe-houses.

In the R.C. divisions this diocese is united as in the Established Church, forming the bishoprick of Down and Connor: in the Bishoprick of Down are 18 parochial districts, containing 37 chapels served by 28 clergymen, 18 of whom are parish priests and 10 coadjutors or curates. The cathedral of the united diocese is at Belfast, where the R.C. bishop resides.

The parish comprises, according to the Ordnance survey, 11,484^1/$_2$ statute acres, of which 125 are water, and there is neither waste land nor bog within its limits; the land is very fertile, and, with the exception of some marshes, is all arable, and in an improved state of cultivation. There are several quarries of rubble stone, which is used principally for building. The scenery is enriched with numerous gentlemen's seats, of which the principal are Hollymount, the beautiful residence of Col. Forde, situated in an extensive demesne, richly planted and well watered; Ballykilbeg House, the residence of J. Brett Johnston, Esq.; and Vianstown, of Mrs. Ward. About two miles from the town is the beautiful lake of Ballydugan; and near it is Ballydugan House,

memorable as the residence of Col. White, who was murdered, and the mansion burnt in the war of 1641. The living is a rectory, in the diocese of Down, formerly united, by royal charter in the 7th of James I., to the rectories of Saul, Ballyculter, Ballee, Bright, and Tyrella, which together constituted the union and corps of the deanery of Down; but under the provisions of the Church Temporalities Act, the ancient union has been dissolved, and by act of council, in 1834, the rectories of Down and Tyrella, seven townlands in the parish of Ballee, one in that of Kilclief, and four in that of Bright, have been made to constitute the incumbency and corps of the deanery, which is in the patronage of the Crown. The gross income of the present deanery amounts to £1,554.15.11^1/$_2$, of which £1,078.11.3 is paid by the parish of Down, £164.15.9 by that of Tyrella; £6.6 is the rental of a small glebe of 1a.0r.7p; £146.7 is received from the townlands of Ballee; £148.2.8^1/$_2$ from those of Bright, and £10.13.3 from that of Kilclief. Out of this income the dean pays £6 to the diocesan schoolmaster, £12.16 for proxies, a quit.rent of £7.9.4^1/$_2$, £100 to a curate, &c., £100 for a residence (there being no deanery or glebe-house), and £127.7.10^1/$_2$ as a contribution to the cathedral, The parish church, a neat edifice in the Grecian style, was rebuilt on an enlarged scale in 1735, partly at the expense of Mr. Southwell, lord of the manor, and the Rev. – Daniel, then Dean of Down; it was repaired and newly roofed in 1760 and the Ecclesiastical Commissioners have lately granted £200 for its further repair. The R.C. parish is co-extensive with that of the Established Church, and contains two chapels, one in the town (built in 1790) and the other at Ballykilbeg, three miles distant. There are also two places of worship for Presbyterians, one in connection with the Synod of Ulster (completed in 1827, at an expense of £900, and now about to be enlarged), and of the second class; and the other with the presbytery of Antrim of the first class; and one each for Wesleyan Methodists, Methodists of the new connection, and Primitive Methodists.

The diocesan school, founded in the 12th of Elizabeth, appears to have fallen into decay until the year 1823, when it was united to that of Dromore, and an excellent school-room and residence for the master were erected at the end of Saul-street, in this town, in 1829, at an expense of £1,000, defrayed by the county at large, on a site given by Lord de Clifford. It is free to all boys of both dioceses, and is endowed with £50 per annum from the diocese of Dromore, and £40 from that of Down, of which one-third is paid by the bishops and two-thirds by the clergymen, being a per centage on the net value of their livings; it is also further supported by a contribution of £10.10 per ann. from the lay impropriators, a rent-charge of £20 on the estate of the late Lord de Clifford, and the rental of the land on which the school premises at Dromore were situated, amounting to £4.4. The master is appointed by the lord-lieutenant, on the recommendation of the bishop. A parochial school conducted on the Lancasterian plan, and an infants' school, established in 1832, are supported by voluntary contributions; in connection with the Presbyterian meeting-house of the Synod of Ulster, is a large school-house for girls, and the trustees intend immediately to erect another for boys; at Hollymount are schools for boys and girls, supported by Lady Harriet Forde; and there are other day and Sunday schools supported by subscription. The number of children on the books of these day schools is 646, namely, 440 boys and 206 girls; and in the private pay schools are 340 boys and 200 girls. On a gentle eminence, a short distance southward from the town, stands the county infirmary, a large and handsome building erected in 1832, comprising a centre and two wings, which extend rearward, and containing 11 wards, in which are 40 beds, 20 for males and 20 for females. Near it is the fever hospital, also a large and well-arranged building, erected in the same year, and divided into 8 wards, containing 20 beds: these two buildings cost £6,500. In English-street is an hospital founded in 1731 by the Rt. Hon. Edward Southwell, ancestor of the late Lord de Clifford, who endowed it with £237 per ann. payable out of the lands of Listonder and Ballydyan, in the parish of Kilmore, now the property of David Ker, Esq. The building, which is of brick, underwent a thorough repair in 1826, at an expense of £1,000, defrayed by Lord de Clifford: it comprises a centre and two wings, the former occupied as an asylum for six aged men and six aged women, who have two rooms and a garden and £5 per ann. each; and the latter as schools for ten boys and ten girls, who are clothed and educated for four years, and receive £3 per ann. each towards their support, and on leaving the school at the age of 15 are apprenticed: the schoolmaster receives a salary of £15, with house, garden, and fuel, and the schoolmistress £12, with similar advantages. In the same street are four good houses for clergymen's widows of the diocese, of which two were founded in 1730 by the Rev. H. Leslie, Rev. J. Mathews, and Rev. J. Hamilton, who endowed them with £40 per annum from lands in Ballybranagh; and two in 1750, by the Rev. Edward Mathews, D.D., who endowed them with £42 per ann. from lands in Tubermony, Grangetown, and Ballywarren, all in this parish: the management is vested in the Dean and Chapter. John Brett, Esq., in 1810, bequeathed £300 in trust, the interest to be distributed annually among the poor of the town. A society for clothing the poor in winter, and a mendicity society for assisting the aged and infirm and preventing vagrancy, have been established. Besides the abbey founded by St. Patrick, there were, prior to the dissolution, a priory of regular canons, called the priory of the Irish, founded in honour of St. Thomas, in 1138, by Malachy O'Morgair, Bishop of Down; the priory of St. John the Baptist, called the priory of the English, founded by John de Courcy for crossbearers of the order of St. Augustine; an abbey of Cistercian monks, founded in the 12th century by – Bagnal, and a Cistercian nunnery, of both which no further particulars have been recorded; a Franciscan friary, founded about 1240 by Hugh de Lacy, or, according to some writers, by Africa, daughter of Godred, King of Man, and wife of John de Courcy;

and an hospital for lepers, dedicated to St. Nicholas, which in 1413 was, with the hospital of St. Peter at Kilclief, granted in trust to certain individuals by royal charter: there are no remains of these ancient establishments, even their sites can scarcely be distinctly traced. There are several forts and raths in the parish; the most noted are the large rath or doon near the cathedral, which gave name to the town and county, and one at Ballykilbeg, finely planted by J.B. Johnston, Esq. In 1825, the head and horns of an elk of large size, the latter measuring 5 feet 11 inches between their extremities, and the head of a spear, were found in a marl-pit near the town. The celebrated Duns Scotus was born here in 1274: he was educated at Oxford, and in 1307 was appointed Regent of Divinity in the schools of Paris; his works are very voluminous. For a discription of the Struel wells, see the county article.

DROMARAGH, or ANNESBOROUGH, a post-town and parish, partly in the barony of KINELEARTY, partly in that of LOWER IVEAGH, but chiefly in that of UPPER IVEAGH, county of DOWN, and province of ULSTER; 5 miles (E.S.E.) from Dromore, and 72 miles (N. by E.) from Dublin, on the road from Banbridge to Ballynahinch; containing, with the district of Maghera hamlet, 10,129 inhabitants. It contains part of the lands granted by patent of Queen Elizabeth, in 1585, to Ever Mac Rorye Magennis, which were forfeited in the war of 1641, and afterwards granted by Chas. II. to Col. Hill; they are included in the manor of Kilwarlin. According to the Ordnance survey, it comprises 21,192$^3/_4$ statute acres, of which 6,027$^1/_4$ are in Lower Iveagh, 7,024$^1/_2$ are in Kinelearty, and 8,141 are in Upper Iveagh. The greater part is arable land, and about 91$^3/_4$ acres are under water; considerable improvement has been made in agriculture, and many even of the mountain tracts have been brought under tillage. The village, which is small, is called Annesborough, or Annesbury, in a patent which granted a weekly market on Thursday, and a fair for three days in Sept.; the market has been changed to Friday, and is held chiefly for the sale of butter and linen yarn; and the fairs are now held on the first Friday in Feb., May, Aug., and Nov., for farming stock and pedlery. Petty sessions are held in the village every fourth Monday: here is a sub-post-office to Dromore and Comber. Woodford, formerly the residence Jas. Black, Esq., has extensive bleach-works, and was once the seat of a flourishing branch of the linen manufacture. Dromaragh, with part of the rectory of Garvaghey, constitutes a union and the only prebend in the cathedral of Christ the Redeemer at Dromore, in the patronage of the Bishop: the tithes of the parish amount to £620.17.5, and of the union, to £937.4.3. The glebe-house was erected in 1821, for which a gift of £100 and a loan of £1,125 was obtained from the late Board of First Fruits. The ancient glebe, consisting of one moiety of the townland of Dromaragh, which was granted to the rector in pure alms by Jas. I., is now in the possession of the Marquess of Downshire; 20 acres of the same, held at a rent of £42 per ann., constitutes the present glebe. The church is a small handsome edifice, with a tower and clock in good repair, built in 1811, at the expense of the parishioners. The Ecclesiastical Commissioners have recommended that this union be dissolved on the next avoidance of the prebend, and that Garvaghey be separated from it, and consolidated with its vicarage, and the 9½ townlands now forming the perpetual cure of Maghera hamlet be constituted a distinct parish, leaving the remainder of Dromaragh to form the corps of the prebend. The R.C. parish is co-extensive with that of the Established Church, with the exception of the district of Maghera hamlet, which is united to the R.C. parish of Magheradroll: the chapel is a large handsome edifice at Finnis, built in 1833. At Artana is a meeting-house for Presbyterians of the first class, in connection with the Synod of Ulster. Here are 10 public schools, two of which are aided by an annual donation from Capt. Maginnis; also 11 private and eight Sunday schools. On the mountain of Slieve Croob is a cairn, having a platform at the top, on which eleven smaller cairns are raised; and in the townland of Finnis is a remarkable artificial cave, 94 feet long, 6 feet wide, and upwards of 5 feet in height, with a transept near the centre, 30 feet long; the walls are rudely arched near the top, which is covered with slabs of granite: in 1833, the Rev. H. Elgee Boyd, rector of the parish, caused it to be cleared out and an iron door fixed up to protect it from injury.

DROMORE, a market and post-town, a parish, and the seat of a diocese, in the barony of LOWER IVEAGH, county of DOWN, and province of ULSTER, 16 miles (W.N.W.) from Downpatrick, and 66½ (N.) from Dublin, on the mail coach road to Belfast, from which it is 14 miles distant; containing 14,912 inhabitants, of which number, 1942 are in the town. Its name, anciently written Druim-mor, signifies 'the Great Ridge,' Druim being the term applied to a long ridge-shaped hill, such as that above Dromore. Its origin may be traced from St. Colman, who founded here an abbey for Canons Regular, which afterwards became the head of a see, of which he was made the first bishop. This abbey had acquired extensive possessions early in the 10th century, and was frequently plundered by the Danes; it also suffered materially from the continued feuds of the powerful septs of the O'Nials, Magennises, and Macar-tans, In the 14th century, Sir J. Holt and Sir R. Belknap, being convicted of treason against Rich. II., were condemned to death, but on the intercession of the clergy, were banished for life to the ville of Dromore, in Ireland. At the Reformation the cathedral was in ruins, and the town had greatly participated in the devastations of the preceding periods; in this situation it remained till 1610, when Jas. I. refounded the see by letters patent, rebuilt the cathedral, and gave to the bishop extensive landed possessions in this and several adjoining parishes, which he erected into a manor called 'Bailonagalga,' corrupted into Ballymaganles, a denomination or townland on which the town stands, with a court leet, twice in the year, a court baron every three weeks for pleas under £5, a free market every Saturday, and two fairs. An episcopal palace was commenced by Bishop Buckworth,

but previously to its completion, the war of 1641 broke out, and the cathedral, the unfinished palace, and the town were entirely destroyed by the parliamentarian forces. From this time the town remained in ruins till the Restoration, when Chas. II. gave the see in commendam to the celebrated Jeremy Taylor, with Down and Connor, by whom the present church, which is also parochial, was built on the site of the ruined cathedral. In 1688, a skirmish took place near the town between a party of Protestants and some of the Irish adherents of Jas. II.

The town consists of a square and five principal streets, and contained, in 1831, 396 houses. There are two bridges over the Lagan; one, called the Regent's bridge, was built in 1811, and has a tablet inscribed to the late Bishop Percy, recording some of the leading traits of his character. Several bleach-greens were formerly in full work in the vicinity, and among others, that occupied by the late Mr. Stott, whose poetical effusions under the signature of Hafiz, in the provincial newspapers, attracted much attention; but all are now unemployed except one, in the occupation of Thos. McMurray and Co., connected with which is a manufacture of cambrics, and also a linen manufacture, established in 1832; another linen-factory was established at Ashfield, in 1828. The market is on Saturday, and is well supplied with all sorts of provisions, farming stock, and linen; and fairs are held on the first Saturday in March, May 12th, Aug. 6th, Oct. 10th, and Dec. 14th. A constabulary police force is stationed here; courts leet and baron are held for the manor, and petty sessions occasionally. In the bishop is vested, among other privileges, the power of appointing a coroner, escheator, and clerk of the market, and a bailiff.

The BISHOPRICK of DROMORE is supposed to have been included in that of Armagh till the 13th century, as the only bishops whose names are recorded prior to 1227 are St. Colman, the founder; Malbrigid Mac Cathesaige, and Rigan. About 1487, the Archbishop of Armagh, in a letter to Hen. VII., states that the revenues of this see did not exceed £40 per annum Irish, which was less by a third than sterling money, so that none would remain upon the bishoprick. Under the Church Temporalities Act, on this bishoprick or that of Down and Connor becoming vacant, they are to be united, and the remaining bishop is to be Bishop of Down, Connor, and Dromore; the temporalities of the see will then be vested in the Ecclesiastical Commissioners. It is one of the ten dioceses that form the ecclesiastical province of Armagh, and is 35½ English miles in length by 21½ in breadth, including an estimated area of 155,800 acres, of which 1,500 are in Antrim, 10,600 in Armagh, and the remainder in Down. The Earl of Kilmorey claims exemption from the bishop's jurisdiction for his lordship of Newry, as having been extra-episcopal before the Reformation; it belonged to the monastery at Newry, which was granted by Edw. VI. to Sir Nicholas Bagnal, one of this nobleman's ancestors; yet in the Regal Visitation book of 1615, Nova Ripa alias Nieu Rie is among the parishes under the jurisdiction of the see of Dromore. In the ecclesiastical court at Newry, marriage licences, probates of wills, &c., are granted by Lord Kilmorey's authority under the ancient monastic seal. The bishop's lands comprise 18,424 statute acres; and the annual revenue of the bishoprick, on an average of three years ending Dec. 31st, 1833, was £4,219.12. The ancient chapter consisted of a dean, archdeacon, and prebendaries, but was remodelled by Jas. I., and made to consist of a dean, archdeacon, precentor, chancellor, treasurer, amid the prebendary of Dromaragh, to which offices several rectories and vicarages were annexed. The consistorial court, held at Dromore, consists of a vicar-general, two surrogates, a registrar, apparitor, and two proctors. The diocesan school, which was united with that of Down in 1823, is described in the article on Downpatrick, where it is situated. The total number of parishes in the diocese is 26, exclusively of Newry, and of benefices 25, including 2 perpetual cures, of which the deanery is in the patronage of the Crown; the vicarage of Donaghmore is in the gift of the Lord Primate, and the vicarage of Aghalee in that of the Marquess of Hertford; the remainder are in the patronage of the Bishop. There is a church in each benefice, and two in Dromaragh and Clonallon; and five other places have been licensed for public worship by the bishop: the number of glebe-houses is 23. In the R.C. divisions the diocese is a separate bishoprick and one of the nine suffragan to Armagh. It comprises 17 parochial benefices, containing 34 chapels, which are served by 27 clergymen, 17 of whom, including the bishop, are parish priests, and 10 are coadjutors or curates. The bishop's parish is Newry, where he resides, and in which is a handsome cathedral.

The parish comprises, according to the Ordnance survey, 20,488$^1/_4$ statute acres, of which 18,212 are applotted under the tithe act. The lands are generally of good quality, and almost all are either under tillage or in pasture, and in a tolerable state of cultivation, or enclosed within demesnes: there is not more bog than is requisite to furnish a supply of fuel. Not far from the town is the episcopal palace, the residence of the Lord Bishop, the grounds of which were richly planted by Bishop Percy, who also clothed the surrounding hills with the flourishing woods that now ornament them: Shenstone's celebrated seat at Leasowes was the model on which he designed his improvements: St. Colman's well is in the demesne. Near the town also is Gill Hall Castle, the mansion and demesne of the Earl of Clanwilliam. This extensive property was originally granted by Chas. II. to Alderman Hawkins, who, during the civil war, procured food, raiment, and lodging, in London, for 5,000 Irish Protestants who had been driven from their country, and by his exertions £30,000, raised by subscription in England, was expended in

clothing and provisions, which were sent over to Ireland for such as could not effect their escape. With the aid of four other gentlemen, he also raised a sum of £45,000 for the help of the distressed Irish both at home and in England; he afterwards resided for some time in Ireland, where he became possessed of the town of Rathfriland, forfeited with other property by the Magennisses, Lords of Iveagh, in the war of 1641. The other seats are Islanderry House, the residence of J.G. Waddell, Esq.; Altafort, of W.C. Heron, Esq.; Clanmurry, of W. McClelland, Esq.; the Villa, of J. Vaughan, Esq.; Quilly House, of R. Vaughan, Esq.; and Islanderry, of S. Fivey, Esq. The living is a rectory and vicarage, forming the corps of the treasurership in the cathedral church of Christ the Redeemer, Dromore, in the patronage of the Bishop. The tithes amount to £910; there is neither glebe-house nor glebe. The church, situated on the north bank of the Lagan, close to the town, is a plain neat edifice, and was constituted the cathedral church by act of the 21st of Geo. II.; it was thoroughly repaired, enlarged, and modernised in 1808, when the tower was taken down, and the original oaken roof replaced with one of slate, chiefly at the expense of Bishop Percy: the Ecclesiastical Commissioners have lately granted £145 for its repair. Beneath the communion table is a vault, in which Dr. Taylor and two of his successors are interred, but the only inscription is on a small mural tablet to Bishop Percy, author of the key to the New Testament, translator of the Northern Antiquities, and editor of the 'Reliques of Ancient English Poetry,' who presided over the see from 1782 to 1811: his remains are deposited in a vault in the transept added to the cathedral, where also are interred those of Mrs. Percy, the 'Nancy,' to whom his beautiful ballad is addressed. In the R.C. divisions the parish is the head of a union or district, comprising also the parish of Garvaghy, in each of which is a chapel. There are places of worship for Presbyterians in connection with the Synod of Ulster and the Remonstrant Synod, both of the first class, and for Wesleyan Methodists. Nearly 1,500 children are educated in the public schools of the parish, of which one is chiefly supported by Mrs. Saurin, and one by Mr. Douglass; and there are also eight private schools, in which are about 430 children, and twelve Sunday schools. Near the church are two good houses for clergymen's widows, erected in 1729, and endowed by the bishop and clergy of the diocese. The Countess of Clanwilliam, who died in 1817, bequeathed to the poor a sum now producing £10.3, and a further sum to the dispensary, producing £3.7 per annum. Near the town are the remains of an ancient castle, built by William Worsley, son-in-law to Bishop Tod, for the bishop's protection, being one of the conditions on which a considerable extent of the see lands was alienated to Worsley, and which led to the act for restraining bishops from leasing lands beyond a term of 21 years. At the eastern extremity of the town is a remarkable earthwork, called the 'Great Fort' (or 'folkmote,' as such works are called by Spenser,): it has a treble fosse on the north or land side, and a strong out-post to the south, continued in a regular glacis to the water's edge; and near Gill Hall is a fort of different character, and smaller, evidently erected to defend the pass of the river. In 1817 a cavern was discovered near the castle, hewn out of the solid rock, of rectangular form, and about $4^1/_2$ feet high, 24 feet long, and $2^1/_2$ feet wide; on the floor were several broken urns of coarse brown clay, charcoal, and calcined human bones. At Islanderry was found a canoe cut out of a solid oak, and near it a pair of oars. Celts, spear and arrow-heads of flint, with other ancient weapons of stone, brass, and bronze, have been found at Skeogh, among which were stone hatchets; many were in the museum of Bishop Percy, and many are now in the possession of Mr. Welsh, of Dromore. During the prelacy of Bishop Percy, a large and very perfect skeleton of an elk was found in one of the adjacent bogs; the distance between the tips of the horns was 10 feet 3 inches; it was placed in the bishop's palace, where it was carefully preserved. The valuable library belonging to Bishop Percy was purchased, after his death, by the Earl of Caledon, for £1,000. Dromore formerly gave the title of Viscount to the Farnshaw family.

DRUMBALLYRONEY, a parish, in the barony of UPPER IVEAGH, county of DOWN, and province of ULSTER; on the road from Newry to Downpatrick; containing, with a part of the market and post-town of Rathfriland, 8,544 inhabitants. It comprises, according to the Ordnance survey, $12,338^1/_2$ statute acres, of which 1896 are bog, 80 mountain and water, and 10,445 are applotted under the tithe act, all of which is arable or pasture land in excellent cultivation. Here is a lake, called Lough Ballyroney, in the centre of which is a small island. The manufacture of linen and drugget is extensively carried on. The living is a vicarage, in the diocese of Dromore, united from time immemorial to that of Drumgooland, and in the patronage of the Bishop; the rectory is part of the corps of the deanery of Dromore, The tithes amount to £482, of which £321.6.8 is payable to the dean, and the remainder to the vicar; the gross tithes of the benefice amount to £630.9.9. The church, a small neat edifice with a tower, was erected by aid of a gift of £500, in 1800, from the late Board of First Fruits. The glebe-house was built by aid of a gift of £200, and a loan of £300, in 1821, from the same Board: the glebe, given

Drum church. From supplement to The Dublin Penny Journal, *vol.4, 1836.*

by the Countess of Clanwilliam in 1820, comprises 20 acres, subject to a rent of 15s. per acre. In the R.C. divisions the parish forms part of the union of Annaghlone, and has a small chapel near the Diamond. There is a place of worship for Presbyterians of the first class, in connection with the Synod of Ulster, and one for Covenanters. About 170 children are taught in two public schools, and there are eight private and four Sunday schools. The fine ruin of Seafin castle, which was for ages the strong hold of the Magennises, is situated on the Bann; and there are several other fortresses.

DRUMBEG, a parish, partly in the barony of UPPER BELFAST, county of ANTRIM, but chiefly in that of UPPER CASTLEREAGH, county of DOWN, and province of ULSTER, $^3/_4$ of a mile (N.E.) from Lisburn, on the road to Belfast; containing 2,883 inhabitants. According to the Ordnance survey it comprised 2,704$^3/_4$ statute acres, of which 11,863. were in Down, and 1,518 in Antrim; of these, 2,627 were applotted under the tithe act, and valued at £3,367 per ann.: but a portion of the parish of Drumboe having been lately added to it under the Church Temporalities' Act, it now comprises 6,868 acres. The soil differs greatly in quality, from a sandy loam to a stiff clay, but is very fertile. The Lagan navigation from Belfast to Lough Neagh passes through the parish. The principal seats, besides those noticed under the head of Dunmurry (which see), are Glenburn, the residence of F. Crossley, Esq.; Wilmont, unoccupied; Finaghey, of J. Charley, Esq.; Larkfield, of Henderson Black, Esq.; Drumbeg Rectory, of the Rev. J.L.M. Scott; Drum House, of W.H. Smyth, Esq.; and Belvidere Cottage, a neat and commodious residence, lately built on the property of A. Durham, Esq. Ballydrain, the beautiful demesne of Hugh Montgomery, Esq., though not in this parish, is within 200 yards of the church, and with the adjoining grounds of Lakefield, the residence of Miss Richardson, and Lismoyne, of Mrs. Callwell, presents one of the finest landscapes in the neighbourhood of Belfast. A court leet and court baron are held every third week at Four Land Ends, for the manor of Drumbracklin, by a seneschal appointed by Narcissus Batt, Esq., lord of the manor, with jurisdiction for the recovery of debts under £20, extending over the townlands of Doneight and Lisnoe in the parish of Hillsborough, Ballyaulis in this parish, and Ballycairn, Ballylesson, Molough, and Knockbreccan in Drumboe. The living is a rectory, in the diocese of Down, and in the gift of the Bishop; a part of the rectorial tithes is impropriate in W. Charley, A. Durham, and Narcissus Batt, Esqrs., as lessees under the Marquess of Donegal. The tithes now amount to £336.16.6, of which £94.13.6$^1/_2$ is payable to the impropriators, and the remainder to the incumbent: the glebe-house was built in 1826, by a gift of £415 and a loan of £46 (British) from the late Board of First Fruits, exclusively of £450 expended by the incumbent in building and improvements; the glebe comprises eight statute acres. The church was rebuilt by subscription in 1795, by aid of a gift of £461 (British) from the same Board: it has a tower surmounted by a spire,

which having been blown down in 1831, was rebuilt at the expense of J. Charley, Esq. About 300 children are educated in five public schools, two of which are on Erasmus Smith's foundation.

DRUMBOE, a parish, in the barony of UPPER CASTLEREAGH, county of DOWN, and province of ULSTER, 4 miles (N.E.) from Lisburn, on the river Lagan, and on the old road to Belfast; containing 6,429 inhabitants. Twelve townlands of the ancient parish having been lately annexed to Drumbeg, it now comprises 9,629 statute acres, chiefly arable, with a very small proportion of woodland, and, except lands belonging to gentlemen who farm their own property, in a very indifferent state of cultivation, though lately much improved: there is a large tract of bog. The weaving of cotton is carried on for the manufacturers of Belfast; and at Edenderry is a bleachgreen. The Lagan opens a communication with Belfast, Lisburn, and Lough Neagh, The principal seats are Edenderry, the residence of W. Russel, Esq.; Edenderry House, of C. Dunlop, Esq.; Belvidere, of A. Durham, Esq.; New Grove, of J. Russel, Esq.; and the elegant lodge and greater part of the demesne of Purdysburn, the splendid residence of Narcissus Batt, Esq. The living is a rectory, in the diocese of Down, and in the patronage of the Bishop; the tithes amount to £517, The glebe-house was built in 1816, by a gift of £415 (British), and a loan of £46, from the late Board of First Fruits, exclusively of £200 expended by the incumbent: the glebe comprises 6$^1/_2$ acres. The church, a handsome Grecian edifice with a lofty tower surmounted by a copper dome, was erected, in 1788, by subscription, aided by a grant of £500 from the same Board, a donation of 150 guineas from Mr. Hull, of Belvidere, and of 100 guineas from the Marquess of Downshire. There are places of worship for Presbyterians, Independents, and Primitive and Wesleyan Methodists. Nearly 600 children are educated in the several public schools of the parish; that at Purdysurn was built at the expense of Mr. Batt, who supports the school and also provides residences for the

Giant's Ring, Parish of Drumbo. From The Dublin Penny Journal, *vol.3, 1834.*

master and mistress, who have about 150 pupils; and the master of a school at Ballymacbrennard receives £20 per annum from the trustees of Erasmus Smith's fund, and has an acre of land given by the Marquess of Downshire. There are also six private schools, in which are about 400 children. Not far from the church is the Giant's Ring, a circular entrenchment enclosing more than 8 plantation acres, perfectly level; in the centre of the enclosure is a large cromlech, or Druids' altar, consisting of seven upright stones supporting a table stone of nearly circular form and sloping towards the east: the land is now let, and the earth-work is being removed for the purpose of cultivation, In the burial-ground close to the supposed site of the ancient church was an abbey, said to have been founded by St. Patrick, and of which St. Mochumna was the first abbot; there is also an ancient round tower. In the parish are eight large raths, the most conspicuous of which, on the summit of Tullyard, is constructed of earth, loose stones, and vitrified substances, similar to the cairns of Scotland. It is supposed by some writers that there was anciently a fortified town here.

DRUMGATH, a parish, in the barony of UPPER IVEAGH, county of DOWN, and province of ULSTER, on the road from Downpatrick to Newry; containing, with the greater part of the post-town of Rathfriland (which is separately described), 4,448 inhabitants. According to the Ordnance survey, it comprises 5,330^1/$_2$ statute acres, of which about 100 are bog. It is a vicarage, in the diocese of Dromore, and patronage of the Bishop; the rectory forms part of the union of Clonallon, and corps of the chancellorship of Dromore cathedral. The tithes amount to £258, of which £168.13.4 is payable to the chancellor, and £89.6.8 to the vicar. There is a glebe-house, with a glebe of 150 acres. The church, which is in Rathfriland, is a neat building, for the repair of which the late Board of First Fruits lent £150, in 1829, and the Ecclesiastical Commissioners have recently given £119. The R.C. parish is co-extensive with that of the Established Church, and has chapels at Rathfriland, Barnmeen, and Drumgath. In Rathfriland is a large and handsome meeting-house for Presbyterians, in connection with the Synod of Ulster, of the first class, and a second is now being built; there is also one in connection with the Seceding Synod, of the second class, and one each for Covenanters, Wesleyan Methodists, and the Society of Friends. About 350 children are educated in two public and two private schools. Some ruins of the ancient church exist in a large burial-ground, and a curious antique bell was found in a bog in 1764.

DRUMGOOLAND, a parish, in the barony of UPPER IVEAGH, county of DOWN, and province of ULSTER, 4 miles (N.E.) from Rathfriland, on the road from Castlewellan to Banbridge; containing 10,281 inhabitants. It comprises, according to the Ordnance survey, 19,653 statute acres, of which, 133^3/$_4$ are under water, 3,240 are mountain and bog, and the remainder is cultivated with great labour and expense, and in some parts is very productive: many of the

inhabitants are employed in linenweaving. Ballyward, a large handsome house, situated in a beautiful demesne, is the residence of C.F. Beers, Esq.; the Cottage, of Capt. Tighe; and Ballymacaveny, of the Rev. J.B. Grant. The parish is in the diocese of Dromore: the rectory is partly appropriate to the see and partly to the deanery of Dromore, and partly consolidated with the vicarage, which, from time immemorial, has been united to the vicarage of Drumballyroney, together forming the union of Drumgooland, in the patronage of the Bishop. The tithes amount to £495.3.0^1/$_2$, of which £380.2.8^1/$_2$ is payable to the incumbent, £59 to the bishop, and the remainder to the dean; and the gross value of the benefice, tithe and glebe inclusive, is £570.16.0^1/$_2$. The church is a large handsome edifice, in the early English style, erected, by aid of a gift of £900 from the late Board of First Fruits, in 1822; it contains a handsome monument erected by the parishioners to the memory of the Rev. T. Tighe, forty-two years rector of this parish. There is another church in Drumballyroney, where there is a good glebe-house, and a glebe of 20 plantation acres, valued at £30 per annum. In the R.C. divisions the parish forms two unions or districts, called Upper and Lower Drumgoo land: the chapel for the former is at Leitrim; in the latter there are two, one at Gargary, the other at Dechamet. There are two meeting-houses for Presbyterians in connection with the Seceding Synod, one at Drumlee (of the first class), the other at Closkilt. There is a school for boys and girls at Ballyward, built and principally supported by C.F. Beers, Esq.; the parochial school, adjoining the ruins of the old church, is supported by the vicar and Miss Beers; and there are six other public, and five private, schools, also three Sunday schools. In this parish are several large and nearly perfect raths and forts; at Legananney is a large cromlech, of which the table stone is supported by three large upright stones; at Mullaslane are four large upright stones; a fifth, but smaller, stands not far off, and in the adjoining field is a single upright stone of enormous size. In the gable of the school-house at Drumgooland is a large, perfect, and ancient stone cross, which formerly stood in the churchyard, but, having been thrown down and broken, it was built into the wall by the late rector: the shaft and cross are of porphyry, and the plinth of granite.

DUNDONALD, a parish, in the barony of LOWER CASTLEREAGH, county of DOWN, and province of ULSTER, 4 miles (E.) from Belfast, on the mail coach road to Newtown-Ardes; containing 1,669 inhabitants. This parish, which is called also Kirkdonald, comprises, according to the Ordnance survey, 4,635 statute acres of fertile land, principally under tillage and in a high state of cultivation. Every improvement in the mode of tillage and the construction of farming implements has been eagerly adopted; there is neither bog nor waste land in the parish, The principal seats are Stormont, that of S. Cleveland, Esq.; Summerfield, of R. Gordon, Esq.; Rose Park, of Major Digby; Bessmount, of T.S. Corry, Esq.; and Donleady, of A. McDonnel, Esq. Near the village is an extensive bleach-green, where 5,000 pieces of linen are annually finished. The living is a rectory, in the diocese of Down, and in the patronage of S. Cleveland, Esq.; the tithes amount to £205. The glebe-house, a handsome residence, was built in 1820 by a gift of £300 and a loan of £500 from the late Board of First Fruits; the glebe comprises 15^1/$_2$ acres. The church, a small edifice, was rebuilt on the site of a former church in 1771, and a tower was added to it in 1774. In the R.C. divisions the parish forms part of the union of Newtown-Ardes. There is a place of worship for Presbyterians in connection with the Synod of Ulster, of the second class, to the poor of which congregation Mr. John Crane, of London, bequeathed the interest of a sum of money. About 50 children are taught in the parochial school, which is aided by the rector; and there is a private school, in which are about 45 children. A large and handsome school-house has been built and endowed at Church Quarter, by David Gordon, Esq., the principal proprietor of the parish. In the demesne of Summerfield is a chalybeate spring; and close to the church is a large circular fort surrounded by a moat, from which the parish is supposed to derive its name. A little below, in the same ground, is a cave continued to the fort and passing under its base. Near the bleach-green is a conical hill, or rath, contiguous to which, at the mouth of a small rivulet, is a stone pillar 10 feet high. Gilbert Kennedy, a distinguished Presbyterian divine, was interred in the church in 1687.

DUNDRUM, a maritime village, in that part of the parish of KILMEGAN which is in the barony of LECALE, county of DOWN, and province of ULSTER, 1^1/$_2$ mile (S.) from Clough, on the road from Newry to Downpatrick: the population is returned with the parish. This place is situated on an inner bay, about 1^1/$_2$ mile long by ^{1}/$_4$ of a mile broad, at the head of the larger one to which it gives name; and was distinguished for its ancient castle, of which though twice besieged and taken by the lord-deputy, and finally demolished by Cromwell, there are still considerable and very interesting remains. It is said to have been built by Sir John de Courcy for Knights Templars, who kept possession of it till the suppression of their order in 1313, when it was transferred to the Prior of Down. On the dissolution of the monasteries, the castle, with several townlands, was given to Gerald, Earl of Kildare, and subsequently to the Maginnis family, on whose attainder it was forfeited to the Crown and granted to the Earl of Ardglass; it afterwards became the property of Viscount Blundell, from whom it descended to the Marquess of Downshire, its present proprietor. The village, which previously consisted of one narrow street, containing only a few houses very indifferently built, has been recently much improved by the Marquess of Downshire, who has widened the old street and opened several new lines of road, and has promoted the erection of many neat and comfortable dwelling-houses. He has also built a spacious and commodious hotel, hot and cold baths, and adjoining the latter a lodging-house for himself, which is occasionally let to strangers during the summer. The principal

trade is the export of grain, for which a small but convenient quay has been constructed by his lordship, who has also built warehouses and stores for grain. Fairs are held on Jan. 3rd, Feb. 5th, May 12th, Aug. 6th, and Oct. 10th. The larger bay, which affords great facilities for bathing, extends from the foot of the mountain of Slieve Donard to St. John's Point, a distance of nine miles, and nearly four miles inland. The ground is mostly clean and the depth moderate; but the bay is exposed to severe gusts of wind from the Mourne mountains; the south, and south-east winds send in a heavy sea, and vessels should never remain here unless when the wind is from the north or northeast. The ground immediately outside the larger bay is said to be one of the best fishing grounds in the British seas, affording always in their respective seasons large supplies of excellent haddock, cod, whiting, plaice, sole, and turbot. The western shore is a continued range of sand hills, through which is an inlet deep enough to admit vessels of 50 tons laden with coal, lime, and slate to the quay at the village, In the inlet, during the summer months, there are large shoals of sand eels, to take which several hundreds of the neighbouring peasantry assemble every tide, and provide themselves with an. abundant supply for some months. The remains of the castle consist chiefly of a lofty circular tower of more than 30 feet internal diameter, built on the summit of a rock overlooking the bay; the walls and the winding staircase leading to the battlements are nearly perfect, but the roofs and the floors of the several stories have fallen in; and the vault or dungeon, deeply excavated in the rock, is exposed. The tower is surrounded by a deep fosse hewn in the solid rock, and on the east are the remains of two lofty bastions: the walls of the ancient gatehouse are still standing. Dr. Thomas Smith, consecrated Bishop of Limerick in 1695, was a native of this place. – See KILMEGAN.

DUNSFORD, or DUNSPORT, a parish, in the barony of LECALE, county of DOWN, and province of ULSTER, 3^1/$_2$ miles (E.S.E.) from Downpatrick; containing 1,680 inhabitants. This parish, which is situated near the southern entrance to Strangford Lough, comprises, with Guns island, according to the Ordnance survey, 4,239 statute acres, all under cultivation, except 40 acres of bog, and very fertile, much grain being exported from the stores at Ballyhornan, where small vessels land coal. Guns island lies off the coast, which is bold and rocky, and includes Killard Point. The parish is in the diocese of Down, and is a rectory, forming the corps of the prebend of Dunsford in the cathedral of the Holy Trinity, and in the patronage of the Bishop: the tithes amount to £382, of which £263 is payable to the incumbent and £139 to the impropriators. The church is a small plain edifice with a bell tower. In the R.C. divisions it is the head of a union or district comprising this parish and Ardglass, and containing two chapels, of which the one for Dunsford is at Ballydock. About 350 children are educated in four public schools.

GARVAGHY, a parish, partly in the barony of LOWER, but chiefly in that of UPPER IVEAGH, county of DOWN, and province of ULSTER, 4 miles (S.E.) from Dromore, on the western branch of the river Lagan, and on the road from Banbridge to Downpatrick; containing 5,036 inhabitants, This parish comprises, according to the Ordnance survey, 10,256³/₄ statute acres, which with the exception of about 50 acres of bog and 26 of water, are wholly under tillage; the system of agriculture is greatly improved, and the lands are well fenced and generally in a high state of cultivation. There are some quarries of stone of good quality, which is extensively worked for building, repairing the roads, and other purposes. The principal seats are Carniew, the residence of R.D. Macredy, Esq.; the Cottage, of W. Cosby, Esq.; Ballyely, of R. Maginnis, Esq.; Lion Hill, of H. Waugh, Esq.; the glebe-house, of the Rev. H.S. Hamilton, Esq.; and Waringsford, the property of J. Heron, Esq. The living is a vicarage, in the diocese of Dromore, and in the patronage of the Bishop; the rectory is partly appropriate to the see, and partly constitutes the corps of the prebend of Dromeragh in the cathedral of Dromore. The tithes amount to £514, of which £185 is payable to the bishop, £129 to the prebendary, and £200 to the vicar. The Ecclesiastical Commissioners have recommended the re-annexation of the rectorial tithes to the vicarage on the next avoidance of the prebend. The glebe-house, a handsome residence, was built by aid of a gift of £400, and a loan of £400, from the late Board of First Fruits, in 1820; the glebe comprises 74 acres. The church, a small edifice in the Grecian style, built in 1699, was thoroughly repaired in 1780, when the chancel was taken down In the R.C. divisions the parish forms part of the union or district of Dromore; the chapel at Ballineybeg is a small edifice, erected in 1822. There are places of worship for Presbyterians in connection with the Seceding Synod (of the first class), and Antiburghers. The parochial school is on the glebe, near the church; at Carniew is a school, with a residence for the master attached, to which the Rev. C. Hamilton, in 1814, gave an acre of land; there are also a national and five other public schools. About 250 children are taught in four private schools, and there are six Sunday schools. At Ballineybeg, and also at Knockgorman, are some remains of cromlechs.

GILFORD, a post-town, in the parish of TULLYLISH, barony of LOWER IVEAGH, county of DOWN, and province of ULSTER, 11 miles (N.) from Newry, and 65¹/₂ (N.) from Dublin, on the river Bann, and the road from Loughbrickland to Tanderagee and Portadown; containing 529 inhabitants. In 1772, a body of insurgents, calling themselves 'Hearts of Oak,' committed frequent outrages in this neighbourhood, and on the 6th of March attacked Gilford Castle, the residence of Sir R. Johnston, Bart., and in the assault the Rev. S. Morell, Presbyterian minister, was shot while attempting to reason with the assailants from a window of the castle; it is now the residence of Sir W. Johnston, Bart. The town is situated on both sides of the river, over which is a handsome stone bridge of two arches, and in the vicinity are a large spinning establishment, some extensive bleach-greens, flour-mills, and

chemical works. The canal from Lough Neagh to Newry passes within a mile of the town, and on its banks at that place is a wharf with some good warehouses. Fairs are held on the 21st of June and November; they are toll free and well attended. There is a constabulary police station, and petty sessions are held on alternate Wednesdays. There is a chalybeate spring, the water of which has the same properties as those of Pyrmont. Several gentlemen's seats in the neighbourhood are noticed in the account of Tullylish, which see.

GREY-ABBEY, a post-town and parish, in the barony of ARDES, county of DOWN, and province of ULSTER, 6 miles (S.E.) from Newtownards (to which it has a sub-post-office), and 95 (N.N.E.) from Dublin, on the road from Newtownards to Portaferry; containing 3,700 inhabitants. This place derives its name from a monastery founded here in 1192, by Afric, wife of John de Courcy, and daughter of Godred, King of Man, in honour of the Blessed Virgin, for monks of the Cistertian order, who were brought hither from the Abbey of Holme-Cultram, in Cumberland. The establishment continued to flourish till the dissolution, and had ample possessions in Great and Little Ardes. Towards the close of the reign of Elizabeth it was nearly destroyed, in the rebellion raised by Tyrone; and in the 3rd of Jas. I. the site and precincts, together with all its possessions, were granted to Sir James Hamilton. The village is pleasantly situated on Lough Strangford, and on the road from Portaferry to Belfast; and the neighbourhood is embellished with some elegant seats and beautiful scenery. Mount Stewart, the splendid residence of the Marquess of Londonderry, is a spacious mansion, situated in an extensive demesne richly wooded and pleasingly diversified with water. On the summit of an eminence in the grounds is an elegant building, a model of the Temple of the Winds at Athens, erected under the personal superintendence of J. Stewart, Esq., whose skill and taste in Grecian architecture have procured for him the appellation of the Athenian Stewart; it is built of stone from the quarries of Scrabo, and the floors, which are of bog fir found in the peat moss on the estate, are, for beauty of material and elegance of design, unequalled by any thing of the kind in the country; nearly adjoining the village is Rosemount, the residence of Mrs. Montgomery. According to the Ordnance survey the parish, with some small islands in Strangford Lough, comprises 7,689 statute acres, nearly equally divided between tillage and pasture, the land on the shore being good, but in the interior boggy and rocky; very little improvement has been made in agriculture. Excellent slate is found in the townland of Tullycaven, but the quarry is not judiciously worked. There is a very extensive bog, which supplies the inhabitants with abundance of fuel, and beneath the surface are found large oak and fir trees lying horizontally at a depth of 15 and 20 feet; the fir is in a fine state of preservation, exceedingly hard, and susceptible of a very high polish. A great quantity of calico and muslin is woven here by the peasantry at their own dwellings, and many of the females are employed in tambour-work. It is a perpetual

Greyabbey monastery. Drawn by R.O'C Newenham and engraved by J.D. Harding. From R.O'C Newenham, Picturesque views of the antiquities of Ireland, *vol.1, (London, 1830).*

curacy, in the diocese of Down, and in the patronage of W. Montgomery, Esq., in whom the rectory is impropriate: the tithes are included in the rent, and the perpetual curate's stipend amounts to £96.19.10$^1/_2$, of which £13.16.11 is paid by the impropriator. £9.4.7$^1/_2$ by the Marquess of Londonderry, £4.12.4 by A. Auchinleck, Esq., and £69.6 by the Ecclesiastical Commissioners out of Primate Boulter's fund. The church is a small neat building, erected in 1778, and contains some handsome monuments of the Montgomery family. There is a place of worship for Presbyterians in connection with the Synod of Ulster, of the third class. There is a school of Erasmus Smith's foundation, for which the school-house was built by the late Marchioness of Londonderry, and 60 of the children are supported and clothed by the present Marchioness; and a male, female, and an infants' school, to which Mrs. Montgomery annually contributes £6, £12, and £6 respectively. In these and six other schools about 460 children are educated. The remains of the abbey are beautiful and picturesque; the eastern gable is nearly entire; and contains five lancet-shaped windows, of which the stone work is quite perfect; there are also a window of the same character on the north and south sides of the choir; the nave, which till 1778 was used as the parish church, is tolerably entire, and is now the mausoleum of the family. There are

the remains of several ancient monuments, and within the choir are two recumbent effigies, said to be those of John de Courcy and his wife, finely carved in freestone. There are also several other walls remaining, serving to give an idea of the former extent of the buildings, which appear to have been in the purest style of early English architecture. A very large tumulus was opened in 1825, by Dr. Stephenson, and found to contain 17 stone coffins, formed by placing together several flagstones on edge, and covering them with one large stone; one of these in the centre was larger than the rest, and in each of them was found an urn of baked clay, containing granular earth of a dark colour.

GROOMSPORT, a village, in the parish of BANGOR, barony of ARDES, county of DOWN, and province of ULSTER, 1$^1/_2$ mile (N.E. by E.) from the sea-port town of Bangor, on the coast road to Donaghadee; containing 408 inhabitants. It is situated on the south side of Belfast Lough, and has a harbour for small craft chiefly engaged in fishing. Here is a station of the coastguard. forming part of the district of Donaghadee. On the 13th of August, 1689, the advanced army of Wm. III., consisting of about 10,000 troops under the command of Duke Schomberg, disembarked at this place from 70 transports, and encamped for the night: on the following day the Duke proceeded to invest Carrickfergus.

HILLSBOROUGH, an incorporated market-town (formerly a parliamentary borough), and a parish, in the barony of LOWER lVEAGH, county of DOWN, and province of ULSTER, 16 miles (W.N.W.) from Downpatrick, and 70¹/₄ (N.E.) fromDublin; containing 6,386 inhabitants, of which number, 1,453 are in the town. This place, originally called Cromlyn, derived its present name from a castle erected by Sir Arthur Hill in the reign of Chas. I., which at the Restoration was made a royal fortress by Chas. II., who made Sir Arthur and his heirs hereditary constables, with 20 warders and a well-appointed garrison. The castle is of great strength and is defended by four bastions commanding the road from Dublin to Belfast and Carrickfergus: it is still kept up as a royal garrison under the hereditary constableship of the present Marquess of Downshire, a descendant of the founder, and is also used as an armoury for the yeomanry. At the time of the Revolution, the army of Wm. III. encamped under its walls: and during the disturbances of 1798, the royal army encamped on Blaris moor, within two miles of this place. The town, which is built on the summit and declivities of a hill, consists of one principal and three smaller streets, and contains 214 houses, many of which are of handsome appearance; it is well paved, partially lighted, and amply supplied with water conveyed by pipes from the neighbouring bills. The approach from the Dublin road has been widened, one of the old streets near the castle has been removed, and other considerable improvements have been made. Races, established under the management of the horse-breeders of the county of Down, incorporated by charter of Jas. II., are held in this neighbourhood and at Downpatrick alternately, and are kept up with great spirit. The course, called the Maze, about two miles from the town, winds round the base of a hill, from the summit of which the spectators have an excellent view of the races, and an elegant stand has been erected. The manufacture of linen and cotton is carried on, chiefly for the Belfast merchants; an extensive ale brewery was established in 1810, and a very large distillery in 1826, which has three stills worked by one fire; in these works, which belong to Messrs.

Dedicated to the Marquis of Downshire, the print shows the grand fête and dinner given at Hillsborough Castle on 18 Oct. 1837 for 4,000 of the principal tenants on his Co. Down estates in celebration of the marriage of his son and heir, the Earl of Hillsborough, to the Hon. Caroline Stapleton Cotton. After sketches 'taken on the spot and upon recollection of the scene by J.I.R Esq' and 'drawn on stone by John Johnston, deaf and dumb pupil of Claremont in the employment of messrs Allen'. Printed at Allen's Lithographic Press, Trinity St., Dublin.

Bradshaw and Co., 40 men are regularly employed, and 2,000 tons of grain are annually consumed. The Lagan canal from Belfast to Lough Neagh passes within a mile of the town, and a wharf has been constructed on its bank for landing coal and other necessaries. The market is on Wednesday, and fairs are held on the third Wednesday in Feb., May, Aug., and Nov.; the market-place is spacious, and shambles and grain stores have been erected. Great agricultural improvements have been carried on in the neighbouring district by the present Marquess during the last twenty-five years. By charter of Chas. II. the corporation consists of a sovereign, 12 burgesses, and an indefinite number of freemen, assisted by a recorder (who is also town-clerk), a serjeant-at-mace, and inferior officers. The sovereign is annually elected, from the burgesses, and with his deputy is coroner, and, during his year of office and for one year after, justice of peace within the borough; the burgesses are chosen, as vacancies occur, by a majority of their own body, by whom the recorder and other officers are appointed, and the freemen admitted by favour only. The borough returned two members to the Irish parliament till the Union, when the elective franchise was abolished, and the £15,000 awarded as compensation was paid to Arthur, Marquess of Downshire. A borough court and court of record were formerly held, but have been long discontinued. Courts leet and baron are held every three weeks by the seneschal of the Marquess, for the manor of Hillsborough with jurisdiction to the amount of £2 extending over upwards of 26,000 acres in the parishes of Hillsborough, Blaris, Anahilt, Dromara, Dromore, and Moira; and a court of record for the same manor, for pleas to the amount of £200. Petty sessions are held here every Wednesday, and the quarter sessions for the county alternately here and at Newtownards. The court-house, a handsome building of freestone in the centre of the market-place, was erected by the present Marquess: a district bridewell has been built under the provision of an act of the 7th of Geo. IV.; and a chief constabulary police force has been stationed in the town.

The parish comprises, according to the Ordnance survey, 8,484³/₄ statute acres, of which 62¹/₂ are water and the remainder good arable and pasture land, the principal part of which is under tillage and in a high state of cultivation. Hillsborough Castle, the seat of the Marquess of Downshire, situated at the west end of the town, is in a demesne richly embellished with wood; in the grounds is a fine lake, and the scenery is pleasingly diversified and highly picturesque. At the east side of the town is the park, enclosing a space of 1,500 statute acres, surrounded by a wall: it also is beautifully situated, richly wooded, and has a fine lake. Within it is the fort above-mentioned, erected by Sir Arthur Hill, in the centre of the west side of which is a castellated mansion, supposed to have been built as a residence for the constable. King William slept in it when his army was encamped in the neighbourhood. It is entered by an arched gateway, which is the only passage into the fort except a sally-port in the eastern

side. It was from this place that King William issued his declaration to grant the Regium Donum to the Presbyterian ministers of Ulster. The other seats are Culcavy Cottage, the residence of H. Bradshaw, Esq.; Eglantine, of Capt. Moore; Carnbane, of H. Moreland, Esq.; Shamrock Vale, of Lieut. Clarke, R.N.; and Blaris House, of Col. Hawkeshaw. The living is a rectory, in the diocese of Down, formerly the head of a union comprising also the parishes of Drumbeg, Drumboe, and Kilclief, together constituting the corps of the archdeaconry of Down, but since the dissolution of the union under the Church Temporalities' act, consequent on the demise of the Rev. R.M. Mant, in 1834, it has solely formed the corps of the archdeaconry: the tithes amount to £550. The glebe-house is a handsome residence, and the glebe comprises 22 acres, subject to a rent of £31.7.8; attached to the archdeaconry are also 235 acres of glebe in the parish of Kilclief. The church, a spacious cruciform structure in the later English style, with square embattled towers at the extremities of the transepts, and a similar tower at the west end surmounted by an octagonal spire, was erected in 1774, at the sole expense of the late Marquess. The interior is finely arranged; the windows are embellished with stained glass, and a powerful and sweet-toned organ was presented by the late Marquess, and has been enlarged and much enriched in tone by the present Marquess, by whom also the church is kept in repair, and the salaries of the organist, choristers and vergers paid. In the R.C. divisions the parish forms part of the union or district of Lisburn, and has a chapel in the town. There are also places of worship for Presbyterians, the Society of Friends, and Moravians. Nearly 300 children are taught in five public schools, of which the parochial schools are supported by the Marquess and Marchioness of Downshire; and there are four private schools, in which are about 200 children, and a dispensary. Hillsborough gives the inferior titles of Earl and Viscount, and Kilwarlin the title of Viscount, to the Marquess of Downshire.

HILLTOWN, a village, in the parish of CLONDUFF, barony of UPPER IVEAGH, county of DOWN, and province of ULSTER, 2 miles (S.) from Rathfriland, on the road from Newry to Downpatrick; containing 39 houses and 170 inhabitants. It is a handsome village, with a small but remarkably well kept inn, strikingly indicating the care which its noble proprietor, the Marquess of Downshire, has bestowed on the improvement of his estates, and the fidelity with which his lordship's views have been promoted by his agent, W.E. Reilly, Esq. In the grant of it to the Hillsborough family it is called Carquillan. There is a market on Saturday, and a large fair for cattle and linen yarn on the second Tuesday in every month. It is a chief constabulary police station, and has a good inn. The parish church of Clonduff having been destroyed in the war of 1641, a church was built here in 1766. It is a large and handsome edifice with a tower, erected by aid of a gift of £338 from the late Board of First Fruits, and recently repaired by a grant of £230 from the Ecclesiastical

Commissioners. Here is also the glebe-house, with a glebe of 21 acres; a Presbyterian meeting-house, in connection with the Synod of Ulster, of the third class; a R.C. chapel, and the parochial school, for which a house was built in 1824 by the Marquess of Downshire, who has endowed it with £10 per annum.

HOLLYWOOD, a post-town and parish, in the barony of LOWER CASTLEREAGH, county of DOWN, and province of ULSTER, 4 miles (N.E.) from Belfast, and 84 (N.) from Dublin; containing 4,693 inhabitants, of which number, 1,288 are in the town. In the year 1200, Thomas Whyte founded at this place a Franciscan priory, which was amply endowed, and continued to flourish till the dissolution. Among its possessions were the Copeland Isles, and the Isle of Rathlin or Raghery, to the north of the county, which, with its other endowments, were granted to Sir Jas. Hamilton in the 3rd of Jas. I. On the 8th of April, 1644, a meeting of the Presbyterian clergy and laity was held here, at which several persons entered into 'a solemn league and covenant for the defence of the reformed religion, the safety of the king, and the peace, happiness, and security of the three kingdoms, and to secure and hold fast the league and covenant with England;' the original document, signed by 32 gentlemen, is preserved in the museum at Belfast. The village, which is delightfully situated on the eastern shore of Carrickfergus bay, and on the road from Belfast to Bangor, previously to 1800 contained only about 30 dwellings, chiefly poor cabins; but from its proximity to Belfast, and its fine sandy beach, it has since been greatly extended, and is now become a favourite place of resort for sea-bathing. It contains at present 225 houses, mostly well built; bathing-lodges have been erected for the accommodation of visiters, a new road has been made along the shore, and a daily mail has been established. There are several good lodging-houses in the village and its environs; and from the increasing number of visiters, several houses in detached situations, and chiefly in the Elizabethan style of architecture, are now in progress of erection on the Cultra estate, by Thomas Ward, Esq., after designs by Millar. These houses are sheltered with thriving plantations, and beautifully situated on a gentle eminence commanding a richly diversified and extensive prospect of Carrickfergus bay, the Black mountain, Cave Hill, the Carnmoney mountains, and the town and castle of Carrickfergus, terminating with the basaltic columns of Black Head. Close to the shore is an extensive muscle bank; and about a mile to the north-west of the town, in the lough, is a sand bank, called the Hollywood bank, the greater part of which is dry at low water, but which vessels may easily avoid by sailing nearer to the northern shore. It is a constabulary police station, and also a coast-guard station, forming part of the district of Donaghadee. Fairs, principally for cattle and horses, are held on the first Monday in each quarter. A court leet and baron is held every three weeks by the seneschal of the manor, for pleas in civil bill cases to the amount of £10, and pleas of record and attachment of goods

and chattels to the amount of £20; its jurisdiction extends over 27 townlands in the parish of Hollywood, Knockbreda, Dundonald, and Ballymacarett; but the prison not being now used for that purpose, defaulters are sent to the county gaol.

The parish comprises the two ancient parishes of Ballymechan, or Columbkill, and Craigavad, both rectories, one belonging to Hollywood priory, and the other to the abbey of Bangor, which were united in 1626, under the name of Hollywood. It contains, according to the Ordnance survey, 8,064¹/₄ statute acres, principally under an improved system of tillage and in a high state of cultivation. Freestone of excellent quality and coal may be obtained, but the mines are not worked to any extent. The surrounding scenery is finely varied, and embellished with numerous gentlemen's seats; among which are the episcopal palace of the Bishop of Down; Cultra, the seat of H. Kennedy, Esq.; Ballymenock, of T. Gregg, Esq.; Rockport, of I. Turnley, Esq.; Craigavad, of A. Forbes, Esq.; Garnerville, of Capt. Garner; Hollywood House, of J. Macartney, Esq.; Turf Lodge, of J. Kane, Esq.; Knocknagoney, of Mrs. Kennedy; Bloomfield, of J. Agnew, Esq.; Clifton, of Dr. Halliday; Richmond Lodge, of F. Turnley, Esq.; Wellington, of W. Crawford, Esq.; Marino, of T. Ward, Esq.; Greenville, of I. Stott, Esq.; Glen Carrig, of Miss Symes; and the Spa, of J. Cordukes, Esq. The living is an impropriate curacy, in the diocese of Down, and in the patronage of Viscount Dungannon, in whom the rectory is impropriate. The tithes belong to the proprietors of the soil, and are included in the rent; the patron pays £40 per ann., to the minister, which is augmented to £100 by the trustees of Primate Boulter's fund; the glebe-house was built in 1812, by a gift of £450 and a loan of £50 from the late Board of First Fruits: the glebe comprises 12a. 4p. The church, which is at the eastern extremity of the village, is an ancient building, with several antique heads in the outer wall, which are supposed to have been the corbels of a former church. In the R.C. divisions the parish forms part of the union or district of Belfast, and has a chapel, which was built in 1828. There is a Presbyterian meeting-house in connection with the Synod of Ulster, of the second class, and one belonging to the Presbytery of Antrim. About 230 children are educated in five public schools, one of which is supported by Mr. Turnley; and about 60 in two private schools; there are also two Sunday schools. An establishment for the relief of the poor is supported by subscriptions, in which 15 poor persons constantly reside. The church occupies the site of the ancient priory, of which there are no other remains; and of the churches of Ballymechan and Craigavad not a vestige can be traced; the cemeteries of both were used as places of interment till 1765, and in the former were deposited the remains of Con O'Neil, the last of that powerful sept, whose possessions comprised more than one-third of the county of Down, and an extensive district in the county of Antrim, in which was included the now populous town of Belfast. Some carved stones are preserved at Ballymechan, which are supposed to have

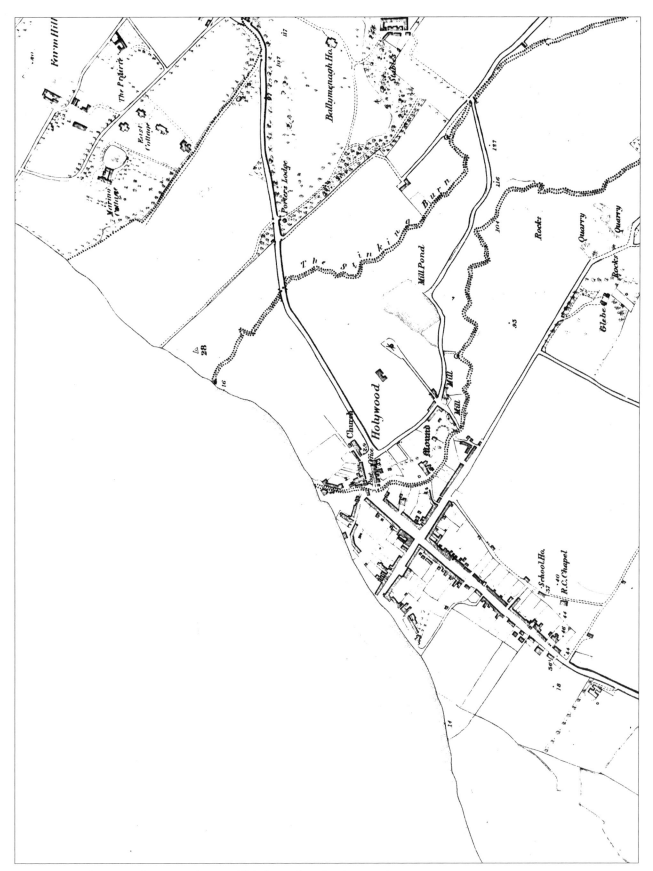

Holywood. Part of O.S. map of Co. Down, sheet 1, published 1835 (reproduced at 140%).

Inch Abbey. Drawn by Andrew Nicholl and engraved by Branston and Wright. From The Dublin Penny Journal, *vol.1, 1833.*

belonged to his tomb, but the sculpture is of an earlier date; the site of that church is now a garden and the churchyard an orchard, and at Craigavad only one solitary stone remains to mark the site of the churchyard, which is now under cultivation. A new species of rose was discovered in this parish by John Templeton, Esq., which by the Dublin Society was called 'Rosa Hibernica,' and afterwards 'Rosa Templetonia,' in honour of the discoverer.

INCH, or INNISCOURCY, a parish, in the barony of LECALE, county of DOWN, and province of ULSTER, $2^1/_2$ miles (N.) from Downpatrick, on the road to Killyleagh; containing 2,857 inhabitants. A Cistertian abbey was founded on a peninsulated portion of this parish, called Inch Island, and subsequently Inniscourcy, by Sir John de Courcy, in 1180, in atonement for having in his wars demolished the abbey of Erynagh, which had been fortified against him. It was dedicated to the Blessed Virgin, and amply endowed by its founder, who transferred to it all the possessions of the abbey of Erynagh, and placed in it monks from Furness in Lancashire; after the dissolution, its site and possessions were granted to Gerald, Earl of Kildare. The parish, which is bounded on the east by Strangford Lough, comprises, according to the Ordnance survey, $6,494^1/_4$ statute acres, of which $80^1/_4$ are water, and 4,731 are applotted under the tithe act; of these, 200 acres are wood and plantations, 1,800 rocky pasture, and the remainder, with the exception of 20 acres of bog, are under tillage and in a high state of cultivation. Over the river Quoile, which here opens into the western branch of Strangford Lough, is a bridge connecting this place with Downpatrick. Adjoining the parish are the very extensive embankments called the water-works, constructed across the lough by Mr. Southwell, in 1748, at which time a large tract of marshy ground was reclaimed. Finnebrogue, the seat of J.W. Maxwell, Esq., is a handsome mansion, situated in a richly wooded and well-watered demesne of 500 acres, embellished with thriving plantations. At Ballanacreg is a lead mine, and near it a slate quarry, both of which have been imperfectly worked. The living is a rectory, in the diocese of Down, formerly united to the rectory of Ardkeen and vicarage of Witter, together constituting the corps of the prebend of

St. Andrew, in the cathedral of Down, but in 1834 separated from those parishes, on the recommendation of the Ecclesiastical Commissioners, and now solely forming the corps of the prebend, and in the patronage of the Bishop: the tithes amount to £286.3.1. The church, erected in 1742, and enlarged and repaired by a loan from the late Board of First Fruits, in 1831, is a handsome structure with a tower and spire, added in 1784, and a transverse aisle added in 1826. In the R.C. divisions the parish forms part of the union or district of Kilmore, or Crossgar; the chapel is a small building near the extremity of the parish. About 100 children are taught in the parochial school, for which a good school-house was built at the joint expense of the rector and J. W. Maxwell, Esq., by whom it is chiefly supported; and there are two private schools, in which are about 150 children, and a Sunday school. There are some remains of the Cistertian abbey, situated in a fertile dell near the southern extremity of the parish, and within a quarter of a mile of the cathedral of Down, from which they are separated by the Quoile river, across which is a ferry; the choir is nearly perfect having three lofty windows at the east end, and two in the north and south walls, with many other interesting details. To the north of the abbey are the ruins of the ancient parish church, a spacious cruciform structure, erected in 1610, partly with the materials of the old abbey; the spacious cemetery is still used as a burial-ground. These ruins, from their style and situation, are exceedingly picturesque.

INNISHARGEY, a parish, in the barony of ARDES, county of DOWN, and province of ULSTER, 1¹/₂ mile (N.) from Kircubbin; the population is returned with the union of St. Andrew's. According to the Ordnance survey it comprises 5,516 statute acres. It is a vicarage, in the diocese of Down, forming part of the union of St. Andrew's; the rectory is appropriate to the Lord-Primate. The church of the union is in this parish, a parish, in the barony of ARDES, county of DOWN, and province of ULSTER, 1¹/₂ mile (N.) from Kircubbin; the population is returned with the union of St. Andrew's. According to the Ordnance survey it comprises 5,516 statute acres. It is a vicarage, in the diocese of Down, forming part of the union of St. Andrew's; the rectory is appropriate to the Lord-Primate. The church of the union is in this parish.

KILBRONEY, a parish, in the barony of UPPER IVEAGH, county of DOWN, and province of ULSTER, on the road from Newry to Kilkeel; containing, with the town of Rosstrevor, 4,257 inhabitants. According to the Ordnance survey it comprises 13,208¹/₄ statute acres, of which 275 are woodland, about 5,000 arable, and the remainder bog and mountain, the latter of which affords excellent pasture. Here are some large bleach-greens, and some lead mines. The principal seats are the Lodge, the residence of D. Ross, Esq.; Brandensburg, of Mrs. Ross; Carpenham, of H. Hamilton, Esq.; Green Park, of Mrs. O'Brien; Amos Vale, of the Ven. Dean Carter; Ballyedmund, of A. Stewart, Esq.; Woodhouse, of Mrs. Reynell;

Old Hall, of Smithson Corry, Esq.; and Crayfield, of W.J. Maguire, Esq. The living is a vicarage, in the diocese of Dromore, and in the gift of the Bishop, to whom the rectory is appropriate: the tithes amount to £155.6.6, of which one-third is pay. able to the vicar, and two-thirds to the Bishop. The church, which is in Rosstrevor, is a handsome cruciform edifice, with a lofty tower and pinnacles: it was built at an expense of £2,000, of which the late Board of First Fruits, in 1814, gave £200 and lent £1,100. The Board also granted £450 as a gift, and £120 as a loan, for the erection of the glebe-house, in 1821: the glebe comprises 11 acres. The R.C. parish is co-extensive with that of the Established Church, and contains two chapels, one in Rosstrevor, the other at Killowen. About 600 children are educated in six schools, to one of which Mrs. Ross contributes £13.16.11, to another Mrs. Balfour contributes £20, and to a third the R.C. clergyman contributes £5, annually. On the acclivity of a mountain is a very large stone, called Cloughmerne, which was formerly part of a cromlech; and near Killowen are the ruins of Green Castle. It was built by Walter de Burgh, Earl of Ulster, destroyed by the Irish in 1343, rebuilt soon after on a large scale, and dismantled by order of Cromwell. Here are also the remains of Castle Roe, or Ross Trevor Castle. On the Hillstown road are the ruins of Kilbroney church, in which a cloghban, or 'white bell,' was some years since discovered; also an ancient stone cross and a holy well. In 1834 a spacious cave was discovered, containing broken urns filled with calcined

Kilclief Castle. Drawn by Andrew Nicholl and engraved by Branston and Wright. From The Dublin Penny Journal, *vol.1, 1833.*

human bones and ashes. A chalybeate spring was formerly much resorted to, but is now almost neglected. – See ROSSTREVOR.

KILCLIEF, a parish, in the barony of LECALE, county of DOWN, and province of ULSTER, 2 miles (S.) from Strangford; containing 841 inhabitants, of which number, 351 are in the village. Here was formerly an abbey under St. Eugene and St. Neill, disciples of St. Patrick; also an hospital for lepers, of which there are still some small remains. The castle of Kilclief, of which also part remains, was anciently the palace of the bishops of Down, to whom the manor belongs. According to the Ordnance survey, the parish contains 2,424^1/$_2$ statute acres: there is no waste or bog, and the land is extremely well cultivated, furnishing much wheat, barley, oats, and potatoes for exportation. The living is a rectory, in the diocese of Down, and in the patronage of the Bishop: the tithes amount to £216. The church is a small plain building on an elevated spot near the sea-shore. There is a glebe-house, for the erection of which £450 was given and £50 lent, in 1816, by the late Board of First Fruits: the glebe comprises 10 acres. In the R.C. divisions the parish is the head of a union or district, including also the townland of Ballyargan, and two others in Ballyculter, and containing a small chapel. About 90 children are educated in the parochial school, which was built in 1804.

KILCOO, a parish, in the barony of UPPER IVEAGH, county of DOWN, and province of ULSTER, 2 miles (S.) from Castlewellan, on the road from Newry to Downpatrick; containing 6,520 inhabitants. It is situated on the eastern coast, at the base of Slieve Donard, and comprises, according to the Ordnance survey, 18,205^1/$_2$ statute acres, of which 15,741 are applotted under the tithe act. The surface is very uneven, and the land, with the exception of that around the village of Bryansford, cold, wet, and unproductive; its cultivation is also much impeded by the great number of stones which are scattered over it in every direction. The mountains of Slieve Donard (which has an elevation of 2,796 feet above the level of the sea) and Slieve Bingian, of 2,449 feet, are within the parish, forming part of a chain rising at Newcastle and extending to Rosstrevor, a distance of 20 miles; the northern sides are here covered with verdure, but the south and west sides present chiefly large tracts of bog. The principal seats are Tollymore Park, the elegant residence of the Earl of Roden, situated in a richly wooded and well watered demesne; Donard Lodge, the handsome mansion of the Earl of Annesley, erected in 1830 on the acclivity of Slieve Donard, and commanding some fine views; Brook Lodge, of W. Beers, Esq.; and Burren Cottage, of the Hon. Gen. Meade: there are also many very good houses at Bryansford and Newcastle (which see), and at Drumlee is the neat cottage of the Rev. J. Porter. The parish is in the diocese of Down, and the rectory forms part of the union of Kilkeel and corps of the treasurership of the cathedral of Down; the tithes amount to £300. The church, with the village of Kilcoo, was burnt in

1641, and in 1712 a church was built at Bryansford, which, being too small for the congregation, was considerably enlarged in 1806, when a handsome tower was added to it; and was repaired by aid of a grant from the late Board of First Fruits, in 1812. There is also a handsome church with a lofty tower at Newcastle, built in the year 1833, at the expense of Earl Annesley, who appoints the minister and pays his stipend. In the R.C. divisions the parish includes the districts of Bryansford and Kilcoo; there are three chapels, situated respectively at Bryansford, Newcastle, and Ballymony; and at Newcastle is also a place of worship for Wesleyan Methodists. A school at Fofeny was founded in 1822, by the Earl of Roden, who also built another for boys, with a house for the master, in 1826, and by whom both are supported. A school for girls at Bryansford, with a cottage for the mistress, was built in 1822, and is supported by the Countess of Roden; and there are schools at Lower Kilcoo, Ballymoney, and Ardaghy. About 650 children are taught in these schools, and there is also a private school, in which are about 40 children. On the western side of the parish, at Lough Island Reavy, a reservoir has been constructed for supplying water to the river Bann in dry weather; it covers an area of 255 acres, and when filled will contain a supply for 13 weeks; the expense to the river Bann Company has been estimated at £20,000. A new quay has been erected at Newcastle, to afford shelter to vessels passing the channel in stormy weather; the expense was defrayed by a grant from government, aided by a subscription from Earl Annesley.

KILKEEL, a post-town and parish, in the barony of MOURNE, county of DOWN, and province of ULSTER, 15 miles (S.E.) from Newry, and 65^3/$_4$ (N.N.E.) from Dublin; containing 14,806 inhabitants, of which number, 1,039 are in the town. According to the Ordnance survey it comprises 47,882^3/$_4$ statute acres, of which about 11,000 are arable and 12,000 pasture; the remainder consists of the Mourne mountains. The only creek in the twelve miles of coast that bounds the parish is Annalong, where a small dock for fishing-vessels has been excavated out of a rock. There are coast-guard stations at Annalong, Cranfield, and the Lee Stone, all in the district of Newcastle; also a constabulary police station. Fairs are held on Feb. 8th, May 3rd, Aug. 2nd, and Dec. 8th; and a manorial court is held in the sessions-house at Kilkeel, once in three weeks, for the manor of Greencastle and Mourne, by a seneshal appointed by the Earl of Kilmorey; its jurisdiction extends over the whole of the barony of Mourne, which is included in this parish, and is the property of his lordship, and pleas to the amount of £10. are determined either by attachment or civil bill. The principal seats are Mourne Park, the splendid residence of the Earl of Kilmorey; Shannon Grove, of J.S. Moore, Esq.; and the glebe-house, of the Rev. J. Forbes Close. The living is a rectory, in the diocese of Down, united, in 1809, by charter of Jas. I., to the rectories of Kilcoo and Kilmegan and the chapelry of Tamlaght (a small townland in Kilkeel), which together form the union of Kilkeel and the corps of the treasurership of the cathedral of Down, in the alternate patronage of the Marquess of Anglesey, and the Earl of Kilmorey. The tithes amount to £800, and of the entire benefice to £1,600. The church was rebuilt in 1818, for which the late Board of First Fruits granted a loan of £2,160. The glebe-house is situated on a glebe of 30 acres, valued at £37.10 per annum, but subject to a rent of £19.7.9, payable to the Earl of Kilmorey. In the R.C. divisions the parish forms two districts, called Upper and Lower Mourne, the former containing a chapel at Ballymaguagh; the latter, one at Glassdrummond and one at Ballymartin. There are a Presbyterian meeting-house in connection with the Synod of Ulster, and one of the third class in connection with the Seceding Synod, also meeting-houses for Wesleyan Methodists, Baptists, and Moravians. About 770 children are educated in eight public schools, to one of which the Earl of Kilmorey contributes £31, and to another, Mrs. Keown £10 annually. Needham Thompson, Esq., built and principally supports the school at Mullartown; and that for girls, at Ballinahatton, was built by the Rev. J.F. Close, who clothes and educates 65 children there. About 450 children are taught in 10 private schools; and there are six Sunday schools and a dispensary.

KILLANEY, or KILLENEY, a parish, in the barony of UPPER CASTLEREAGH, county of DOWN, and province of ULSTER, 4 miles (W. by S.) from Saintfield, on the road from that place to Ballinahinch; containing 1,298 inhabitants. According to the Ordnance survey, it comprises 2,859 statute acres, of which 68¼ are water: the land is good, and under an excellent system of cul tivation, producing abundant crops. The living is a vicarage, in the diocese of Down, and in the patronage of the Marquess of Downshire, in whom the rectory is impropriate: the tithes amount to £85. There is neither church, glebe-house, nor glebe. The church was greatly injured in 1641, and is now in ruins, but divine service is regularly performed in the parochial school-house. There is a Presbyterian meeting-house. The parochial school is supported by the Marquess of Downshire and the vicar. The school-house was built by subscription; about 30 children are educated in it and 100 in a private school; and there is a Sunday school.

KILLINCHY, a post-town and parish, partly in the barony of DUFFERIN, but chiefly in the baronies of UPPER and LOWER CASTLEREAGH, county of DOWN, and province of ULSTER, 9 miles (N.) from Downpatrick, and 92 (N.N.E.) from Dublin, on the road from Downpatrick to Belfast: containing 7,820 inhabitants, of which number, 199 are in the town. According to the Ordnance survey it comprises 13,686 statute acres, of which 6,437¼ (including the islands of Duncey and Island More, in Strangford Lough, and 75¾ acres in that lough), are in the barony of Dufferin; of the remainder, 3281 are in Lower Castlereagh and 4,147¾ (including 50½ of water) are in Upper Castlereagh. The land is chiefly in tillage, and in a high state of cultivation; there is no waste land and but little bog; clay-slate abounds, and a

thin seam of coal is visible at the lough. There are several corn-mills, and fairs are held in the town on Jan. 5th, April 6th, July 6th, and Oct. 5th. It is a constabulary police station, and has a sub-post office to Comber and Killyleagh. Petty sessions are held in the court-house on alternate Saturdays. At the White rocks is a small but excellent harbour and a small pier, at which vessels of 80 tons can load, and from which a considerable quantity of agricultural produce is exported. Here is Ardview, the residence of T. Potter, Esq. The living is a rectory, in the diocese of Down, and in the alternate patronage of Viscount Bangor and the Earl of Carrick: the tithes amount to £800. The church, a large and handsome edifice with a square embattled tower, situated on an eminence, was built in 1830, at an expense of £900, above half of which was raised by subscription. There is a glebe-house, with a glebe of 12 acres. In the R.C. divisions the parish forms part of the union or district of Saintfield and Killinchy, and has a chapel at Carrickmannon. There is a meeting-house for Presbyterians in connection with the Synod of Ulster, of the first class. The parochial schools, in which are about 140 children, are principally supported by the rector; the school-house, built in 1825, is a good plain edifice, containing separate school-rooms for boys and girls, and residences for the master and mistress. There are also eight other public schools, some of which are aided by annual donations from Lord Dufferin, D. Gordon, Esq., and the rector; they afford education to about 600 children; and about 70 children are educated in a private school. The Earl of Limerick, about 1730, gave part of the townland of Killinchy, which now produces £300 per annum, to the Incorporated School Society; and in 1810, Major Potter bequeathed £100 to the poor members of the Presbyterian meeting-house, among whom the interest is divided every Christmas. Here are the remains of Balloo fort, near which many silver coins of the reigns of John and other monarchs were found in 1829. The ancient castle of the family of White stood on the site of Killinchy fort, and in 1802 many silver and copper coins were found in its vicinity. In the churchyard is the tomb of the ancient family of Bruce.

KILLOUGH, or ST. ANNE'S PORT, a sea-port and post-town, in the parish of RATHMULLEN, barony of LECALE, county of DOWN, and province of ULSTER, 5 miles (S.E.) from Dowapatrick, and 78¾ (N.) from Dublin; containing 1,162 inhabitants. This place is situated on the harbour to which it gives name, on the eastern coast, in lat. 54° 15' (N.) and long. 5° 37' 30" (W.) The town contains 247 houses, built along the margin of the bay, and carries on a considerable coasting trade with the principal ports in the Irish channel. The chief exports are corn and live cattle, of the former of which very great quantities are shipped; and the principal imports are coal and salt. A lucrative fishery is carried on off the coast; haddock and whiting are taken in great quantities, and from 12 to 20 boats are daily employed during the year. The manufacture of salt is also carried on upon a small scale. The harbour is about half a league to the east of St. John's

Point, and affords safe shelter for coasting-vessels and for merchant-ships of 150 tons burthen; there is a good roadstead in offshore winds for vessels navigating the channel, and it is the rendezvous of a considerable portion of the numerous fishing-vessels that frequent this part of the coast. The pier and quays extend on both sides of the entrance to the bay, and have been greatly improved by Viscount Bangor, at an expense of more than £18,000. Fairs are held on the first Friday (O.S.) in February, June 9th, Aug. 17th, and Nov. 12th, for live stock and pedlery; and a manorial court is held on the first Tuesday in every month.

The living is an impropriate curacy, in the diocese of Down, and in the patronage of the Incumbent of Rathmullen. The church, which had been rebuilt in 1716, and had subsequently fallen into a state of dilapidation, was again rebuilt in 1802, by the munificence of the Rev. J. Hamilton, who died in 1797, and bequeathed £1,200 for that purpose. It is a neat edifice, on the site of the former, in the early English style, with a tower surmounted with an octangular spire, affording an excellent landmark for mariners entering the port. The glebe-house, towards the erection of which the late Board of First Fruits granted £450 as a gift and £50 as a loan, is a comfortable residence. The stipend of the curate is £100, of which £20 is paid by Lord Bangor, as impropriator of Rathmullen, and £80 by the trustees of Primate Boulter's augmentation fund. The R.C. parochial chapel is in the town, and there is also a place of worship for Wesleyan Methodists. At St. John's Point are the ruins of a preceptory of Knights Hospitallers; and about a quarter of a mile from the town, on the shore, is a beautiful grotto, in which is a well, seven feet deep, supplied with water oozing through a mass of tufa at the top of the cavern. About half a mile from the town, on the road to Downpatrick, is a copious spring, the water of which is specifically lighter by one-fourth part than spring water in general; and close to the shore is St. Seordin's Well, issuing from a rocky bank, and discharging at the rate of one

hogshead per hour, without any diminution in the driest weather. Not far from this is a hole in the rock, which at the ebbing and flowing of the tide emits a sound resembling that of a huntsman's horn.

KILLYLEAGH, a market and post-town, and a parish, partly in the barony of CASTLEREAGH, but chiefly in that of DUFFERIN, county of DOWN, and province of ULSTER, 5 miles (N.E.) from Downpatrick, arid 78³/₄ (N. by N.) from Dublin, on the mail coach road from Belfast to Downpatrick; containing 5,712 inhabitants, of which number, 1,147 are in the town. This place, which is situated on the western shore of Strangford Lough, was a port of some eminence previously to the conquest of Ireland by the English; and, with the adjoining barony of Kinalearty, formed part of the territories of the native sept of the McCartans. It was afterwards granted to De Courcy, who, in order to protect it from the attacks of that powerful chieftain, erected castles on every advantageous site round the shores of the lake, among which the principal was the Castle of Dufferin. In 1356, Edw. III. appointed John De Mandeville, warden of this castle, which subsequently fell into the hands of the O'Nials, who maintained possession of it till 1561, when the adjoining territory was by Elizabeth granted to Hugo White, who shortly afterwards erected a castle at Killyleagh, into which he removed his warden from Castle Dufferin. Shane O'Nial besieged the newly erected castle in 1567, and meeting with a powerful resistance, set fire to the town; but a league being subsequently made between the McCartans and the O'Nials, they jointly attacked the castle, dispossessed the family of White, and usurped the uncontrolled dominion of the entire country. On the suppression of the Tyrone rebellion at the close of the 16th century, the possessions of the McCartans were confiscated, and the manor and district of Killyleagh were subsequently granted by Jas. I. to Sir James Hamilton, who restored and considerably enlarged the castle, which, after his elevation to the peerage by the title of Lord Claneboy, he made his principal residence. The castle was besieged and taken by Gen. Monk for the parliament, in 1648, and was partly demolished in the war of that period, but was substantially repaired in 1666, and in it was born Archibald Hamilton Rowan, Esq., whose grandson, a minor, is now the proprietor. It is a large and strong pile of building, in the later English style, occupying an eminence which commands the town, but affords no protection to the harbour.

The town is pleasantly situated on a gentle eminence on the western shore of Strangford lough, and consists of two nearly parallel streets, intersected by a longer street, which forms the principal thoroughfare; it contains 207 houses, built principally of clay-slate found in the parish, and is the property of Lord Dufferin and Archibald Hamilton, Esq. The cotton manufacture is carried on upon a very extensive scale. Some large mills were built upon a copious stream, in 1824, by Messrs. Martin and Co., and were greatly enlarged in 1828: in these works are 13,798 spindles, employing 186 persons,

Killyleagh Castle. From The Dublin Penny Journal, *vol.2, 1833.*

and 244 power-looms attended by 156 persons, constantly engaged in weaving printers' cloths for the Manchester market; and connected with this manufactory are more than 2,000 hand-looms in the neighbouring districts. The buildings, which are very spacious and six stories high, are lighted with gas made on the premises, and the proprietors have erected a steam-engine of 35 horse power. The trade of the port is limited, and consists principally in the exportation of wheat, barley, oats, potatoes, butter, kelp, and cotton goods; and in the importation of cotton, wool, coal, iron, salt, and general merchandise. The harbour is well sheltered, and is accessible to vessels not drawing more than 10 feet of water. The quay and basin are very commodious, and were completed in 1833, at an expense of more than £1,000, defrayed solely by Lord Dufferin. The market is on Friday, and the fairs are on April 10th, Trinity-Monday, Oct. 11th, and Dec. 11th. A constabulary police force is stationed in the town, and there are barracks for the North Down militia, of which this place is the headquarters. The inhabitants received a charter from Jas. I., in the 10th year of his reign, by which they were incorporated by the designation of the 'Provost, Free Burgesses, and Commonalty of the Borough of Killileagh.' By this charter the corporation consists of a provost (annually elected), 12 free burgesses, and an indefinite number of freemen, assisted by a town-clerk, two sergeants-at-mace, and other officers, all of whom are chosen by the provost and free burgesses, by whom also freemen are admitted. The corporation, under their charter, continued to return two members to the Irish parliament till the Union, when the borough was disfranchised, and the £15,000 awarded as compensation was paid to Sir James Stevenson Blackwood, Bart., now Lord Dufferin. The court of record for the borough, which had jurisdiction to the extent of five marks, has long been discontinued. The seneschal of the manor, who is appointed by Mr. Hamilton, holds a court every three weeks, for the recovery of debts not exceeding £10, and a courtleet annually; and a court of petty sessions is held every alternate week.

The parish, according to the Ordnance survey, comprises 11,759$\frac{1}{4}$ statute acres (including 123$\frac{1}{2}$ under water), of which 988$\frac{1}{4}$ are in the barony of Upper Castlereagh, and the remainder in that of Dufferin. The soil is generally fertile and the system of agriculture improved; there is very little waste land, and the bogs are productive both of turf and of bog fir. There are extensive quarries of basalt and clay-slate, from which has been taken the whole of the stone of which the town is built. The principal seats are Delamont, the residence of R. Gordon, Esq.; Ringdufferin, of J. Bailie, Esq.; Killyleagh Castle, of Mrs. Hamilton; Tullyvery House, of 3. Heron, Esq.; Ardigon House, of R. Heron, Esq.; Shrigley, of J. Martin, jun., Esq.; Gosean of A.H. Read, Esq.; and the handsome residence of the Hon. Hans Blackwood, in the town. The living is a rectory, in the diocese of Down, and in the patronage of the Provost and Fellows of Trinity College, Dublin: the tithes

amount to £795. The church, a handsome cruciform structure, with a tower surmounted by a spire of good proportions, was built in 1640, but becoming dilapidated, was rebuilt, and the tower and the spire added, by Lord Dufferin, at an expense of more than £5,000, exclusively of a loan of £2,000 from the late Board of First Fruits in 1812. It contains some handsome monuments to the Blackwood family, including one to the memory of Capt. Blackwood, who fell at Waterloo; another to Capt. Blackwood of the North Downshire militia, and a third to the Rev. James Clewlow; and in the churchyard is the sepulchral vault of the Dufferin family, recently erected, in which Admiral Blackwood was interred, and near it a monument erected by the parishioners to the Rev. Peter Carlton, the late rector. The glebe-house, towards the erection of which, in 1815, the late Board of First Fruits contributed a gift of £100 and a loan of £1,350, is a very handsome residence; the glebe comprises 14 acres. In the R.C. divisions the parish forms part of the union or district of Kilmore: the chapel, a small neat building, was erected in 1832. There is a place of worship for Presbyterians in connection with the Synod of Ulster, of the first class. About 450 children are taught in six public schools, of which three were built and are supported by Lord and Lady Dufferin, D. Gordon, Esq., and the Rev. A.R. Hamilton; and there are four private schools, in which are about 140 children, and three Sunday schools. The remains of the ancient parish church are still visible in a low marshy meadow to the north-west of the town: the eastern gable, perforated with two narrow lancet shaped windows, is yet standing. Sir Hans Sloane, the celebrated physician and naturalist, was born here in 1660. The barony, of which this place is the head, gives the title of Baron to the family of Blackwood, Barons of Dufferin and Claneboy.

KILMEGAN, a parish, partly in the barony of KINELEARTY, partly in LECALE, but chiefly in UPPER IVEAGH, county of DOWN, and province of ULSTER; containing, with the post-town of Castlewellan (which is described under its own head), 6,921 inhabitants. It comprises, according to the Ordnance survey, 13,971$\frac{3}{4}$ statute acres, of which 1,793 are in Kinelearty, 5,983$\frac{1}{2}$ (of which 22$\frac{1}{4}$ are water) in Lecale, and 6,195$\frac{1}{4}$ (of which 107 are water) in Upper Iveagh. Of these about 500 are woodland, 800 pasture, 150 bog, and the remainder arable land. The greater part of the townland of Murlough is covered with sand, which is constantly drifted in from Dundrum bay: the land near Castlewellan is stony, cold, and marshy, but in other parts of the parish it is rich and well cultivated. There are several quarries of granite; lead ore has been found in different parts, and there are mines of lead and zinc in Slieve Croob and the hill above Dundrum, which see. Slieve Croob, situated on the northern boundary of the parish, rises, according to the Ordnance survey, 1,755 feet above the level of the sea. The principal seats are that of Earl Annesley at Castlewellan lake; Bally willwill, the residence of the Rev. G.H. McDowell Johnston; Mount Panther, of 3. Reed Allen, Esq.; Wood Lodge, of H. Murland, Esq.; Woodlawn, of

J. Law, Esq.; Greenvale, of J. Steele, Esq.; Annsbro', of J. Murland, Esq.; and Clanvaraghan, of T. Scott, Esq. It is a rectory, in the diocese of Down, forming part of the union of Kilkeel; the tithes amount to £500. The church is a large handsome edifice, for the repairs of which the Ecclesiastical Commissioners have recently granted £109: divine service is also performed in the market-house at Castlewellan. In the R.C. divisions the parish is the head of a union or district, called Castlewellan, and has chapels at Castlewellan, Aughlisnafin, and Ballywillwill. At Castlewellan is a meeting-house for Presbyterians of the Seceding Synod, of the second class, and one for Wesleyan Methodists. The parochial school, near the church, is supported by the Marquess of Downshire and the rector; his lordship has given the master a house, a garden, and an acre of land; he also supports a school at Dundrum. There are four other public schools, one aided by Earl Annesley, and three in connection with the National Board of Education, one of which is patronised by J. R. Allen, Esq., another by J. Murland, Esq., and the third is under the charge of trustees: there are male and female teachers in each school. There are also five private schools, in which latter about 360 children are educated. At Sliddery ford, near Dundrum, is a cromlech, of which the table stone is flat on the upper surface, and convex beneath, resting upon three upright stones, each four feet high; near it is a circle of upright stones, of which the entrance is marked by two stones larger than the rest. On a hill called Slieve-na-boil-trough, and near a small lake, is another cromlech, consisting of a table stone of rough grit, in the shape of a coffin, ten feet long and five feet in the broadest part resting on three supporters, about 6$^1/_2$ feet from the ground.

KILMORE, a parish, partly in the barony of KINELEARTY, but chiefly in that of UPPER CASTLEREAGH, county of DOWN, and province of ULSTER, 4 miles (E. by S.) from Ballinahinch, on the road from Downpatrick to Belfast; containing 6602 inhabitants. According to the Ordnance survey it comprises 12,854 statute acres, of which 6,387$^3/_4$ are in the barony of Kinelearty, and 6,466$^1/_4$ in Upper Castlereagh. Of these, 94 are water, 60 bog, 400 waste, 250 woodland, 600 pasture, and the remainder arable land in a high state of cultivation, and producing a great quantity of barley. The living is a vicarage, in the diocese of Down, and in the patronage of the Bishop; the rectory is appropriate to the see. The tithes amount to £714, of which £394 is payable to W. Sharman Crawford, Esq., lessee under the bishop, and the remainder to the vicar. The glebe-house was erected in 1794, at an expense of £461.10, towards which the late Board of First Fruits gave £92. The glebe comprises 29a.1r.17p, statute measure, valued at £22 per ann., and subject to a rent of £8.5. The church is a small edifice, built about 1792, principally at the expense of the family of the present W.S. Crawford, Esq. In the R.C. divisions the parish is the head of a union or district, comprising the parishes of Kilmore, Inch, and Killileagh, and has two chapels in Kilmore, and

one in each of the other parishes. Here is a meeting-house for Presbyterians in connection with the Remonstrant Synod, of the second class, in the burial-ground of which Dr. Moses Nelson, who was minister here, and his son, Dr. William Nelson, are interred; also meeting-houses for Presbyterians in connection with the Synod of Ulster, of the first class, and with the Seceding Synod, of the second class. There are four public schools, in which about 360, and nine private schools, in which 310, children are educated; also seven Sunday schools, one of which, held at Crossgar House, is supported by Miss McNeil Hamilton.

KILMUD, or KILMOOD, a parish, in the barony of LOWER CASTLEREAGH, county of DOWN, and province of ULSTER, contiguous to the post-town of Killinchy, on the road from Belfast to Downpatrick; containing 2,219 inhabitants. This parish, called also Kilmoodmanagh, together with an extensive manor having various important privileges, formed part of the possessions of the ancient monastery of Comber. It comprises, according to the Ordnance survey, 46,344 statute acres, of which about 34 are water, 38 consist of plantations in the demesne of Florida, from 40 to 50 are bog, and 3,613 are applotted under the tithe act. The soil is generally fertile, and the land in a high state of cultivation: there is very little waste land; and the bog, as it becomes exhausted, is brought into cultivation. In almost every part of the bog are found numbers of oak, birch, and fir trees of full growth, which last especially are in high preservation; they are sawn with difficulty, and the timber, said to be more durable than oak, is much used in building. The oaks are large, some measuring 30 feet in girth, and are found beneath the fir at a depth of 26 feet, but in general much decayed. Florida manor-house, the elegant mansion of David Gordon, Esq., D.L., is the principal seat in the parish. A court leet and baron is held every third week by the seneschal of the manor, at which debts under 40s. are recoverable, and of which the jurisdiction extends over the whole of this parish and the townland of Drumreagh in the parish of Killinchy. Petty sessions are also held on alternate Saturdays in the manor court-house, a handsome building erected in 1822. During the disturbances of 1798, the manor of Florida raised a battalion of yeomanry; the men still retain their arms and accoutrements, but of late have been seldom called out by government to exercise. The living is a vicarage, in the diocese of Down, and in the alternate patronage of the Marquess of Downshire and David Gordon, Esq., in the latter of whom the rectory is impropriate. The tithes amount to £151.12.8, of which £65.12.8 is payable to the impropriator. and the remainder to the vicar. A handsome glebe-house has been erected by the patrons, aided by a gift of £415 and a loan of £129 from the late Board of First Fruits; and Mr. Gordon has given 10 acres of land as a glebe, and endowed the vicarage with a rent-charge of £40 payable out of his estate of Florida. The church, after the dissolution of the monastery of Comber, fell into decay, and the tithes were annexed to those of the parish of Hillsborough, 14 miles distant; but in 1819, the present church, an elegant structure in the later English style, with a handsome tower and spire rising to the height of 120 feet, was erected near the site of the ancient ruins, at the joint expense of the lord of the manor and the Marquess of Londonderry, aided by a gift of £900 from the late Board of First Fruits. The interior is handsomely fitted up with Riga oak; the east window, of large dimensions and elegant design, appears to have been copied from that of Salisbury cathedral, and in the churchyard is a splendid mausoleum belonging to the Gordon family. In the R.C. divisions the parish forms part of the union or district of Saintfield. About 200 children are taught in four public schools; of these one, for which a handsome school-house was erected by Mr. Gordon and the Marquess of Londonderry, is supported by the trustees of Erasmus Smith's charity, who pay the master £30 per ann.; and one at Drumnahirk was built and is supported by Lord Dufferin. There are also two private schools, in which are about 150 children. A mendicity society has been established, for raising funds to be applied to the relief or maintenance of the poor, which are distributed at their own dwellings monthly; and an extensive religious lending library is kept in the court-house for the use of the poor.

KIRCUBBIN, a market and post-town, in the parish of ST. ANDREW, barony of ARDES, county of DOWN, and province of ULSTER, 8³/₄ miles (S.E.) from Newtown-Ardes, and 96¹/₄ (N. by E.) from Dublin, on the road from Belfast to Portaferry; containing 537 inhabitants. This town, which is situated on the shore of Strangford lough, is of very recent origin, having been built since the year 1790, previously to which time there were not more than five houses in the place. The present town contains 117 houses, for the greater part neatly built, and the inhabitants carry on a small but prosperous trade. The manufacture of straw hats and bonnets, of which great numbers are sent every year into the interior, affords employment to most of the industrious female population of the town and adjoining parishes; great quantities of kelp are burned and sent annually to Liverpool, and corn and potatoes are shipped hence for the Liverpool and Glasgow markets to a considerable extent. The situation of the town, close to which is an excellent landing-place, affords every facility of conveyance by land and water. The market is held every third Wednesday, and is well supplied with provisions of every kind and with brown linens. Fairs are held on the 28th of April, May, Aug., and Nov. A neat market-house, with a brown linen hall in the rear of it, was erected by the late Hon. Robert Ward; the same family are about to expend a considerable sum in the erection of quays for the greater convenience of shipping the produce of the neighbourhood. A court leet and baron is held every three weeks by the seneschal of the manor, in which pleas are entertained to the amount of £20, with jurisdiction over all the parishes of the union; and the magistrates hold a petty session here every alternate Monday.

KNOCKBREDA, or KNOCK-with-BREDA, a parish, partly in the barony of LOWER, but chiefly in that of UPPER CASTLEREAGH, county of DOWN, and province of ULSTER, 2³/₄ miles (S.S.E.) from Belfast, on the road to Downpatrick; containing 3,900 inhabitants. The ancient fortress called Castle-Reagh, or 'the royal castle,' which gives name to the barony, was formerly the baronial residence of a branch of the O'Nials. It is said to have been erected in the reign of Edw. III. by Aodh Flann, whose descendants possessed the Great Ardes, Toome, Massereene, Shankill or Belfast, and Carrickfergus. By inquisition in the reign of Elizabeth it appeared that Con O'Nial, the last of that powerful sept, possessed this castle, together with 224 townlauds, which were all freehold, and also many others held by various tenures. In 1602, O'Nial having exhausted his cellars during a grand banquet which he gave here, sent some of his soldiers to Belfast to procure more wine; and there meeting with a party of the Queen's soldiers, a battle ensued, and O'Nial was sent prisoner to Carrickfergus castle, but was liberated the year following by the master of a Scottish trading vessel and conveyed to Scotland, where Sir Hugh Montgomery, in consequence of a surrender of most of his lands, obtained a pardon for him from Jas. I., who had just ascended the English throne. After the decease of O'Nial, the castle fell into decay, and with the adjoining lands was purchased by the Hillsborough family; there are now no vestiges of it. The parish is bounded on the north and west by the river Lagan, over which are two bridges connecting it with the parish of Belfast, and is intersected by the great Scottish road by way of Donaghadee. It comprises, according to the Ordnance survey, 8,098¹/₄ statute acres, of which 6,968³/₄ are in the Upper and 1,129¹/₂ in the Lower barony; the lands are chiefly under tillage, and in a high state of cultivation; there is neither bog nor any wasteland. Large quantities of tobacco were grown previously to its cultivation being prohibited. There are extensive quarries of clay-slate for building and for repairing the roads; and on the townland of Gillinahirk has been opened a fine quarry of basalt, of which a bridge is now being built at Belfast over the river Lagan, which is navigable along the whole boundary of the parish. The surrounding scenery is richly diversified, and within the parish are Ormeau, the seat of the Marquess of Donegal; Belvoir Park, the residence of Sir R. Bateson, Bart.; Purdysburn, the splendid mansion of Narcissus Batt, Esq., built after a design by Hopper, in 1825, in the Elizabethan style; Orangefield, of J.H. Houston, Esq.; Fort Breda, of W. Boyd, Esq.; Cherry Vale, of J. Stewart, Esq.; and Ravenhill, of H.R. Sneyd, Esq. Previously to 1658 there were two separate parishes, called respectively Knock and Breda, both rectories; but the church of the latter being in ruins, they were united into one rectory at the restoration of Chas. II. The two villages have long since disappeared, and a parish church was, in 1747, built in the village of Newtown-Breda, which see. The rectory is in the diocese of Down, and in the patronage of Sir R. Bateson, Bart., who purchased the advowson in 1825; the tithes amount to £586.5.7¹/₂. The glebe-house was built in 1816, by a gift of £100 and a loan of £825 from the late Board of First Fruits: the glebe comprises nearly 20 statute acres. The chapel of Ballymacarrett was formerly in this parish, from which that townland was separated by act of parliament in 1825, and made a distinct parish. There are places of worship for Presbyterians in connection with the Synod of Ulster, Covenanters, and Seceders. About 130 children are taught in three public schools, of which one is supported by Mrs. Blakeston; and there are five private schools, in which are about 170 children, and four Sunday schools. Six almshouses, built by subscription in 1810, are endowed with £100 by the Rev. Mr. Pratt, late rector, who also bequeathed £100 to the poor, to whom Lady Midleton, in 1747, left £50. On an eminence near the south-eastern extremity of the parish are the picturesque ruins of Knock church; and near them are the remains of a cromlech, consisting of five large stones, and a Danish rath of conical form. Of Breda church there are no remains, except the cemetery enclosed with a high stone wall in Belvoir park, in which is a small mausoleum built by Arthur Hill Trevor, who was created Viscount Dungannon in 1765.

LAMBEG, a parish, partly in the baronies of UPPER BELFAST and UPPER MASSAREENE, county of ANTRIM, but chiefly in the barony of UPPER CASTLEREAGH, county of

DOWN, and province of ULSTER, 2¹/₂ miles (N.) from Lisburn, on the old road from Belfast to Dublin; containing 1,537 inhabitants, of which number, 175 are in the village. The parish, which is pleasantly situated on the river Lagan, comprises, according to the Ordnance Survey, 1,567 statute acres, of which 376³/₄ are in the county of Antrim. The land is good and the system of agriculture improved; and the surrounding scenery is pleasingly diversified. Lambeg House, the property and residence of A. Williamson, Esq., is a handsome modern mansion, formerly belonging to J. Williamson, Esq., author of an able treatise on the linen trade, and framer of the laws by which it is now regulated throughout Ireland; he was much persecuted for framing those laws, and was driven from his house and his native country by an infuriated mob. Chrome Hill, also a spacious modern mansion, was erected by R. Nevin, Esq., late of Manchester, who established here some extensive works for printing muslin, in which he first applied with success his invention of the 'Ba Chrome,' now universally used, and also introduced the oxyde of ohrome into the ornamental department of the china manufacture, from which circumstance he named his estate. The village is about a mile north of Lisburn, with which and also with Belfast it is connected by houses continued along the road between those towns. The blanket manufacture established by the Wolfenden family, who settled in this part

Ormeau House. Drawn by J.H. Burgess and engraved by Branston. From The Irish Penny Journal, *vol.1, 1841.*

of the country about two centuries since, is still carried on. On the river Lagan are two large bleach-greens; and further down the stream is the extensive printing establishment of Mr. Nevin, the buildings of which are capacious and furnished with every modern improvement in machinery. The living is a perpetual curacy, in the diocese of Connor, and in the patronage of the Bishop, to whom the rectory is appropriate as mensal, but the whole of the tithes, amounting to £103.19.2³/₄, are given by him to the curate. The church occupies the site of an ancient monastery, said to have been founded in the 15th century by Mac Donell for Franciscan friars of the third order; it is a small but handsome edifice in the Grecian style, with a tower at the west end. There is a place of worship for Presbyterians in connection with the Synod of Ulster; also a national school, in which are about 90 children, and a private school of about 120 children. From a part of the churchyard being called the Nuns' Garden, it has been supposed that there was a nunnery here, but no account of such an establishment is extant.

LOUGHBRICKLAND, a post-town, in the parish of AGHADERG, barony of UPPER IVEAGH, county of DOWN, and province of ULSTER, 8 miles (N.E.) from Newry, and 58¹/₂ (N.) from Dublin, on the road from Newry to Belfast; containing 618 inhabitants. This town, which is prettily situated on the lake from which it takes its name, owes its rise to Sir Marmaduke Whitchurch, to whom Queen Elizabeth, in 1585, granted the adjacent lands. Sir Marmaduke built a castle on the shone of the lake, for the protection of a pass where three roads united, and soon after a church and a mill, and laid the foundation of a town, in which a Protestant colony was settled, for which he obtained the grant of a market and two fairs. In 1641 the castle was dismantled and the town and church were destroyed by fire; in this desolate condition it remained till 1688, when the church was rebuilt and the town began gradually to improve. It consists of one principal street, from which two smaller streets branch off, and contains 123 houses, most of which are well built and of handsome appearance; the whole town has a cheerful and thriving aspect. The lake, which is supposed to have taken its name from the speckled trout with which it is said to have formerly abounded, comprises an area of about 90 Irish acres, and is bordered on its western side by the road from Dublin to Belfast; it forms the summit level of the Newry canal, to which its waters are conveyed through Lough Shark, and is itself supplied from a spring within, its superfluous water escaping through a sluice at the north-western extremity. Fairs are held here on the third Tuesday in every month, for horses, cattle, pigs, and pedlery. There are several handsome seats in the immediate neighbourhood, which are noticed under the heads of their respective parishes. The parish church, a handsome edifice, with a square tower and octagonal spire, is situated in the centre of the town; and nearly opposite to it is the R.C. chapel, in the later English style, built at an expense of £1,700 on a site presented by N.C. Whyte, Esq., who also

gave £400 towards its erection, There are also places of worship for Presbyterians and Primitive Methodists. On the shore of the lake is a modern house, erected in 1812 on the site of the ancient castle, which was then taken down. The Danes, who had ravaged the north of Ireland, were defeated here by the Irish under Mac Lorniagh, in 1187. – See AGHADERG.

LOUGHIN-ISLAND, a parish, in the barony of KINELEARTY, county of DOWN, and province of ULSTER, on the road from Newry to Downpatrick; containing, with the post town of Clough and the villages of Seaford and Anadorn (which see), 6,574 inhabitants. The parish, according to the Ordnance survey, comprises 12,485³/₄ statute acres, of which 124³/₄ are water, and 9,767 are applotted under the tithe act; about one-half of the land is of the richest quality, and of the remainder, with the exception of a small proportion of waste and bog, the greater part is tolerably fertile. There are some quarries of stone, which is used for building and mending the roads; and near the mountains some very good slate for roofing is obtained. The principal seats are Seaforde House, the splendid mansion and demesne of Col. M. Forde, noticed in the article on Seaforde; Ardilea, of the Rev. W. Annesley, a handsome residence near Clough; and Draper Hill, of J. Cromie, Esq., about halfway between Ballynahinch and Castlewilliam. The linen manufacture was established here in 1815 by Mr. Cromie, and not less than 42,000 webs are annually made from English mill-spun yarn, affording employment to more than 3,000 persons. The living is a rectory, in the diocese of Down, constituting the corps of the precentorship of the cathedral, and in the patronage of the Bishop: the tithes amount to £550. The church, situated at Seaforde, is a handsome edifice in the Grecian style, with an octagonal spine of wood covered with copper; it was built in 1720, and has been recently repaired by a grant of £362 from the Ecclesiastical Commissioners; the approach to it is through a fine avenue of trees. In the R.C. divisions the parish is partly in the union or district of Ballykindlar, and the remainder forms the head of the district of Loughin-Island; the chapel is a plain building, and there is also a chapel at Drumaroad for the union of Ballykindlar. There is a place of worship at Clough for Presbyterians in connection with the Synod of Ulster, of the third class, and at Seaforde for Presbyterians in connection with the Seceding Synod, of the second class, About 570 children are taught in seven public schools, of which one, for which a house was built by the governors and Col. Forde, at an expense of £600, is supported by the trustees of Erasmus Smith's fund, who pay £30 per ann. to the master, who has also an annual donation from the rector, and a house and garden with two acres of land; and a female school was built in 1816, and is endowed with £14 per ann. by Col. Forde: in these two schools 95 children are annually clothed by Col. and Lady Harriet Forde, by whom two other schools are also endowed with £8 per ann.; and there are two national and three Sunday schools. Mrs. McKenny, in 1832, gave £50 to the poor of Clough, the interest of which is annually divided among them; and there is an annual fund of £24 for the purchase of blankets to be distributed among the poor in the winter. Near Seaforde are the ruins of Drumcaw church, formerly a separate parish: near it is a perfect circular fort, and at the termination of the townland is a very ancient bridge of one lofty arch over the Moneycarry river. At Clough are the ruins of an old castle within an ancient fort on the summit of a hill commanding a full view of two separate lines of forts, and the whole of Dundrum bay and castle. At Anadorn is a mound, called Castle Hill, on which was the castle of the McCartans, ancient proprietors of the country; near it is a cairn, 60 yards in circuit, having in it a kistvaen, in which were found calcined bones and ashes. There are some remains of the ancient church with its cemetery, of the old church built in 1547, and of the cell of St. Fynian, afterwards a private chapel and the burial-place of the ancient family of the McCartans.

MAGHERA, a parish, in the barony of UPPER IVEAGH, county of DOWN, and province of ULSTER, 2 miles (S.W.) from Castlewellan, on the road from Bryansford to Downpatrick; containing 1,514 inhabitants, of which number, 167 are in the village. This parish, which is bounded on the east by a branch of the inner bay of Dundrum, comprises, according to the Ordnance Survey, 3,214$\frac{1}{4}$ statute acres, of which 2,384 are applotted under the tithe act. The soil is various; in some parts extremely fertile, and in others sandy, with detached portions of marsh and bog; the marshy grounds afford good pasture. The principal seats are Tollymore, that of Mrs. J. Keowen, and Church Hill, of the Misses Montgomery, both handsome residences. The living is a vicarage, in the diocese of Down, and in the patronage of the Bishop, to whom the rectory is appropriate: the tithes amount to £210, of which £130 is payable to the see, and the remainder to the vicar. The glebe comprises 19$\frac{1}{4}$ statute acres, valued at £36 per annum. The church, towards the erection of which the late Board of First Fruits gave £830.15.4$\frac{1}{2}$, in 1825, is a small neat edifice, about a quarter of a mile from the village. In the R.C. divisions the parish forms part of the union or district of Bryansford, or Lower Kilcoo. About 40 children are educated in the parochial school, which was founded in 1826, by the late J. Keowen, Esq., who built the school-house on the glebe, and endowed it with £5 per ann.; and at Tollymore is a neat school-house, built and supported by Mrs. Keowen, in which about 50 children are gratuitously instructed and some of the females clothed. There are also two Sunday schools. Near the church are the ruins of the ancient church, of which the western gable and the south wall remain; the beautiful Norman arch at the western entrance is in good preservation; the windows in the south wall are narrow and of elegant design. Near the new church also are the remains of an ancient round tower, the upper part of which, from the height of 20 feet above the base, was thrown down by a storm in 1704, and lay in an unbroken column on the ground; the doorway, in that portion which is still erect, is towards the

east and about 7 feet from the ground. About a mile from the church are the remains of a large cromlech, the table stone of which is supported on three upright pillars; in a narrow lane to the west is an upright stone, 13 feet high and having 5 sides; and in an adjoining field is a large block of granite, capped with a conical stone of grauwacke.

MAGHERA-HAMLET, an ecclesiastical, district, in the barony of KINELEARTY, county of DOWN, and province of ULSTER, 3 miles (S.) from Ballynahinch, on the road from Dundrum to Dromore; containing 3,223 inhabitants. This district, formerly called Templemoile, and sometimes Kilwilk, is situated within a mile of the Ballynahinch baths, and comprises 1844 statute acres, of which 753 are mountainous, and of the remainder, which is tolerably good land, a small portion is rocky pasture: the system of agriculture is improving. There are quarries of good slate, and of building stone, which is raised chiefly for building and for the roads. Part of the Slieve Croob mountain is within its limits, and in it is the source of the river Lagan, which, after flowing by Dromore and Lisburn, discharges itself into Belfast lough. The living is a perpetual curacy, in the diocese of Dromore, and in the patronage of the Prebendary of Dromaragh; the stipend arises from the tithes of 1,200 acres applotted under the act, amounting to £75, and an augmentation of £23.2 from Primate Boulter's fund. The glebe-house, towards which the late Board of First Fruits gave £450 and granted a loan of £50, was built in 1830; the glebe comprises 7 acres, bought by the same Board from Col. Forde, for £450, and subject to a rent of £7.7. The church, a neat edifice with a square tower, situated at the extremity of the district, with a view to accommodate the visiters of Ballynahinch spa, was erected at a cost of £500, wholly defrayed by the late Board of First Fruits, in 1814. The Ecclesiastical Commissioners have recommended, on the next avoidance of the prebend of Dromaragh, that the townlands now forming the perpetual curacy be separated from the prebend and formed into a distinct benefice. In the R.C. divisions this is the head of a union or district, comprising also the parishes of Magheradroll and Anahilt, and called also the union of Dunmore, in which are two chapels, one at Dunmore in this district, and one at Ballynahinch, in that of Magheradroll. There is a place of worship for Presbyterians in connection with the Seceding Synod, of the third class. About 150 children are taught in a school supported by Col. Forde, who also built the school-house; and there are three private schools, in which are about 200 children, and three Sunday schools. At Dunmore is an extensive deer-park, the property of Col. Forde, encompassed by a wall.

MAGHERADROLL, a parish, partly in the barony of LOWER IVEAGH, but chiefly in that of KINELEARTY, county of DOWN, and province of ULSTER, on the road from Dromore to Saintfield; containing, with the post-town of Ballinahinch (which is separately described), 7,530 inhabitants. This parish, according to the Ordnance survey, comprises 12,552 statute acres, of which 628$\frac{1}{2}$ are in the barony of Lower Iveagh, and the remainder in Kinelearty; 176³/₄ acres are water, and of the remainder, about two-thirds are land of the richest quality and in the highest state of cultivation; the other portion, though inferior, is still fertile, and there is scarcely any wasteland. Slate of excellent quality is found in the townland of Ballymacarne, but not worked. Nearly in the centre of the parish is Montalto, formerly the seat of the Earl of Moira, by whom it was built, and now the property and occasional residence of D. Kerr, Esq.: the mansion is spacious and the demesne extensive. During the disturbances of 1798, a party of the insurgents took up a position in the park, from which they were driven by the king's forces with great loss. The weaving of linen, cotton, and muslin is carried on extensively, and there are two large bleach-greens in the parish. The living is a vicarage, in the diocese of Dromore, and in the patronage of the Bishop, to whom the rectory is appropriate: the tithes amount to £775.3.8¹/₂, of which £200 is payable to the vicar, and the remainder to the bishop. The glebe-house, towards which the late Board of First Fruits granted a gift of £400 and a loan of £400, in 1817, is a handsome residence; and the glebe comprises 42 acres, valued at £86 per annum, and some gardens let to labourers at £5 per annum. The church, built in 1830 at an expense of £850 advanced on loan by the same Board, is a neat edifice with a tower and spire, and is situated close to the town of Ballinahinch. In the R.C. divisions the parish forms part of the union or district of Dunmore, or Maghera-Hamlet; the chapel at Ballinahinch is a large and handsome edifice. There are places of worship for Presbyterians in connection with the Synod of Ulster, of the first class, and with the Seceding Synod, of the first and second classes. About 650 children are taught in seven public schools; the parochial school-house was built in 1824, by aid of a grant from the lord-lieutenant's school fund; and there are six private schools, in which are about 180 children, and six Sunday schools. The late S.M. Johnstone, Esq., bequeathed one-third of the profits of a work entitled the 'Medley,' published in 1802, amounting to about £4.3.4 per annum, which is annually distributed among the poor at Christmas. There are some remains of the ancient church, about a mile from the town, with a large cemetery, in which are interred several of the ancient and powerful family of the Magennises of Kilwarlin.

MAGHERALIN, or MARALIN, a parish, partly in the barony of O'NEILLAND EAST, county of ARMAGH, but chiefly in that of LOWER IVEAGH, county of DOWN, and province of ULSTER, 1¹/₂ mile (S.W.) from Moira, on the river Lagan, and at the junction of the roads from Armagh to Belfast, from Moira to Lurgan, and from Banbridge to Antrim; containing 5,058 inhabitants. Here stood the monastery of Linn Huachuille, (one townland in the parish being yet called by that name), the remains of which are by some thought to be the massive walls on the north side of the churchyard; it was founded by St. Colman, or Mocholmoc, who died in 699. The ancient palace of the bishops of Dromore was close to the village, on the site now occupied by the parochial school; the last prelate who resided in it was the celebrated Jeremy Taylor. The parish contains, according to the Ordnance survey, 8,293¹/₂ statute acres, of which 486¹/₄ are in the county of Armagh, and the remainder in the county of Down. The lands are all in tillage, with the exception of a proportion of meadow and about 200 acres of exhausted bog, which latter is fast being brought into cultivation: the system of agriculture is improved. Here are extensive quarries of limestone and several kilns, from which lime is sent into the counties of Antrim, Armagh, and Down; this being the western termination of the great limestone formation that rises near the Giant's Causeway. There are also good quarries of basalt much used in building, which dresses easily under the tool; and coal and freestone are found in the parish, but neither has been extensively worked. A new line of road has been formed hence to Lurgan, a distance of 2¹/₂ miles, and an excavation made through the village. An extensive establishment at Springfield, for the manufacture of cambrics, affords employment for 250 persons; and at Milltown a bleach-green annually finishes upwards of 10,000 pieces for the English market. The principal seats are Grace Hall, the residence of C. Douglass, Esq.; Drumnabreagh, of M. Stothard, Esq.; Newforge, of Cosslett Waddell, Esq.; Springfield, of J. Richardson, Esq.; Kircassock, of J. Christie, Esq.; and the rectory, of the Rev. B.W. Dolling. The living is a rectory and vicarage, in the diocese of Dromore, forming the corps of the precentorship of Dromore, in the patronage of the Bishop. The tithes amount to £453.1.7, exclusively of a moiety of the tithes of four townlands in the parish of Donaghcloney amounting to £17.19; the gross value of the precentorship, tithes and glebe inclusive, is £684.17. There is an excellent glebe-house on a glebe of 66 acres, valued at £138.12.0 per annum. The church is an ancient edifice, having a tower and low spire, and has lately been repaired at a considerable expense; it was long used as the cathedral of Dromore, and the bishop's throne yet remains in it. In the R.C. divisions this parish and Moira form the union or district of Magheralin and Moira, in each of which there is a chapel. About 280 children are educated in four public schools, of which the parochial school in the village is aided by an annual donation of £10 from the incumbent; the school-house is large and commodious, with a residence for the master, and was erected at an expense of £350. There are also schools at Rampark and Grace Hall, the former built and supported by C. Douglass, Esq., and the latter, for females, by Mrs. Douglass. In six private schools about 220 children are educated. The late Mr. Douglass, of Grace Hall, made a charitable bequest for clothing the poor in winter; and there are some minor charities. A sulphureous chalybeate spring on the lands of Newforge, is said to equal in efficacy the waters of Aix-la-Chapelle.

MAGHERALLY, a parish, in the barony of LOWER IVEAGH, county of DOWN, and province of ULSTER, 3 miles (E.) from Banbridge, on the road to Downpatrick; containing

3,189 inhabitants. This parish, called also Magherawley, comprises, according to the Ordnance survey, 5,243³/₄ statute acres, of which 22¹/₂ are water, and the remainder, with the exception of about 150 acres of bog, good arable and pasture land; the soil is fertile, and the system of agriculture improving. The principal seats are Tullyhenan, the residence of J. Lindsay, Esq.; and the glebe-house, of the Rev. M. Sampson. Many of the inhabitants are employed in weaving linen for the manufacturers at Banbridge. The living is a rectory and vicarage, in the diocese of Dromore, the rectory forming part of the union of Aghaderg and of the corps of the deanery of Dromore, and the vicarage in the patronage of the Bishop. The tithes amount to £190.14.6, of which £60.10 is payable to the dean, and £130.4.6 to the vicar; the gross revenue of the benefice, including tithes and glebe, and an augmentation from the Ecclesiastical Commissioners of £31.8.0, is £191.12.6. The glebe-house was built in 1780, at an expense of £276.18.5¹/₂, of which one-third was a gift from the late Board of First Fruits, and the remainder paid by the incumbent; the glebe comprises 20 acres, valued at £30 per ann., held under the see of Dromore at 5s. per annum. The church, a small but handsome modern edifice with a tower and spire, towards which the late Board of First Fruits gave £276.18.5¹/₂, is situated on an eminence. In the R.C. divisions the parish forms part of the union or district of Tullylish. There is a place of worship for Presbyterians in connection with the Synod of Ulster, of the second class. About 160 children are taught in the parochial school, built in 1828, and now in connection with the New Board of Education; since that period schools have been established at Corbet, Ballymoney, and Mullaghfernaghan. There are also three private schools, in which are about 260 children. Numerous forts are scattered over the parish, but they are rapidly disappearing in consequence of the advancement of agriculture.

MOIRA, MOYRAGH, or ST. INNS of MOIRA, anciently called MOIRATH, a post-town and parish, in the barony of LOWER IVEAGH, county of DOWN, and province of ULSTER, 13 miles (S.W.) from Belfast, on the road to Armagh, and 71¹/₂ (N.) from Dublin; containing 3,801 inhabitants, of whom 787 are in the town. In 637, a sanguinary battle between the exiled Congal Cloan and Donald, King of Ireland, is said to have been fought here, which terminated in the defeat of Congal. The parish, which is on the river Lagan and the Belfast and Lough Neagh canal, comprises, according to the Ordnance survey, 6,096¹/₄ statute acres, all rich arable land, under an excellent system of cultivation. It is at the western termination of a ridge of white limestone; there are many kilns always at work, and vast quantities of the stone in its natural state are annually sent away by the canal, and by land carriage, to distant parts. There are also quarries of excellent basalt, in great request for building; freestone is found of superior quality; and there are thin seams of coal in several parts, which are not worked. An excellent line of

road has recently been opened hence to Lisburn, and other improvements are in progress. Moira was at one time celebrated for the manufacture of linen, large quantities having been made, sold, and bleached in the town and neighbourhood: its improvement was greatly attributable to the fostering care of Sir John Rawdon, and to the first Earl of Moira, who gave premiums, and otherwise encouraged the manufacture; but it has long been on the decline, and little is done in the market, the brown webs being chiefly sent to the market of Lisburn: yet there are some extensive manufacturers in and near the parish, who give out the yarn as piece-work. The town, though small, is well built, and remarkably clean; it is the property of Sir R. Bateson, Bart., and consists of one long spacious street, containing a court-house, a large handsome building, erected by the proprietor, in which a manor-court is held, every three weeks, for the recovery of debts under £5, by civil bill and attachment; petty sessions are also held here on alternate Mondays, and it is a constabulary police station. Fairs take place on the first Thursday in February, May, Aug., and Nov., for black cattle, pigs, agricultural produce, pedlery, &c. The principal seats are Waringfield, the residence of T. Waring, Esq.; and the glebe-house, of the Rev. W.H. Wynne. The Moira demesne is very extensive and well wooded, possessing many large and rare trees planted by the first Earl of Moira, with a noble avenue leading to the site of the castle, long since demolished: the demesne is now the property of Sir R. Bateson, whose residence is at Belvoir Park, in the adjoining county of Antrim.

The living is a rectory, in the diocese of Dromore, and in the patronage of the Bishop: the tithes amount to £351.15.7. The glebe comprises 17 acres, valued at £51 per ann.; the glebe-house, a handsome building, was erected in 1799, at an expense of £710.3, British currency. This was formerly part of the parish of Magheralin, and was made a distinct parish about 1725, shortly after which the church was erected, at the joint expense of Sir John Rawdon and the Earl of Hillsborough: it is a large and handsome Gothic edifice, with a square tower surmounted by a spire, in excellent repair, and, from its situation on an eminence above the town, forming a beautiful object in this rich and well-planted district. In the R.C. divisions the parish is the head of a union or district, comprising Moira and Magheralin, in each of which is a chapel. There is a meeting-house for Presbyterians in connection with the Remonstrant Synod, of the third class; also one for those of the Seceding Synod, of the second class; and there are places of worship for Wesleyan and Primitive Methodists. There are parochial schools at Moira and Lurganville, supported by Sir R. Bateson, Bart., and the rector; a school for females at Moira, established in 1820 by Lady Bateson, who built the school-house, a large and handsome edifice with a residence for the mistress attached, and by whom also the children are principally clothed; and at Battier is a national school. These schools afford instruction to about 200 children: in a private school are about 80 children, and

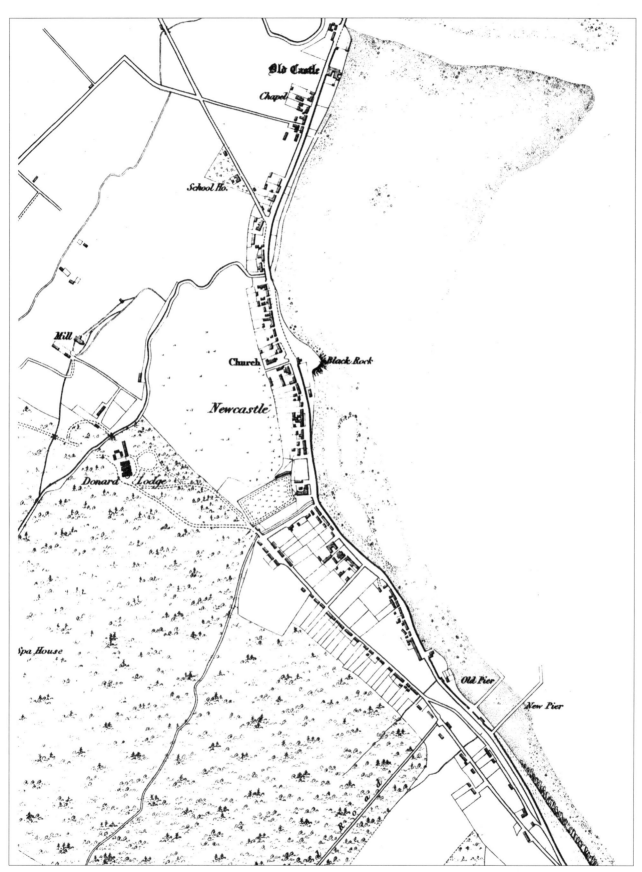

Newcastle. Part of the O.S. map of Co. Down, sheet 49, published 1835 (reproduced at 140%).

there is also a Sunday school. The interest of £200, equally bequeathed by Jasper and Samuel Waring, Esqrs., is distributed by the churchwardens to the poor housekeepers of this parish. The first Earl of Moira bequeathed a sum of money, which, with some other legacies, amounts to nearly £400, the interest of which is annually distributed among poor housekeepers. Moira gives the inferior title of Earl to the Marquess of Hastings; the castle was formerly the family residence, and was the birth-place of the late Marquess, whose father was buried here. He is said to have had the largest funeral procession ever seen in Ireland; it was attended by upwards of 800 carriages of various kinds, with a train of 4,000 people, among whom 2,000 hatbands and scarfs were distributed.

MOYALLON, a village, in the parish of TULLYLISH, barony of LOWER IVEAGH, county of DOWN, and province of ULSTER, 1 mile from Gilford, on the road from Banbridge to Portadown: the population is returned with the parish. It is situated in one of the best-cultivated and most beautiful districts in the county, and appears to have originated in the settlement of a colony of the Society of Friends, about 1698. Among these was Mr. Thos. Christy, who, about 1710, commenced the bleaching of linen on the river Bann, which flows through the vale of Moyallon; he appears to have established a bleach-green here prior to the institution of the Linen Board in Dublin; the Moyallon linens obtained a celebrity above those of other districts. The bleach-green is capable of finishing 15,000 pieces of linen annually; and in the vicinity is a chemical laboratory for preparing bleaching acids. The meeting-house of the Society of Friends, erected about 1723, is a small but neat edifice: there is also a meeting-house for the Wesleyan Methodists. The school was established in 1788, and was supported by the Society of Friends, until 1832, since which period it has been aided by an annual donation from the National Board: about 140 children are here educated and partially clothed, Of the numerous seats in the vicinity, the principal are Moyallon, the residence of Thos. Christy Wakefield, Esq.; and Moyallon House, of T.C. Wakefield, Jun., Esq., embosomed in plantations, and commanding picturesque views of the adjoining county of Armagh. On the elevated grounds of Ballynacarnick are traces of the extraordinary remnant of antiquity called the 'Danes Cast'.

NEWCASTLE, a small sea-port town, in the parish of KILCOO, barony of UPPER IVEAGH, county of DOWN, and province of ULSTER, 3¹/₂ miles (S.E.) from Castlewellan; containing 987 inhabitants. This place, which is situated on the shore of Dundrum bay, in the Irish sea, derives its name from a castle erected here by Felix Magennis, in the memorable year of the Spanish Armada; and though only an inconsiderable fishing village previously to the year 1822, it has since been gradually increasing in importance. In addition to its trade as a port, it has made great advances as a fashionable place for sea-bathing, and is now nearly a mile in length, containing several large and handsome private

dwelling-houses, and numerous comfortable and respectable lodging-houses. The castle, built by Magennis close to the sea shore, has been taken down, and on its site Earl Annesley has erected a spacious and elegant hotel, from a design by Mr. Duff, of Belfast, at an expense of £3,000, which is fitted up with superior accommodations, including hot and cold baths, and every requisite arrangement. The house is beautifully situated and commands a most extensive prospect, embracing the isle and calf of Man in the foreground, and in the rear the lofty mountains of Mourne. Earl Annesley has also built an elegant marine residence, called Donard Lodge, at the foot of Slieve Donard; the demesne is laid out with great taste, and within its limits is a chalybeate spa, to which the public has free access. The other seats are Tollymore, the residence of Mrs. Keowen, situated near the town; Brook Lodge, of W. Beers, Esq.; and the residence of John Law, Esq., a handsome mansion in the Elizabethan style. The environs are of pleasing character, and abound with interesting scenery; they afford many agreeable walks and rides, and within two miles of the town are Tollymore Park, the handsome seat of the Earl of Roden, and the beautiful village and church of Bryansford. The trade of the port consists chiefly in the export of oats, barley, and potatoes, of which large quantities are sent to Dublin and Liverpool. A commodious pier has been erected on an extensive scale, at an expense of £30,000; it is accessible at high water to vessels of large burden, and has been very beneficial to the trade of the town. Granite of very fine quality abounds in the neighbourhood; the quarry was first opened, in 1824, by J. Lynn, Esq., and the stone is conveyed from the mountain by a railroad to the pier, and large quantities of it are shipped. From this quarry was raised the stone for the court-house, new prison, infirmary, and fever hospital of Downpatrick, the chapel of ease in this town, and the spire of Inch church. Newcastle is the head of a coast-guard district, which extends from Strangford to Warren Point, including the stations of Gun Island, Ardglass, St. John's Point or Killough, Leestone, and Cranfield, comprising a force of one resident inspector, seven officers, and 66 men, A penny post has been established to Castlewellan, and a constabulary police force has been stationed here. The chapel of ease is a handsome building, with a spire at the east end; it was erected at an expense of £1,500 by Earl Annesley, who pays the curate a stipend of £100. In the mountains and streams near the town are found fine specimens of rock crystal, of the various hues of beryl, emerald, amethyst, and topaz, some of which have brought high prices. Sand eels are found in great numbers on the beach at particular seasons. Within a mile and a half is a place called the Giant's steps, near which is a cavity of great depth, resembling the shaft of a mine, and called Armour's Hole, from the circumstance of a man of that name having been thrown into it, whose body was found next day at St. John's Point, about ten miles distant. At a small distance from it is a cavern resembling a tunnel, supposed to have been excavated in the rock by the incessant action of the waves.

NEWRY, a sea-port, borough, market and post-town, and a parish, partly in the barony of O'NEILLAND WEST, and partly in that of UPPER ORIOR, county of ARMAGH, but chiefly constituting the lordship of NEWRY, in the county of
DOWN, and province of ULSTER, 30 miles (S.W.) from Belfast, and 50 (N.) from Dublin, on the road to Armagh, and on the great northern road to Belfast; containing 24,557 inhabitants, of which number, 13,134 are in the town. It was a place of some importance from a very remote period. The Annals of the Four Masters notice a monastery in it, in which was a yew tree planted by St. Patrick. The next intimation of its existence is the foundation of a Cistercian abbey, in 1157, by Maurice Mac Loughlin, King of Ireland, the charter of which is extant, and has been published by Dr. O'Conor in his work on the Irish writers. In this charter the place is named Jubhar-cin-tracta, 'the pass at the head of the strand,' or Jubhar-cinn-tracta, 'the flourishing head of a yew tree,' the former being traced from the position of the town, the latter from the circumstance respecting St. Patrick; by the Latin writers of that day it is called Monasterium Nevoracense, and in after times Monasterium de Viridi Ligno; it was also named Na-Yur, and at a still later period, The Newrys. The charter of Mac Loughlin was renewed and enlarged by Hugh de Lacy, Earl of Ulster, in 1237, by which the head of the house was made a mitred

abbot with episcopal jurisdiction within the precincts of the lordship. When Sir John de Courcy took possession of this district, he secured the pass, justly considered as very important, being the only road through the mountains between Ulster and Leinster, by a castle, which was destroyed by Bruce, on the retreat of the Scotch after their defeat at Dundalk in 1318. After several changes of masters, during which the place was frequently in the possession of the O'Nials, chieftains of Ulster, a second castle was built in 1480, which was demolished by Shane O'Nial, who then held a strong castle at Feedom, now Fathom. Marshal Bagnal restored the castle, rebuilt the town and peopled it with Protestant settlers; for which Jas. I., in 1613, granted the entire lordship, together with the manors of Mourne, Greencastle, and Carlingford, in fee to him and his heirs for ever. At the breaking out of the civil war in 1641, Sir Con Magennis took the town and castle, destroyed the church and slew many of the inhabitants. It was shortly after recovered by Lord Conway, who did not hold it long, as O'Nial surprised it by night, and regained possession of it. In 1642, Munroe invested the town and took it by storm, After the Restoration, the town recovered from the sufferings inflicted on it, and continued to flourish till 1689, when it was burned by the Duke of Berwick in his retreat from Duke Schomberg: the castle and six houses only remained.

The town is advantageously situated on the Newry water. The western part, called Ballybot and sometimes Southwark, in Armagh county, is connected with the eastern, in the county of Down, by four stone bridges and a swivel bridge. The

Newry from Trevor Hill. Drawn by T.M. Baynes and engraved by Percy Heath. From G.N. Wright, Ireland illustrated *(London, 1831).*

general appearance of the place, as seen from without, is cheerful and prepossessing: the old town, on the eastern side, situated on the side of a bill, with its church and spire rising above the houses, leads to an expectation of a correspondence of character in the interior; but the reverse is the case. Like other old towns, the streets are narrow, precipitous and inconvenient; but the modern part of the town, generally called 'the Low Ground,' is very elegant; the houses lofty and built of granite; the streets wide, well formed, and paved, with flagged footways. Marcus-square, with several lines of new buildings, presents very elegant specimens of domestic architecture. A great number of excellent springs issuing from the rocks eastward of the town, and more than 200 wells, have been formed in various parts, but no artificial means have yet been adopted to provide a supply of water on a scale commensurate with the domestic and manufacturing demands of the population. The streets and public buildings are lighted with gas supplied by works established by a company in 1822. Much has been done within the last few years to improve the general appearance of the town and neighbourhood; a new line of road has been opened, and an excellent approach formed from Warren point, where the river expands into the bay: the north road has been widened and improved, and several very handsome terraces and detached villas have been built: among the bridges, already noticed, is one of a single arch of elegant proportions, called Needham bridge; and an iron swivel bridge is about to be thrown across the canal, which, when completed, will open a communication from the Monaghan road to the very centre of the town. The assembly, news, and coffee rooms were built by subscription in 1794; the assembly-rooms are spacious and elegant; the news-room is well furnished with newspapers and periodical publications, and is open on the most liberal terms to strangers: the offices of the Commissioners of Police and of the Savings' Bank are in this building. Two newspapers are published here, each twice in the week. A. barrack affords accommodation for 44 officers and 670 non-commissioned officers and privates of infantry, and 10 horses, with an hospital for 30 or 40 patients.

Newry is much more a commercial than a manufacturing town. There are two iron-foundries, each on an extensive scale, for light castings. The manufacture of flint glass is also carried on largely; a distillery in Monaghan-street consumes annually 25,000 barrels of grain, the produce of which is consumed in the counties of Down, Armagh, Louth, and Monaghan: there are also large manufactories of cordage and of spades, shovels, and other kinds of ironmongery. One of the most complete and extensive bleach-greens in the country is at Carnmeen; and at Bessbrook is a mill for spinning linen yarn. The Newry flour-mills, worked by water, consume 900 tons of wheat annually, and there are several others in the immediate neighbourhood, the produce of which is mostly shipped to Liverpool. An oatmeal-mill grinds 17,000 barrels of grain annually, which is wholly purchased for the Liverpool and

Manchester markets; and in the neighbourhood there are several others equally extensive.

The trade of Newry, now of much importance, has gradually risen to its present height from the protection afforded to the merchants by Wm, III. Prior to that time the river was not navigated above Warren point; Newry being then considered as a creek to Carlingford, which was the port for all this part of the coast. But during the reigns of that monarch and his successors, several grants were made for clearing and embanking the river and improving the harbour. At length, in consequence of the many obstructions arising from the nature of the river, and the advantageous situation of the town as a central mart for the introduction of foreign commodities into the interior of Ulster, it was determined to form a line of inland navigation from Newry to Lough Neagh. The communication is carried on from the Newry water by an artificial cut by Acton, Scarva, Tanderagee, and Gilford to Portadown, where it is connected with the Bann, whence it proceeds in the bed of that river to the lake. It was commenced in 1730, and connected with Lough Neagh in 1741, but in consequence of the inconveniences arising from the accumulation of mud and sand in the mouth of the river, near Newry, it was deemed adviseable to prolong the navigation towards the bay to Fathom: this portion of the work, which is two miles in extent, was completed in 1761; the entire length of the navigation, including that of Lough Neagh, is 36 miles, and the total expense was £896,000. In 1726, the customhouse was removed from Carlingford to Newry: the amount of the first year's customs paid here was only £1,069.12, and there were then but four trading barks belonging to the port; the gross amount of customs' duties for 1836 was £58,806.2.6. About 1758, a very considerable trade was carried on with the West India islands, and although at that time the vessels trading with foreign countries were prohibited from sailing direct to the Irish ports, being compelled to land their cargoes in some place in Great Britain, the Newry merchants succeeded in establishing a very lucrative traffic with the most celebrated commercial marts in other countries. This branch, however, was afterwards nearly lost by the competition of the superior capital of Great Britain, until it again revived after the restrictions were taken off the commerce of Ireland, in 1783. The port is very favourably situated for trade at the inner extremity of Carlingford bay, an arm of the sea extending nine miles south-east, and two miles in breadth at its mouth between Cooley point, in the county of Louth, and Cranfield point, in that of Down. Vessels of the greatest draught can come up to Warrenpoint, within five miles of the town, where they can ride in from 6 to 8 fathoms of water in all states of the tide in perfect security. Proceedings are also in progress by D. Logan, Esq., in pursuance of a plan recommended by Sir John Rennie, for deepening and securing the channel from Narrowwater, and scouring it by a steam dredge and other means calculated to facilitate the admission of vessels of a larger class than those which at present come up to the quays: the total expense of these improvements has been estimated at £90,000. The despatch of business is also facilitated by the construction of a line of quays on the eastern bank of the canal, bordered by stores and warehouses, at which vessels can unload: farther north are basins or floating docks, where boats navigating the canal can take in and discharge their cargoes. The custom-house, a neat and commodious building, is situated on the quay, in a position well adapted for business, and has extensive yards and stores for bonding goods adjoining it.

The most important branch of the commerce is the cross-channel trade, which has increased to a great magnitude since the introduction of steam navigation. The principal exports in this department are linen cloth, grain, live stock, butter, and eggs. In 1834 there were exported to Liverpool, of linen cloth, 4,965 boxes; butter, 92,000 firkins; wheat, 4,166 tons; barley, 6,698 tons; oats, 38,000 tons; flour, 9,163 tons; oatmeal, 18,654 tons; flax, 868 tons; eggs, 4,688 crates; oysters, 482 hogsheads; horned cattle, 7,115; pigs, 65,498; and horses, 498; besides which, large consignments of most of these articles were made to the Clyde. The principal imports in the same trade are tea, sugar, iron, salt, British hardware and soft goods, and general merchandise. Three steamers are employed in the Liverpool trade, and two in that with Glasgow; a steamer also trades regularly to Dublin. The average time of the passage to Liverpool is 16 hours; to Glasgow, 14; and to Dublin 12. The chief branch of foreign trade is with the United States and British North America. The chief exports are linen cloth, blue, starch and whiskey; the imports, timber, staves, tobacco, ashes, flax, and clover seed. The Baltic trade consists of the importation of timber, tallow, ashes, flax, and hemp: hides and tallow are imported from Odessa; mats, tar, pitch, flax and flax seed from Archangel; and wine, fruit, oil, lime juice, brimstone and barilla from the Mediterranean. The number of vessels belonging to the port is inadequate to the extent of its commerce, a great portion of which is carried on in vessels of other countries: the Baltic trade is carried on exclusively in foreign bottoms; the United States' trade in American vessels, the trade to British America and Russia in British ships, and the coal trade chiefly in Whitehaven vessels. The market day, under the patent, is Thursday, but a market is held on Tuesday for grain, and on Saturday for meat. The principal market-house is near the site of Bagnal's castle; there are also separate markets for butchers' meat, meal, potatoes, grain and hides, and two for linen yarn. Fairs are held on April 3rd and Oct. 29th.

The present flourishing state of Newry may be attributed originally to the favour shewn by Edw. VI. to Marshal Bagnal, to whom the abbey and surrounding territory were granted, with very extensive privileges, in consequence of his services in Ulster, and were continued to him by Jas. I., vesting the ecclesiastical and municipal authority in the proprietor, who, by virtue of these grants, appointed the vicar general, seneschal, and other inferior officers. A charter of the 10th of

Jas. I. (1612) made the town a free borough, by the name of 'the provost, free burgesses, and commonalty of the borough of Newry,' granting the provost and 12 free burgesses the power of sending two members to parliament, and making the provost judge of a court of record, to be held weekly on Mondays, with jurisdiction to the amount of five marks. A charter granted by Jas. II., in 1688, is not considered to be of any validity. A grant of Jas. I., in 1613, to Arthur Bagnal, empowered a court to be held before the seneschal of the manor, for pleas to the amount of 100 marks: the jurisdiction of this court extends over the borough, and a number of other townlands in Down and Armagh, comprehending 9,664 acres in the former, and 11,434 acres in the latter, of these counties, The court is held every third Wednesday: the seneschal limits his jurisdiction by civil bill to £10; he also holds a court leet, once or twice in the year, at which constables are appointed. All the provisions of the act of the 9th of Geo. IV., c. 82, for watching, lighting, cleansing, paving and improving towns were introduced here shortly after the enactment of that statute: the number of commissioners was fixed at 21. The police of the borough is principally attended to by the constabulary forces of the counties of Down and Armagh: the leading streets are kept in repair by county presentments. These arrangements have tended much to the improvement of the neatness, cleanliness, and good order of the town: the expenditure is defrayed by a local tax, amounting to about £1,150 annually. The elective franchise, conferred by Jas. I., was altered at the Union, when the representation of the borough was limited to a single member, which continues to be the present arrangement. It was a scot and lot borough, but the right of election is now vested in the £10 and certain of the £5 householders; the privilege of the latter cannot be perpetuated, but expires with the lives of the few remaining electors of this class, or with their removal from the premises occupied at the period of the general registration: the seneschal of the manor is the returning officer. The borough includes within its limits a large rural district, comprehending 2,500 statute acres, the precise limits of which are detailed in the Appendix. The general quarter sessions for the county of Down are held here alternately with Downpatrick; and those for the Markethill division of the county of Armagh, in Ballybot. Petty sessions are held every Friday. The court-house, built by subscription for a market-house, and converted to its present purpose in 1805, is an unsightly old building in an inconvenient situation. There is a bridewell for the temporary confinement of prisoners until they can be sent to the county prison at Downpatrick.

The parish comprises, according to the Ordnance survey, 22,491 statute acres, of which 968$\frac{1}{2}$ are in O'Neilland West, and 4,501$\frac{3}{4}$ in Lower Orior; the remainder constitutes the lordship, in which is included a small isolated portion, locally in the barony of Upper Iveagh: about 489 acres are covered with water, and about 260 are bog; the remainder is mostly arable, under an excellent system of agriculture, with some

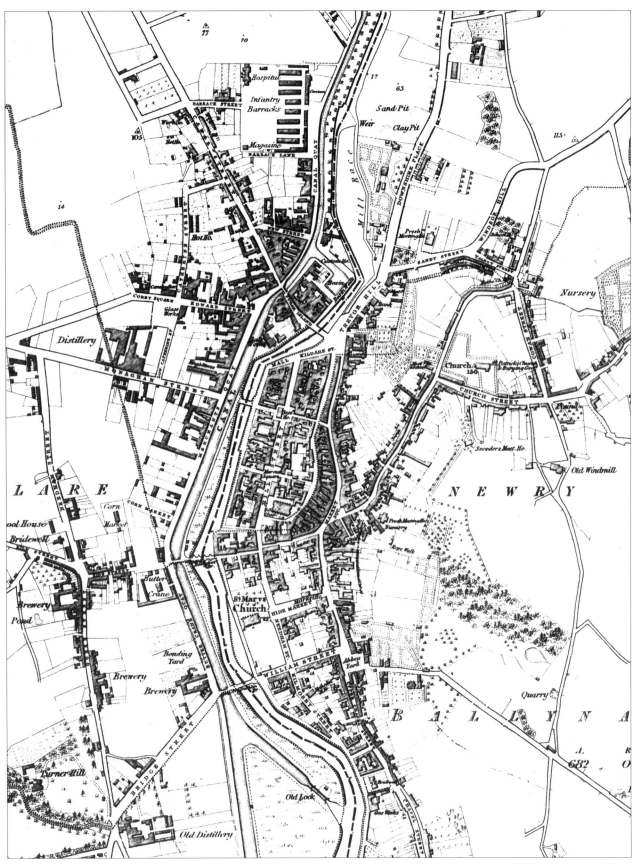

Newry. Part of the O.S. map of Co. Down, sheet 46, published 1835 (reproduced at 140%).

rocky mountain. Though the site of the town is low, as compared with the surrounding country, the climate is pure and salubrious, and the prospects in most parts beautiful and picturesque. The river on which it is built, anciently called the Clanrye, but afterwards the Newry water, flows, after quitting the town, in a south-eastern direction through a highly cultivated tract of rising grounds, well planted and studded with numerous villas and seats, into Carlingford bay, which is bounded on each side by the mountains of Rosstrevor and Fathom: the mountain of Altnaveagh, in the lordship, affords excellent pasturage, and much of it is cultivated; but the greater part of the Fathom range is sterile. The geological features of the district are very striking; it forms the western boundary of the granitic range in this part of Ireland; and granite, sienite, and porphyry are found in it in all their varieties. The old town is almost exclusively built of porphyry; the new of granite. Whyn dykes, in which beautiful specimens of zeolite are frequently found imbedded, penetrate the granite in several directions; in some places layers of quartz are interposed between the strata. Oxyde of manganese is of frequent occurrence; clay-slate, with mica extensively disseminated through it, appears on the Armagh side; and schist to the north of the town. In the townland of Creeve many springs burst out of the granite and quartz rocks, in the streams of which is found a metallic residuum in large quantities, resembling copper, which mixes with the sand and is very heavy; near the toll-gate on the Belfast road is a vein of the newly discovered mineral, trephine; and a still greater body of it was discovered, in 1835, near Mount Kearney. To the north of the town, on the Belfast road, is a very copious chalybeate spring, highly beneficial in scorbutic cases. The principal seats in the vicinity of the town all of which are embellished with rich and flourishing plantations, are Fathom, the residence of – Benson, Esq.; Greenpark, of – Thompson, Esq.; Derramore, of – Smith, Esq.; Drumbanagher Castle, of Lieut. Col. Maxwell Close; Drummantine, of – Ennis, Esq.; and Narrow-water, of Roger Hall, Esq.

The peculiarities of the ecclesiastical arrangements of the lordship proceed from its connection with the monastery already noticed, which, after having risen to a great height of prosperity by the fostering care of many successive kings, underwent the fate of all the other monastic institutions during the reign of Hen. VIII. After the dissolution it was converted into a collegiate church for secular priests, which having soon fallen to decay, the abbey, with all its possessions, was granted by Edw. VI. to Sir Nicholas Bagnal, in as free, full and ample manner as it had been enjoyed by any abbot. Hence, the episcopal jurisdiction previously exercised by its clerical head devolved at once upon its new proprietor, whose representative, the Earl of Kilmorey, exercises it to its fullest extent, as lay abbot; appointing spiritual officers, holding ecclesiastical courts, granting probates of wills and licences of marriage, and performing every other episcopal act with as plenary power as any bishop, being subject only to the Lord-

Primate, as metropolitan. The living is a donative, in the patronage of the Earl of Kilmorey, as lay abbot, who, as such, possesses the whole tithes; yet in the royal visitation book of 1615 it is stated, that Nova Ripa, alias Nieu Rie, is among the parishes under the jurisdiction of the see of Dromore. St. Patrick's church, built by Sir Nicholas Bagnal in 1578, burnt in the civil wars, and restored after the Revolution, was originally the parochial church; but, in 1811, being much dilapidated and too small for the increasing congregation, an act was obtained under the provisions of which a new church was built on an enlarged scale and on a new site, to be henceforth the parish church of St. Mary's, Newry. This church, built in the Gothic style, with a tower and spire 190 feet high, was finished in 1819, at a cost of £12,566.15.4$^1/_2$, British currency, exclusively of £2,469.4.7$^1/_2$ expended in the purchase of the site, and in obtaining two acts of parliament. The funds for liquidating this charge arose from a bequest of £3,138.9.2$^3/_4$ from the late W. Needham, Esq., lord of the manor; a bequest of £1,346.15.4$^1/_2$ from Sir Trevor Corry; a donation of £923.1.6$^1/_2$ from the Earl of Kilmorey, a donation of £461.10.9$^1/_2$ from Gen. Needham; £2,520 raised by the sale of the pews, and £6,646.3.1 by parochial assessment; it is endowed with £300 per ann., payable by the lay abbot in lieu of tithe. In 1829, the old church of St. Patrick was repaired and fitted up as a chapel of ease: the living is a chaplaincy or donative, in the gift of the Earl of Kilmorey, who endowed it with £100 per ann., subject to the peculiar jurisdiction of the vicar-general of Newry. In the R.C. arrangements the parish is the head of the diocese of Dromore, being the bishop's parish or mensal, and is co-extensive with that of the Established Church; containing three chapels, two in the town and one at Shinn, 4 miles distant, which are attended by the same number of curates, The older R.C. chapel, a well-built but plain structure, with three galleries and a spacious cemetery attached to it, was erected in 1789. Being found too small for the accommodation of the numbers that attended it, a new chapel was erected in the low ground, in the pointed Gothic style, 120 feet long, 74 broad, and 46 feet high to the ceiling. The facade consists of a centre and two wings, with a deeply receding doorway, and is highly ornamented. The interior consists of a nave and two side aisles detached by rows of moulded granite pillars, supporting lofty pointed arches, over which are the clerestory windows by which the centre is lighted: the great altar is surmounted by a large window of three lights. This chapel is considered to be the diocesan chapel of the Bishop of Dromore, who resides at Violet Hill, to the north of Newry, where there was formerly a house of lay friars, which has been transferred to the town; in which also is a seminary for preparing the youth of the Catholic church for Maynooth college. A convent of the order of St. Clare was removed hither from Dublin, in 1830: the house, with its appendages, was presented to the community by the Rev. J. Gilmer, of Rosstrevor, since which time the nuns have built a large and handsome chapel in the Gothic style, and also a school-house for the education of female children, which receives aid from the Board of National Education. There are in the town a congregation of Presbyterians in connection with the Synod of Ulster, of the second class, who have a large and elegant meeting-house; one in connection with the Remonstrant Synod, and one with the Seceding Synod, both of the first class; also places of worship for Independents, Primitive and Independent Wesleyan Methodists, and Kellyites. Three schools in the lordship, connected with the Board of National Education, are situated in Newry and at Grinane; there are four in connection with the London Hibernian Society, one of which, founded in 1825, is built on an acre of land given by the Marquess of Downshire; and another, in Ballybot, on land given by Lord Kilmorey. Other schools have been aided by donations from the Marquess of Anglesey, the late Rob. Martin, Esq., who left a bequest of £7 per ann., and J. Dickinson, Esq., who left one of £8 per ann., for their endowment. About 880 boys and 960 girls are educated in these schools: there is also a private school, which affords instruction to about 50 boys and 20 girls.

The Mendicity Association was established in 1820, and is now merged in the workhouse: it is supported by subscriptions and bequests, among which is one of the late Wm. Needham, Esq., who, in 1806, bequeathed £50 per ann. for 50 years to the poor of the parish. A bequest of £30 per ann. by the late W. Ogle, Esq., to the poor is given in equal shares to the vicar, the parish priest, and the Unitarian minister, for the paupers of their respective congregations. The interest of £2,000, bequeathed by Sir Trevor Corry, is distributed by his nephews, Trevor and Smithson Corry, Esqrs., among poor housekeepers. There are six almshouses, erected at the expense of the Rev. J. Pullayn, vicar-general, without any endowment attached to them; the inmates are appointed by the vicar of Newry. Among the more remarkable relics of antiquity may be noticed a large and perfect rath, about 1¹⁄₂ miles from the town, on the Rathfriland road, called Crown Rath. It is an earthwork, 112 feet high, nearly circular at the base, which measures 585 feet in circumference, with a flat top of oblong form, and is surrounded by a fosse 20 feet broad and 10 deep. On the south side of the fosse is a square platform, surrounded with an intrenchment, the glacis of which declines towards the old ford of the river. Many other remains of forts and many cromlechs are to be found in various parts. Newry is said to have been the birthplace of Jarlath MacTrien, who was prior of Armagh in 465; also of Dr. Parry, who was raised to the bishoprick of Killaloe in 1647. It gives the inferior title of Viscount to the Earl of Kilmorey.

NEWTOWN-ARDES, an incorporated market and post-town (formerly a parliamentary borough), and a parish, partly in the barony of LOWER CASTLEREAGH, but chiefly in that of ARDES, county of DOWN, and province of ULSTER, 8 miles (E.) from Belfast, and 88 (N.E.) from Dublin, on the mail coach road from Donaghadee to Belfast; containing, in 1837,

11,000 inhabitants, of which number, 6,000 are in the town. This place has been celebrated from a very early period for the number of religious foundations in its immediate neighbourhood. In 1244, Walter de Burgh, Earl of Ulster, founded a monastery here, in honour of St. Columb, for Dominican friars, which on its dissolution was granted to Lord Clandeboy, by whom it was assigned to Viscount Montgomery of the Ardes; no vestiges of the building can be traced. On the north side of the town was the cell of Kiltonga, which has been supposed to have originally given name to the parish; and within five miles were the abbeys of Bangor, Hollywood, Moville, Greyabbey, Cumber, and the Black priory. Jas. I., after the forfeiture of the surrounding territory by Con O'Nial's rebellion, granted several of the sites and possessions of the neighbouring monasteries to Sir James Hamilton and Sir Hugh Montgomery, from whom they passed to the Mount-Alexander family, and from them, by exchange, into the family of the Marquess of Londonderry. The inhabitants received a charter from Jas. I., in 1613, incorporating them under the designation of the 'Provost, Free Burgesses, and Commonalty of the borough of Newtowne.'

The town is beautifully situated a little beyond the northern extremity of Lough Strangford, which, previously to the reclamation of about 100 acres, now under tillage, formed its boundary on that side; and is surrounded by an amphitheatre of hills. It consists of one spacious square, with several wide streets and others of inferior character, and contains at present about 1,300 houses, many of which are handsomely built. Great improvements have been made under the auspices of the Marquess of Londonderry; a new line of road has been constructed to Belfast, avoiding the hills of Scrabo; and new roads also to Cumber and to Grey abbey, crossing the grounds reclaimed from the Lough: two neat bridges have been built over the river, and various other improvements are contemplated. The first attempt to establish a public brewery, and also a public distillery, was made in this town in 1769; but both failed, and, in 1819, John Johnston, Esq., purchased the premises and rebuilt the brewery on an extensive scale; more than 7,000 barrels of beer are brewed annually, and adjoining are large malting premises for the supply of the brewery and for sale, in which the malt is made from barley grown in the neighbourhood. The weaving of damask is carried on to a small extent; about 600 looms are employed in weaving muslin, and 20 in weaving coarse linen for domestic use. More than 1,000 females are constantly employed in embroidering muslin for the Glasgow merchants, who send the fabrics hither for that purpose. The market is on Saturday, and is amply supplied with provisions of all kinds; and fairs are held on the second Saturday in every month, also on Jan. 23rd, May 14th, and Sept. 23rd, for cattle, horses, sheep, pigs and pedlery.

By the charter of Jas. I. the corporation consists of a provost, twelve free burgesses and an indefinite number of

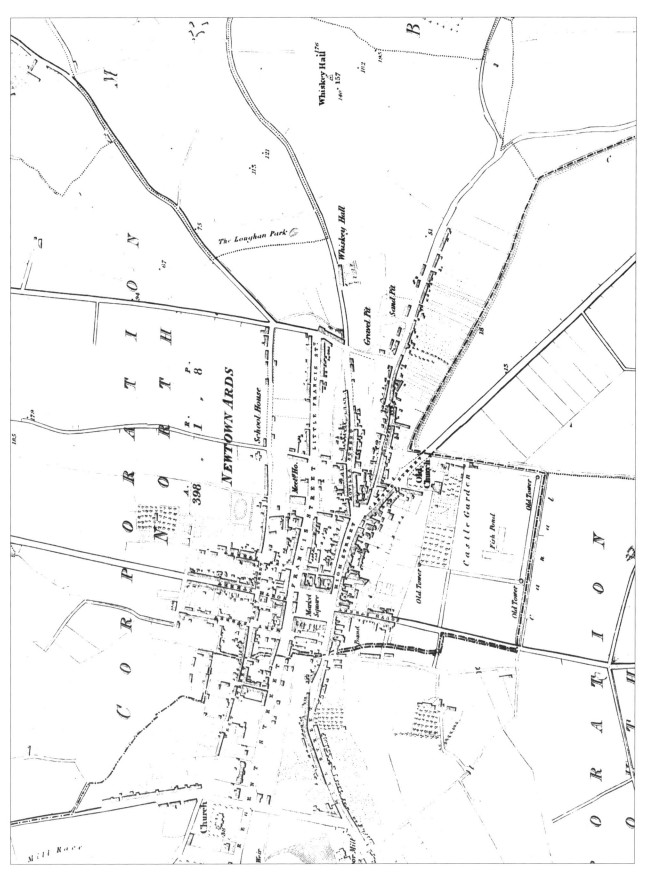

Newtownards. Part of the O.S. map of Co. Down, sheet 6, published 1835 (reproduced at 140%).

freemen, assisted by two serjeants-at-mace. The provost, who is also judge of the borough court of record, and clerk of the market, was to be chosen annually from the free burgesses on the festival of St. John the Baptist, and sworn into office on that of St. Michael; the free burgesses, as vacancies occur, were chosen from the freemen by the provost and a majority of their own body, by whom also the freemen are admitted by favour only; and the serjeants-at-mace are appointed by the corporation. The public business is transacted by a 'Quarter Court,' consisting of 23 inhabitants, who are summoned and sworn by the provost as grand jurors, and act as a court leet in the election of various officers under the corporation, and exercise the power of presentment to be levied on the borough for various purposes. This court, which from its name would appear to have been formerly held quarterly, is now held annually, before the provost, between Michaelmas and Christmas. The corporation, under their charter, continued to return two members to the Irish parliament till the Union, when the borough was disfranchised. The borough court of record, which had jurisdiction to the amount of five marks, has long been discontinued. The provost now is either re-elected annually, or, being once elected, continues to hold his office for life; the burgesses are no longer chosen from the resident freemen, nor has the corporation, since 1821, exercised any municipal functions, except the holding of the Quarter court by the provost. A manor court is held before a seneschal appointed by the Marquess of Londonderry, every third Saturday, for the recovery of debts not exceeding £10; and a court leet annually, at which various officers are appointed for the manor, and also a constable for the borough, whose sole duty it is to assist in preserving the peace. The general sessions for the county are held here, in June and December, before the assistant barrister for the division of Downpatrick; petty sessions are held on the first and third Saturdays in every month, and a constabulary police force is stationed in the town. The church, built by Sir Hugh Montgomery, has been converted into a court-house, recently fitted up by the Marquess of Londonderry, and in which the sessions are held. The town-hall, for the transaction of the corporation business, is a handsome structure in the Grecian Doric style, erected in 1770 by the first Marquess of Londonderry: it is surmounted by a cupola, containing a clock, beneath which is the entrance into an area leading through the centre, on one side of which is the flesh market and on the other a weigh-house and other requisite offices and stores; above is an elegant suite of assembly-rooms, and other apartments, in which the members of the Down hunt hold meetings. A handsome stone cross of octagonal form, decorated with canopied niches, was built by the corporation in the centre of the town, to replace the ancient cross destroyed by the insurgents in 1641.

The parish comprises, according to the Ordnance survey, 14,803 statute acres; the land is of good quality, and the system of agriculture highly improved; there is no waste land,

but about 700 acres of valuable bog, from which the neighbourhood is supplied with fuel. There are two quarries of excellent freestone in the mountain of Scrabo, equal in appearance and superior in durability to that of Portland, besides five others of inferior quality; large quantities are raised for the supply of the neighbouring districts, and several cargoes have been shipped to America. Some extensive lead mines are held under lease from the Marquess of Londonderry by a company in the Isle of Man; the ore is very rich, but the mines are very indifferently worked; the water being imperfectly carried off by a level, the lessees have sunk a new shaft and erected a steam engine to raise the ore and to drain the mine; the ore is shipped at Bangor and sent to Flint, where it is smelted. Under Scrabo are three thin veins of coal, which show themselves in the Lough; but they are at a great depth beneath the surface, and no attempt to work them has yet been made. Regent House, the seat of P. Johnston, Esq., an elegant mansion in the Grecian style, recently erected by its proprietor, is built of polished Scrabostone, and situated in tastefully disposed grounds, commanding a fine view of Lough Strangford and the adjacent country. The living is a perpetual curacy, in the diocese of Down, and in the patronage of the Marquess of Londondenny, in whom the rectorial tithes are impropriate, with the exception of those of the townland of Ballyskeagh, which are appropriate to the see of Down, and are paid by the Marquess. The stipend of the curate is £64.12.3, of which £40.12.3 is payable by the impropriator, and £24 from Primate Boulter's fund: he has also the glebe, which comprises $28^1/_2$ statute acres, valued at £40 per ann,; and the glebe-house, a good residence, situated in the town, and built at an expense of £700, of which £415 was a gift and £46 a loan from the late Board of First Fruits. The church, a handsome cruciform edifice, was built in 1817, at an expense of £5,446, of which £831 was a gift and £3,692 a loan from the same Board; the remainder, £923, was a donation from the late Marquess of Londonderry, In the R.C. divisions the parish is the head of a union or district, comprising also the parishes of Dundonald, Bangor, and Donaghadee; the chapel is a small plain building. There is a place of worship for a Presbyterian congregation in connection with the Presbytery of Antrim, and two for those in connection with the Synod of Ulster, one of which, recently erected in Regent-street, has a handsome hewn stone front of the Doric order; there is also a place of worship for Seceders, another for Covenanters, and two for Methodists. About 620 children are taught in the public schools of the parish, for one of which, on Erasmus Smith's foundation, a spacious house, with residences for a master and mistress, was built at an expense of £1,000, defrayed jointly by the Marquess of Londonderry and the trustees of that charity; and for another a house was lately erected by Francis Turnley, Esq., under the will of his late father, with a house each for a master and mistress, and endowed with £3 per ann. to be distributed in prizes to the children. There are also ten private schools, in which are about

450 children, and four Sunday schools, A house of industry, which has completely suppressed mendicity in this parish, is supported by general subscription, aided by an annual donation of £25 from the Marquess of Londondenny, who also gave the house and premises rent-free. In the bog at Loughriescouse was found, in 1824, at a depth of 23 feet below the surface, the body of a highlander in a good state of preservation; parts of his dress were perfect, but the body crumbled into dust on exposure to the air. The head and horns of a moose deer were, in 1832, dug up on the townland of Ballymagreechan, and are now deposited in the museum at Glasgow. The cemetery of the abbey of Moville is now used for a parochial burial-ground; and near the old church, now the court-house, are the ruins of a private chapel, built by Sir Robt, Colville, In that church were interred the remains of the Earls and others of the family of Mount-Alexander, of several of the Colville family, of the first Marquess of Londonderry, and of his father.

NEWTOWNBREDA, a village, in the parish of KNOCKBREDA, barony of UPPER CASTLEREAGH, county of DOWN, and province of ULSTER, 2 miles (S.) from Belfast, on the road to Saintfield; the population is returned with the parish. It is pleasantly situated on an eminence near the river Lagan, and immediately adjoining Belvoir Park, the seat of

Sir R. Bateson, Bart.; it consists chiefly of small detached white-washed cottages, with gardens in the rear, which give the village an extremely interesting appearance. It is a station of the constabulary police; and petty sessions are held on alternate Saturdays, Fairs are held on July 5th, and Oct. 27th, Here is the parochial church, a small but elegant edifice in the Grecian style, erected in 1747, under the direction of, Mr. Cassels, by the Viscountess Dowager Midleton. The burial-ground, which is the cemetery of several of the most respectable families of the surrounding country, has a very neat and interesting appearance.

PORTAFERRY, a seaport, market, and post-town, partly in the parish of ARDQUIN, and partly in that of BALLYPHILIP, barony of ARDES, county of DOWN, and province of ULSTER, 7 miles (N.E.) from Downpatrick, and 102 (N.N.E.) from Dublin; containing 2,203 inhabitants. It is situated on the eastern side of the inlet to the sea that forms the entrance to Lough Coyne or Strangford Lough, and opposite to the town of Strangford, on the western side of the same inlet, between which two places a constant intercourse is kept up by means of a ferry. The town owes its origin to a castle built by the first of the Savage family who came into this part of the country with John de Courcy, shortly after the arrival of the English, and the place being well secured and garrisoned by that

Belvoir Park House. Drawn by Joseph Molloy and engraved by E.K. Proctor. From Belfast scenery *(Belfast and London, 1832).*

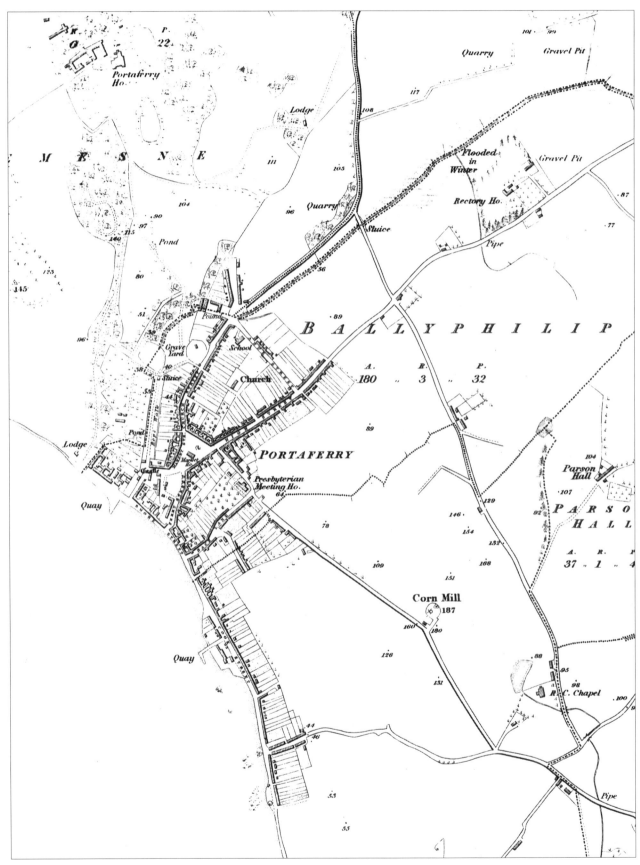

Portaferry. Part of the O.S. map of Co. Down, sheet 25, published 1835 (reproduced at 140%).

powerful family, its situation on the strait made it a post of great importance in all the subsequent wars, during which neither it nor the neighbouring district of the Southern Ardes ever fell into the hands of the Irish; but the town, until lately, was only a small collection of cottages, built under the shelter of the castle, and chiefly inhabited by fishermen. It is now, owing to the exertions of the proprietor, Andrew Nugent, Esq., and the spirit of commercial enterprise in the principal townsmen, a place of considerable business, and increasing yearly in prosperity. It consists of a square and three principal streets, besides a range of good houses on the quay, which is built along the edge of the strait, chiefly at the expense of Mr. Nugent. The only public buildings are the market-house, a substantial old structure in the middle of the square, which in the disturbances of 1798 became a post of defence to the yeomanry of the town, who repulsed a body of the insurgents that attempted to take possession of it; the church of the parish of Ballyphilip, a neat building erected in 1787; a large and commodious Presbyterian meeting house, and another for Wesleyan Methodists: at a little distance from the town is the R.C. chapel (a large building) for the parishes of Ballyphilip, Ballytrustan, Slane, and Witter. The town is a constabulary police and a coast guard station. The market, on Saturday, is well supplied with provisions; fairs are held on Jan. 1st, Feb. 13th, Tuesday after May 12th, and Nov. 13th. There is a distillery; and a brisk trade is carried on, chiefly with Liverpool, Glasgow, Dublin and Belfast, whither it sends wheat, barley, oats, potatoes and kelp, and receives in exchange timber, coal, and general merchandise. The situation of the town gives it the command of a fine prospect southward down the strait to the open sea, and in the contrary direction over the greater part of Lough Coyne, stretching ten miles in land and embellished with numerous thickly planted islands. Adjoining the town, on a rising ground, is Portaferry House, the residence of Andrew Nugent, Esq., a large and handsome building, finely situated in an extensive and highly ornamented demesne. The glebe-house of Ballyphilip, the residence of the Chancellor of Down, stands on the site of the ancient parish church, which is said to have been once an abbey. The first Marquess of Londonderry received his early education in this house. The ancient castle, which for more than half a century has been uninhabited, is rapidly falling to ruin: near it are the ruins of a chapel roofed with stone. A school is maintained here under the patronage of Mr. Nugent, who pays £20 annually to the master.

RATHFRILAND, a market and post-town, partly in the parish of DRUMBALLYRONEY, but chiefly in that of DRUMGATH, barony of UPPER IVEAGH, county of DOWN, and province of ULSTER, 16½ miles (W.) from Downpatrick, and 57¼ (N.) from Dublin, on the mail road from Newry to Downpatrick; containing 200 inhabitants. This town was founded, soon after the Restoration, by Alderman Hawkins, of London, to whom, in acknowledgment of his very important services during the parliamentary war, Chas. II.

granted the whole of the extensive manor, which is now the property of his lineal descendant, Gen. Meade. The benevolent alderman, at his own cost, provided food, clothing, and lodging for 5,000 Protestant royalists, who, during the calamitous progress of the war, had fled to London for protection; collected in England £30,000 for the purchase of corn, wearing apparel, and other necessaries for the support of such as had not been able to effect their escape; and, with the assistance of a few of his friends, raised the sum of £45,000 for the public service and the use of the king. The town is situated on an eminence, previously the site of an ancient fortress, about three miles to the north of the Mourne mountains; and consists of a spacious square, and five principal and several smaller streets, containing together 447 houses, which are in general well built and of handsome appearance, surrounding the crown of the hill. The principal streets communicate with five great roads from different parts of the county, but, from the acclivity of the site, form steep entrances into the town, from which in every direction are extensive and interesting views of the surrounding country. A considerable traffic is carried on with the adjacent district, and the town itself is the residence of numerous respectable families. The market is on Wednesday and is amply supplied; and fairs are held on the second Wednesday in April (O.S.), the Wednesday after Trinity, the second Wednesday in September (O.S.), and the second Wednesday in December. The market-house is a handsome building in the centre of the square; the lower part is appropriated to the use of the market, and the upper part contains accommodation for holding courts. A constabulary police force is stationed in the town, and petty sessions are held on alternate Fridays. The manorial court, with which has recently been incorporated that for the manor of Gilford, is held on the first Tuesday in every month before the seneschal; its jurisdiction extends to pleas of debt to the amount of £100, which may be recovered by civil bill process. The parish church of Drumgath, a small neat edifice with a tower on the north side, is situated on the south side of the square: it was originally founded by Alderman Hawkins, and rebuilt in 1818. There are also in the town a spacious R.C. chapel, and places of worship for the Society of Friends, Presbyterians, Covenanters, and Wesleyan Methodists, and a dispensary. On the very summit of the hill round which the town is built are some slight remains of the ancient castle of the powerful sept of the Magennises, Lords of Iveagh, commanding the entire country for ten miles round; a modern house was erected on the site in 1812, when, in digging the foundation, many small cells were discovered, in some of which were found human bones, pieces of armour, coins, and other relics.

RATHMULLEN, a parish, in the barony of LECALE, county of DOWN, and province of ULSTER; containing, with the post-town of Killough (which is separately described), 2,742 inhabitants. This parish, which is situated on the eastern coast and intersected by the road from Downpatrick, takes its name

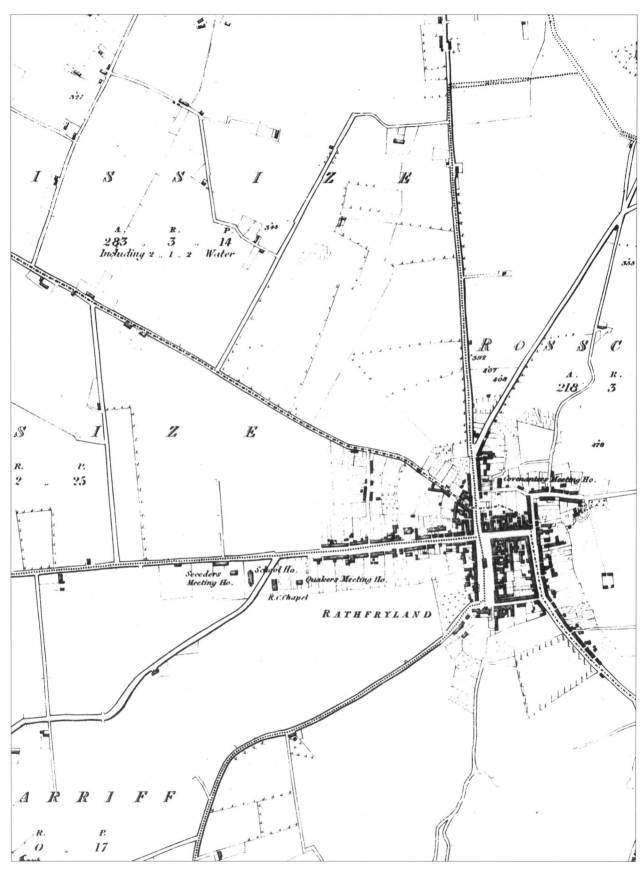

Rathfryland. Part of the O.S. map of Co. Down, sheet 41, published 1835 (reproduced at 140%).

from an ancient rath to the south of the church, near which are still some vestiges of an ancient castle. The parish, which is bounded on the south by Dundrum bay, comprises, according to the Ordnance survey (including detached portions), 3,369³/₄ statute acres, of which 9¹/₂ are water, and the remainder principally under tillage. A considerable tract of sandbank extends along the shore; about 80 acres are marshy land, and there is a small portion of bog; but, with the exception of the town parks, there is very little meadow or pasture. The surface is uneven and in some parts marked by rocky elevations; but the soil in general is rich, and the system of agriculture greatly improved. Coal is supposed to exist in the lands towards the coast, but no attempt has been hitherto made to work it. A lead mine was discovered some few years since, which on examination was found to contain a large proportion of silver. Janeville, the residence of Capt. Browne, is the principal seat; there are also many excellent farm-houses in the parish. During the season, some of the inhabitants are employed in the herring and lobster fishery; and a considerable coasting trade is carried on between Killough and the different ports in the channel, which is highly beneficial to the agricultural interests of the neighbourhood. St. John's Point, in this parish, is the most prominent southern headland between Dublin and the North of Ireland, and together with the adjacent bay of Dundrum has been more disastrous to shipping than any other part of the coast. From the number of wrecks that have occurred here, the erection of a lighthouse is imperatively called for, not only for the safety of trading vessels but also of the numerous fleets of fishing boats which annually rendezvous at Killough and Ardglass. This point is situated in lat. 54° 27' 40" (N.), and lon. 5° 24' 30" (W.); and a coast-guard is stationed here, which is one of the seven stations constituting the district of Newcastle. Fairs are held at Killough, as is also a monthly court for the manors of Killough, Hamilton, and Down, of which the two former are wholly within the parish. The detached townland of Rossglass was, in 1834, separated by act of council from the parish of Kilclief and united to this parish. The living is a vicarage, in the diocese of Down, and in the alternate patronage of the Earl of Carrick and Viscount Bangor; the rectory is impropriate in Viscount Bangor, Stephen Woolfe, Esq., and Miss Hamill, The tithes amount to £343.6.1, of which £113.17 is payable to the impropriators, and £229.9.1 to the vicar. The glebe-house, towards the erection of which the late Board of First Fruits contributed a gift of £450 and a loan of £150, was built in 1817; the glebe comprises 4³/₄ acres, valued at £5.18.9 per annum. The church, a small edifice in the Grecian style, situated on an eminence overlooking the bay, was built in 1701, from the proceeds of forfeited impropriations. At Killough is a chapel of ease, the living of which is a perpetual curacy, in the patronage of the Vicar of Rathmullen. In the R.C. divisions the parish forms part of the union of Bright, and contains chapels at Killough and Rossglass. There are places of worship for Presbyterians and Wesleyan Methodists. About 250 children are taught in two public schools; and there are three private schools, in which are about 100 children, and a Sunday school: the parochial school is about to be rebuilt on a larger scale, at the expense of the vicar. There are several mineral springs, which are warm in winter and cold in summer; one is said to have a petrifying quality, equal, if not superior, to the celebrated waters of Lough Neagh. In various parts of the parish are several small forts: and on a hill to the west of the church is a cave, 34 yards in length, divided into four chambers, of which the farthest is circular and larger than the others. The headland of St. John's Point was anciently the site of a preceptory of the Knights of St. John of Jerusalem. There are still some slight remains of the church on the estate of Capt. Browne, near which several stone coffins of singular form were dug up recently, together with massive gold ornaments and curious coins; the church itself, as far as can be conjectured from its ruins, was of very singular construction, its style of architecture much resembling the Egyptian. There is also a fine spring of clear water, covered over with stones taken from the ruins of the church.

ROSTREVOR, or ROSETREVOR, a sea-port and post-town, in the parish of KILBRONEY, barony of UPPER IVEAGH, county of DOWN, and province of ULSTER, 7 miles (E. by S.) from Newry, and 67 (N.) from Dublin; containing 996 inhabitants. This place was anciently called Castle Roe or Rory, from its original founder, Rory, one of the family of the Magennises, Lords of Iveagh, of whose baronial castle, subsequently occupied by the Trevor family, there are still some remains near the town; it derived its present appellation from Rose, youngest daughter of Sir Marmaduke Whitchurch, after whose marriage with Trevor, Viscount Dungannon, the family seat, Iveagh castle, was invariably called Rosetrevor. The town is beautifully situated in a cove of Carlingford Lough, at the western termination of the Mourne mountains, and contains 185 houses, which are large and handsomely built. The streets are wide and open, and the whole town has a cheerful and attractive appearance. The air is salubrious, and the town is very desirable as a residence from its fine situation on a gentle eminence sheltered by mountains on the north, south, and east, and open on the west to Carlingford bay, the shores of which are richly planted and embellished with numerous seats, handsome villas, and picturesque cottages. The port is principally frequented by fishing boats, for the accommodation of which there is a small quay, from which is a walk nearly a mile in length, thickly shaded with trees; and on the side of the mountain is a stone of very large dimensions, called Cloughmorne, which is frequently visited for the very extensive and beautiful prospect it commands. Between this place and Warrenspoint, in Carlingford Lough, is a large extent of soft ground, on which are two fathoms of water, where large vessels frequenting the port of Newry lie at their moorings. In the vicinity of the town are some salt-works. Fairs are held here on Shrove-Tuesday, Aug. 1st, Sept. 19th,

Rostrevor Pier. Drawn by W.H Bartlett and engraved by R. Brandard. From W.H. Bartlett, Scenery and antiquities of Ireland, *vol.1 (London, 1842).*

Nov. 1st, and Dec. 11th. The parish church, a handsome cruciform edifice with a lofty embattled tower crowned with pinnacles, is situated in the principal street; and near it is a neat R.C. chapel, with a campanile turret. Here are handsome school-houses, with residences for the masters and mistresses; the schools are supported by Mrs. Ross and Mrs Balfour. There are some remains of Castle Roe and Greencastle, and of the old churches of Kilbroney and Killowen; and near the town is a monumental obelisk, erected to the memory of Gen. Ross, who fell in a battle near Baltimore, in America, while leading on the British troops to the victory which they obtained on the 12th of Sept., 1814; on the four sides of the pedestal are recorded the principal engagements in which that gallant officer bore a conspicuous part.

SAINTFIELD, or TONAGHNIEVE, a post-town and parish, in the barony of UPPER CASTLEREAGH, county of DOWN, and province of ULSTER, 9 miles (N.W.) from Downpatrick, and $78^{1}/_{2}$ (N. by E.) from Dublin, at the termination of the mail coach road branching from Dromore, by way of Ballinahinch; containing 7,154 inhabitants, of which number, 1,053 are in the town, which consists of one long street, intersected by a shorter one, comprising 213 houses, the greater number of which are built of stone and slated. At this place the first battle was fought in the north of Ireland during the disturbances of 1798, on June 9th, when the York Fencibles were beaten back and retreated to Cumber. The proprietor and lord of the manor, N. Price, Esq., improved the town in 1802, when he erected a large market-house and hotel, since which time Saintfield has been rapidly improving, and is now one of the most flourishing towns in the county. According to the Ordnance survey, the parish comprises $13,333^{3}/_{4}$ statute acres, 280 of which are roads and waste, and 118 bog; the land is good and nearly all arable, The weaving of fine linen cloth, cotton cords, and hosiery, gives employment to a great number of the working classes at their own houses. Here is a chief constabulary police station; a manor court is held every third Saturday in the court-house, at which debts to the amount of £10 are recoverable; petty sessions are also held in the court-house on alternate Tuesdays. Mr. Price gave premiums for the encouragement of a market and fairs, so that they rank amongst the best in the North of Ireland; the market is held every Monday, and the fairs take place on Jan. 26th, the second Thursday (O.S.) in Feb. and March, the third Thursday in April and May, June 26th, July 30th, Aug. 26th, the third Thursday in Sept., Oct. 26th, the third Thursday in Nov., and the Thursday after Christmas, The principal seats are Saintfield House, the elegant residence of N. Price, Esq., situated on elevated ground near the town, of which it

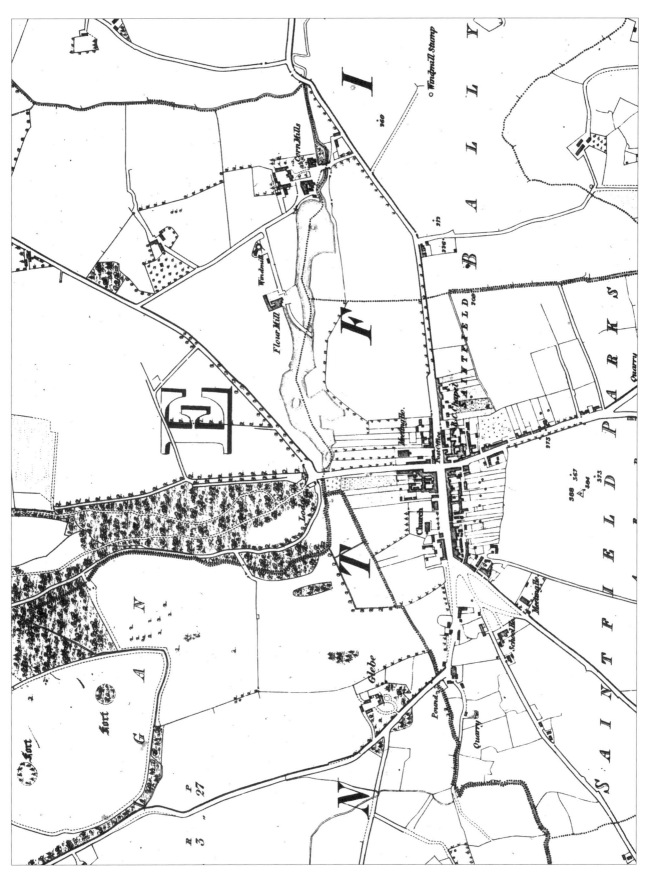

Saintfield. Part of the O.S. map of Co. Down, sheet 16, published 1835 (reproduced at 140%).

commands a fine view; Mill House, of J. McBurney, Esq.; and the glebe-house, of the Rev. H.H. Wolseley; and there are several excellent farm-houses.

The living is a vicarage, in the diocese of Down, and in the alternate patronage of the Earl of Carrick and Viscount Bangor: the rectory is impropriate in the proprietors of the soil, The tithes amount to £612.2.2, of which £175 is payable to Viscount Bangor, £147.1.4 to N. Price, Esq., £9.4.7^1/$_2$ to Lord Dufferin, and £280. 16. 2^1/$_2$ to the vicar. The glebe comprises 20^1/$_4$ acres, valued at £25.6.3 per ann; the glebe-house is a large and handsome building, erected in 1750 at the expense of the then incumbent. The church, in the town, is a large and elegant structure in the early English style, with a square tower, and is in good repair. In the R.C. divisions the parish is the head of a union or district, comprising this parish and that of Killinchy, in each of which is a chapel. The parochial school in the town was built by N. Price, Esq., and endowed by him with an acre of land; there is a female school built by subscription and partially supported by the vicar; and there are 9 other public schools, in all of which are about 560 children; 11 private schools, in which are also about 560 children; and 11 Sunday schools. Hutcheson, the author of a work on Moral Philosophy, was a native of this parish.

SAUL, a parish, in the barony of LECALE, county of DOWN, and province of ULSTER, 1^3/$_4$ mile (N.E.) from Downpatrick; containing 2,119 inhabitants. St. Patrick is said to have founded here an abbey for Canons Regular, and to have constituted his disciple, St. Dunnius, or Modun, abbot thereof: the patron day is May 29th. The founder died here March 17th, 493, in the 120th year of his age, and was interred with great solemnity at Downpatrick. Some years since, the ruins of this establishment were very extensive, but now only a fragment remains. The parish is situated on the south-western branch of Strangford Lough, and comprises, according to the Ordnance survey (including islands and a detached portion), 5,272^1/$_2$ statute acres, of which 2,119 are under tillage, the remainder in pasture. Walsh's-town Castle, the residence of R. Foster Anderson, Esq., is one of many built by De Courcy on the conquest of Ulster, and of twenty-seven around Strangford Lough, this is the only one now inhabited; the ancestors of the present possessor having occupied it ever since the reign of Chas. I. The living was formerly a perpetual cure and part of the deanery of Down, from which, by order of council in 1834, under the Church Temporalities' Act, it was separated, and constituted a distinct rectory, in the diocese of Down and patronage of the Crown: the tithes amount to £386.6. The glebe comprises 6a.0r.20p, valued at £30.12.6 per ann; the glebe-house was built by aid of a gift of £450, and a loan of £50, in 1816, from the late Board of First Fruits. By the order in council the three detached townlands, and the tithes of Whitehill, Ballynarry, and Ballynagarrick were disunited from this parish and annexed to the adjoining parish of Ballyculter, and the clerical duties of those townlands were annexed to the adjoining parish of Kilclief, to which were

also annexed the townland and tithes of Bally. woodan, separated from the parish of Saul. In lieu of such severance the townland and tithes of Ballystokes, severed from Ballee parish, and those of Raholfe and Ballintleave from Ballyculter parish, were annexed to Saul, the clerical duties of the two last-named townlands remaining annexed to Ballyculter. The church, erected about 1770, is a large plain building, without tower or spire, occupying part of the site of the abbey; the Ecclesiastical Commissioners have recently granted £375 for its repair. The R.C. parish is co-extensive with that of the Established Church. There are two schools, aided by annual donations from Dean Plunket and Lady Harriet Forde, in which about 240 children are educated: about 70 are taught in a private school, and there are three Sunday schools. Mrs. Conway bequeathed a rent-charge of £3.7.6 per ann. to the poor of this parish; and Judge Ward gave a rent-charge of 16s. per ann. for ever out of the Castle Ward estate. Near Walsh's-town Castle stood the church of St. Mary, by some supposed to have been parochial, but it seems most probable that it was for the use of the garrison; on levelling the churchyard a few years since, coins of the reigns of Hen. I. and II., Robert Bruce, and Rich. III., were discovered.

SCARVAGH, a village (formerly a market-town), in the parish of AGHADERG, barony of UPPER IVEAGH, county of DOWN, and province of ULSTER, 2 miles (N.W.) from Loughbrickland, on the road to Tanderagee; containing 220 inhabitants. During the civil war of 1641, this place was the scene of many sanguinary struggles: it finally fell into the hands of Gen. Monk, who erected a castle on the summit of a gentle eminence to command the pass, where a garrison was kept for several years. Here the army of Wm. III., under Duke Schomberg, first rendezvoused after landing in Ireland, the camp extending in two lines from Loughbrickland to Scarvagh pass and to Pointz pass; a venerable oak in Scarvagh demesne is still shewn as that under which the royal tent was pitched. In 1783 a battle was fought at Lisnagade fort, between the 'Hearts of Steel,' and the 'Break-of-day Boys,' when several of the former were killed. The village, containing about 50 well-built houses, was founded about 1746 by the late John Reilly, Esq., who obtained a charter for a market and fairs. It is situated on the canal between Newry and Lough Neagh, having a small dock and quayage for lighters; a considerable trade is carried on, particularly in coal and turf, supplying a populous neighbourhood and numerous bleach mills and manfactories with fuel. The market has long been discontinued; but fairs are still held on March 21st, June 19th, Sept. 5th and Nov. 14th, and are well attended. Scarvagh House is the seat of J. Lushington Reilly, Esq.; Union Lodge, of Wm. Fivey, Esq.; and Lisnagade House, of E.H. Trevor, Esq.: the two former are situated in extensive demesnes, on which is some very fine timber; the last is on a lofty eminence, close to the ancient fort from which it is named. Here is a beautiful lake called Loughshark; and not far distant was one more extensive, called Loughadian, which was drained in 1760 by

W. Fivey, Esq.; part of it is cultivated, and the remainder is bog. Here is a male and female school, erected and supported by Mr. Reilly, and also a neat and commodious meeting-house for Seceders. In the vicinity are numerous vestiges of antiquity, which appear to have had some connection with the passes through the bogs, lakes, and forests, which formerly abounded here, although this is now one of the most fertile and beautiful districts in the North of Ireland. In the demesne of Scarvagh is the 'Danes' Cast,' by the native inhabitants known by the name of Gleann na muck duibhe, or 'the glen of the black pig;' it is principally composed of earth, and resembles the Roman wall in Scotland, and Offa's dyke in North Wales; its course is nearly north and south: in some places it consists of a single foss and rampart, in others the rampart is divided by a deep foss, which gives the appearance of a double foss and rampart. It is supposed to extend from Lough Neagh to the sea, near Dundalk, but it is no where so well preserved and unbroken as in this neighbourhood: it traverses south-ward through the demesne of Union Lodge, where it is a single rampart and foss, the rampart being here faced with stone, and it so continues to the reclaimed ground of Loughadian; northward it extends towards the fort of Lisnagade, terminating at a stream that forms the boundary between the townlands of Scarvagh and Lisnagade. Lisnagade, or 'the fort of a hundred,' is one of the most extensive and best-preserved of its kind: it consists of treble ramparts and intrenchinents; the entrance is from the east, leading into an extensive circular enclosure, whence are obtained prospects of the entire country for many miles around, and a great number of forts or raths are seen, from which circumstance it is supposed this fort took its name, being the chief or centre of a hundred others: the fosses on every side are very deep, and it is remarkable that they are all paved at the bottom with rounded pebbles set in clay. In cleaning the fosses, in 1832, Mr. Trevor found a great many silver coins, a brass cauldron, spear-heads, and other relics of antiquity. Great numbers of arrow and spear-heads of flint, stone and brass celts, and other military weapons, have been found in almost every part of the 'Cast.' In 1807 the head and antlers of an enormous elk were found, which are carefully preserved at Scarvagh House: several others were found in the bog marl near Union Lodge; and in draining Loughadian, part of a tiara of gold, brazen swords, skeans, and spear-heads, were discovered, all of which are in the possession of W. Fivey, Esq., of Union Lodge. The greater portion of the ancient castle or tower yet exists at Pointz Pass; some fragments of that at Scarvagh are still seen above the village, and in the centre of Lisnagade fort are the remains of another of the same kind; the floor was discovered entire in 1832, constructed of baked tiles.

SEAFORDE, a village, in the parish of LOUGHIN ISLAND, barony of KINELEARTY, county of DOWN, and province of ULSTER, 1 mile (N.) from Clough, on the roads leading respectively from Downpatrick to Newry, and from Dundrum to Ballynahinch: the population is returned with the parish.

This village, which was anciently called Neaghen, is small but very handsomely built, consisting of one principal street, from the centre of which a smaller street branches off at right angles. At its northern extremity is a very handsome gateway of freestone, consisting of a centre and two side openings; and near it is a chaste Grecian lodge of freestone, forming an entrance into the extensive demesne of Seaforde, the handsome seat of Col. M. Forde; the mansion, which is situated in the centre of the parish, was destroyed by fire in 1816, and rebuilt in 1819 in a style of sumptuous elegance; the demesne, which is finely undulated, comprises 1,060 acres, richly planted and embellished with a large and picturesque lake. The manor of Seaforde extends over the whole of the parish, with the exception only of the townland of Clough; and a court is held every three weeks before the seneschal, in which debts to the amount of £2 are recoverable: petty sessions are also held on alternate Tuesdays, and fairs on March 7th, June 9th, Sept 4th, and Dec. 6th. The parish church, a handsome edifice, is situated in the village; and there is a place of worship for Presbyterians in connection with the Seceding Synod, of the second class. There are also six handsome almshouses, erected in 1828 by Col. Forde, who endowed them with £60 per ann. for six aged widows; and some schools, the particulars of which are stated in the article on Loughin-Island, which see.

SEAPATRICK, a parish, partly in the barony of LOWER IVEAGH, but chiefly in that of UPPER IVEAGH, county of DOWN, and province of ULSTER, on the river Bann, and on the mail coach road from Newry to Belfast; containing, with the post-town of Banbridge, 7,584 inhabitants, This parish comprises, according to the Ordnance survey, 7,582½ statute acres, of which (with detached portions) 3,141 are in Lower and 4,441½ in Upper Iveagh; the whole is rich land in a high state of cultivation. On its border is Lenaderg Cottage, the residence of T. Weir, Esq., built by his ancestor, in 1645, as an asylum for the officers of the royal army. Its connection with the flourishing town of Banbridge has rendered the parish highly important as a seat of the linen manufacture: here are numerous bleach-greens, linen inanufactories, yarn-mills, and depots, with the various other branches connected therewith, which for extent and importance are not excelled in any part of the kingdom; this is mainly attributable to the river Bann intersecting the parish. Upon part of the glebe, extensive manufactories, depots, and handsome houses have been built by F. W. Hayes, Esq. Among the most remarkable gentlemen's seats may be enumerated Millmount, the residence of R. Hayes, Esq.; Brookfield, of Brice Smyth, Esq.; Huntley Glen, of Hugh Dunbar, Esq.; Seapatrick House, of F.W. Hayes, Esq.; Ballyvalley, of the Rev. J. Davis; Ballievy House, of G. and T. Crawford, Esqs.; Edenderry, of W.A. Stewart, Esq.; Banview, of G. Little, Esq.; the residence of F. Welsh, Esq.; and the glebe-house, of the Rev. D. Dickenson.

It is a vicarage, in the diocese of Dromore, and in the patronage of the Bishop; the rectory forms part of the union of Aghaderg and of the corps of the deanery of Dromore. The tithes amount to £390.16.4, of which £119.11.9 is payable to the vicar, and £271.4.7 to the dean. The glebe-house is a commodious old building: the glebe comprises 111³/₄ statute acres, valued at £155.5 per annum. The church, a small building on the eastern shore of the Bann, was erected in 1698 upon the site of the ancient edifice, which had been destroyed in the war of 1641; being incapable of accommodating one-sixth of the population, a large church has been lately built near Banbridge, under the provisions of an order in council, obtained in 1834, at an estimated cost of £2,890, of which £1,500 was given by the Ecclesiastical Commissioners, £600 by the Marquess of Downshire (who also gave the site), and the remainder was raised by voluntary contributions. In the R.C. divisions the parish forms part of the union or district of Tullylish. Near Banbridge is a meeting-house for Presbyterians in connection with the Remonstrant Synod, of the first class; here is also a meeting-house in connection with the Synod of Ulster, of the third class, built in 1830; one in connection with the Seceding Synod, and a chapel each for the Wesleyan and Primitive Methodists. The parochial schools, with residences for the master and mistress, situated on the glebe, are endowed with an acre of land and supported by subscriptions Near Banbridge is a large male and female school-house, comprising a centre and wings, the former the residence of the master and mistress, and the latter the schools; it was built by subscription, to which the Marquess of Downshire contributed £90, and is endowed with an acre and a half of land and £50 per annum. There are also schools at Ballydown, Ballylough, and Banbridge. At Tullyconnaught is a large school-house, founded and endowed by Miss M. Mulligan, by will dated 1824, and built in 1829, at a cost of £150: the interest of the principal bequeathed having accumulated, it furnished a greater surplus than was expected, the interest of which, £15 per annum, is given to the master: it is in connection with the Board of National Education. There are also six private schools in the parish. On the Dromore road is a valuable chalybeate spring, similar in its properties to the waters of Aix-la-Chapelle, and efficacious in scurvy. Baron McClelland was born here, as was also his contemporary, Dr. Dickson, Bishop of Down and Connor.

SLANES, a parish, in the barony of ARDES, county of DOWN, and province of ULSTER, 4 miles (E.) from Portaferry; containing 589 inhabitants, This parish is situated on the eastern coast, and comprises, according to the Ordnance survey, 946¹/₂ statute acres, the whole of which is under cultivation, and produces excellent crops of corn, flax, and potatoes. Here is Slane's Point, between which and Carney Point is a cluster of rocks and shoals, one of which, called the South rock, is three miles (E.N.E.) from Carney Point, and on it there is a lighthouse, called the Kilwarlin Light, erected by the Corporation for the Improvement of the Port of Dublin: it is a revolving light, elevated 52 feet above the sea at high water, with 10 lamps of a bright colour, appearing once in a minute and a half: two bells are also kept tolling in foggy weather, by means of clock work, to warn mariners of their proximity to danger: the rocks and shoals extend a mile at least to the eastward of the lighthouse. Here is a coast-guard station. On the shore are the remains of a large castellated edifice, called Newcastle, which has given name to the district; from this is the communication with the lighthouse, and here are the residences of the keepers. It is a rectory, in the diocese of Down, forming part of the union of Ballyphilip, and of the corps of the chancellorship of Down; the tithes amount to £106.13.5¹/₂. There is no vestige of a church, but the burial-ground remains, where once stood an extensive edifice, traditionally said to have been a wealthy abbey: the Protestants attend divine service at Portaferry church. In the R.C. divisions the parish forms part of the union or district of Upper Ardee.

STRANGFORD, a small sea-port and post-town, in the parish of BALLYCULTER, county of DOWN, and province of ULSTER, 6 miles (N.E.) from Dowinpatrick, and 79³/₄ (N.N.E.) from Dublin; containing 583 inhabitants. In the year 1400, the constable of Dublin city, with divers others, fought a great sea battle at Strangford against the Scotch, in which many of the English were slain. It is situated on the western side of the channel which forms the entrance of the lough to which the town gives name; it is a very small place, having only 119 houses, among which are a chapel of ease to the parish church of Ballyculter, a R.C. chapel, and a Wesleyan Methodist meeting-house: here is also a small quay for the convenience of the fishing boats, and of the passengers crossing the strait to Portaferry. It is a constabulary police station: fairs are held on Aug. 12th and Nov. 8th. The trade is chiefly in coal and timber. A school, in which are about 200 children, is supported by the Hon. W. Fitzgerald De Roos and the Rev. Charles Wolseley. Near this place are the remains of two castles called Welsh's and Audeley's; the former has been converted into the handsome dwelling-house of R.F. Anderson, Esq.; the latter, still in ruins, is on a hill which commands a view of the lough as far as Newtown, and is supposed to have been erected by one of the Audeleys, who settled in this county under John De Courcy. The lough of Strangford was formerly called Lough Coyne: it extends from Killard Point to Newtown, a distance of about 17 miles, from north to south; in some parts it is five and in others three miles in breadth, and at its entrance not quite one. It contains a vast number of islands and rocks. Six of the islands are inhabited; namely, Castle island, in the parish of Saul, containing 118 acres of land under cultivation, and on which are the ruins of a castle; Rea island, in the parish of Tullynakill, containing 103 acres, occupied by a farmer; Wood island, also in the parish of Tullynakill, containing 16 acres, and on which are large beds of shells, from 50 to 60 feet above the level of the sea, that are converted into excellent lime by burning; Tagart island, in the parish of Killyleagh; Islandbawn, in the parish of Killinchy, containing 30 acres of land; and Maghea island,, in the parish of Tullynakill, containing 137 acres of land: it has a small quay, to which brigs can come up, and on it are the ruins of a castle, formerly the summer residence of the Knox family. Strangford Lough is a safe and deep harbour, admitting vessels of the largest draught, but, owing to the great rapidity of the tides and the rocks near its entrance, on which the sea breaks violently, it is not prudent for a strange vessel to attempt to enter. There are two passages to it, divided by a reef nearly in the centre of the channel, and half a mile long, called Rock Angus, corrupted into 'the Rock and Goose,' on which is a stone beacon, and at the south extremity a perch called the Garter, which is dry at half ebb; south-westward from this perch, at a cable's length, are the Pots rocks. The passage on the south side of Rock Angus has $2^1/_2$ fathoms of water, and is navigable only for small vessels. The tide runs in and out of the lough with such velocity as on some occasions to carry vessels against the wind. Strangford gives the title of Viscount to the family of Smythe.

TULLYLISH, a parish, in the barony of LOWER IVEAGH, county of DOWN, and province of ULSTER; containing, with the post-town of Gilford (which is separately described,) 10,501 inhabitants. The parish formerly was part of the property of the powerful family of Maginnis, Lords of Iveagh; it was forfeited in consequence of the part taken by the head of the family in 1641. At the commencement of the war which broke out in that year, a body of Protestant women who were sent by Sir Phelim O'Nial from Armagh to Claneboy, were forced to cross Lough Kernan, in this parish, during a severe frost, when the ice having given way when they were in the middle of it, the whole party perished. In 1685 the townland of Moyallen was granted to a colony of the Society of Friends in England, whose descendants still maintain the settlement and have contributed greatly to the prosperity of the surrounding district. In 1772, a band of the insurgent peasantry, who styled themselves 'Hearts of Oak,' attacked Gilford castle, the seat of Sir R. Johnstone, Bart., who with his family and friends defended the place so gallantly as to repulse the assailants; but the Rev. S. Morell, Presbyterian minister of the parish, who had joined in the defence, was killed during the engagement. The parish, which comprises 11,707 statute acres, according to the Ordnance survey, of which 6,920 are applotted under the tithe act, is situated in the west of the county, on the border of Armagh, from which county it is separated by the Newry canal; it is intersected by the roads from Loughbrickland to Lurgan, from Banbridge to Portadown, and from Gilford to Dromore. The river Bann passes through it in a winding course of five miles from east to west, passing by the town of Gilford, which is nearly in the centre of the parish: the only sheet of standing water is Lough Kernan, near Banford, which covers about $433^1/_4$ acres. The soil is fertile in a highly improved state, and cultivated according to the best systems; there is no wasteland and the bogs have been mostly reclaimed. There are some good quarries of building stone: numerous indications of coal have

led to several unsuccessful attempts to discover a productive vein: ironstone is found in quantities near Gilford: the scenery is highly picturesque, the whole of the surface being studded with numerous and well-planted seats and with many bleachgreens. The district of Moyallen is one of the richest and most beautiful in the county; its numerous elegant houses, lawns, plantations and greens, with the fine river Bann winding tranquilly among them, indicate a high degree of comfort and prosperity, owing chiefly to the linen manufacture, which was introduced into the parish in 1725, and has since continued to be the main source of its wealth. The bleaching of the cloth is the process peculiarly attended to: in the numerous bleach-greens which border the Bann in its progress through the parish upwards of 138,000 pieces of linen were finished for the market in 1834. A thread-manufactory, carried on at Miltown on an extensive scale, gives employment to 170 persons, a mill at Coose for spinning fine linen yarn employs 200: each is worked by a combination of steam and water power: another for linen yarn is now being erected at Gilford on an extensive scale. Large works for manufacturing the chemical ingredients required in the various processes of the fabrication of linen-cloth have been established at Moyallen and at Coose. At Banford there is a very large flour-mill. The vicinity of the canal, which skirts the parish on the west, and on which there is a wharf and stores about a mile from Gilford, contributes to the increase of this prosperity, by affording a vent for the manufactured articles throughout a large extent of inland country both to the north and south, and to the two great shipping ports of Belfast and Newry. The parish is in the manor of Gilford and was subject to the jurisdiction of the court held there with the exception of two townlands which belong to the Bishop of Dromore's manor of Bailonagalga; but it is now united to that of Rathfriland, and is within the jurisdiction of the court there. Petty sessions are held in Gilford and two fairs annually. The seats are very numerous; among them are Gilford castle, the residence of Sir W. Johnstone, Bart.; Tullyhish-House, of H. Hamilton, Esq.; Milltown, of John Smyth, Esq.; Banville, of Jas. Foote, Esq.; Hazelbank, of S. Law, Esq.; Springvale, of Thomas Upritchard, Esq.; Lawrencetown, of – Bowen, Esq.; Banford, of B. Haughton, Esq.; Mount Pheasant, of I. Stoney, Esq.; Tullylish House, of Mrs. Hamilton; the glebe, of the Rev. W.H. Wynne; Fannymount, of the Rev. John Johnstone; Stramore House, of R.J. Nicholson, Esq.; Stramore, of J. Christy, Esq.; Moyallon, of T.C. Wakefield, Esq.; Gilford Villa, of W. McCreight, Esq.; Mill Park, now unoccupied; Banvale, of J. Upritchard, Esq.; and Lennaderg, of the Rev. H.H. Madden, where also is a house built in 1645 for the accommodation of the officers of the royal army, who were stationed on the Bann water during the war of 1641; it is still a handsome cottage and the residence of Thos. Weir, Esq., by whose ancestor it was erected.

The living is a rectory and vicarage, in the diocese of Dromore; the rectory partly forms a portion of the union of

Aghaderg and the corps of the deanery of Dromore, the rectorial tithes of 15 townlands being payable to the dean; and is partly united with the vicarage, and in the patronage of the Bishop; the incumbent receiving the rectorial tithes of the four remaining townlands. The tithes amount to £496.2.10, of which £269.11.8 is payable to the dean and the remainder to the vicar. The glebe-house is situated about a mile from the church, on a glebe of 40 acres, valued at £60 per ann,: it was erected in 1789 by aid of a gift of £100 from the late Board of First Fruits; offices were added in 1803, at an expense of £120 British, and in 1808 £424 was further expended in additions. The church, which is situated at Banford, on the southern bank of the river, over which is an excellent stone bridge, was built in 1698, upon one of the outer defences of an ancient fort or field-work, raised to defend the pass of the river, on the site of the former edifice, which had been destroyed in 1641: a large circular aisle was added to it on the north side, in 1827, by aid of a loan of £800 from the late Board of First Fruits, and at the same time a square pinnacled tower: the church is now about to be again enlarged, to enable it to afford sufficient accommodations for the still increasing numbers of the congregation. In the R.C. divisions the parish is the head of a union or district, comprising this parish and those of Seapatrick (which includes the town of Banbridge), Magherally, and Donaghcloney, in which are two chapels, both of large dimensions; one near the bridge at Coose was greatly enlarged and improved in 1834; the other is on the townland of Clare. Near the village of Hall's Mills is a place of worship for Presbyterians in connection with the Synod of Ulster, of the first class: in it is a handsome monument to the memory of the Rev, Samuel Morell, who was buried here. At Moyallen is a meeting-house of the Society of Friends: there are also places of worship for Seceders and Methodists. A male and female parochial school at Knocknagan is supported by subscriptions; there are also male and female schools at Clare and at Park, a female school at Gilford, and schools at Bleary, Mullabrack, Moyallen, Coose, and Gilford, all in connection with different societies and the last three with the National Board of Education: in all these there are about 260 boys and 130 girls. There are also 12 private schools, in which are about 270 boys and 330 girls. The remains of several ancient forts are still to be traced: the largest is that at Banford, on which the church is built, of which, though a road now passes through it, and the ramparts are nearly levelled, the general outline can still be distinctly traced. At Tullyhoa are extensive ruins, supposed by some to be those of an abbey.

TULLYNAKILL, a parish, in the barony of CASTLEREAGH, county of DOWN, and province of ULSTER, 3 miles (S.S.E.) from Comber, on the western shore of Strangford Lough, and on the road from Downpatrick to Belfast; containing, with the village of Ardmillan, 1,386 inhabitants. It comprises, according to the Ordnance survey, 2,923^1/$_4$ statute acres, including several islands in the lake. The whole of the land is arable and of excellent quality, and it is under a highly improved system of cultivation, producing fine crops of grain, potatoes and turnips. Some large limestone quarries, in which fossil remains abound, are extensively worked: the stone, which resembles porphyry, is conveyed both by land and water to all parts of the surrounding country. A manorial court with extensive jurisdiction and peculiar privileges was formerly held here, but it has fallen into disuse for many years. The living is a vicarage, in the diocese of Down, and in the patronage of the Bishop, to whom the rectorial tithes of the whole of the parish, which is bishop's land, are payable, and have merged in the rental; the vicarial tithes amount to £110.10.1. The church, erected in 1825, at an expense of £830, a gift from the late Board of First Fruits, is a very neat edifice in the early English style. The ruins of the old church, built, or according to some accounts, rebuilt in 1636, are still visible. A private school affords instruction to 37 boys and 35 girls.

TYRELLA, a parish, in the barony of LECALE, county of DOWN, and province of ULSTER, 4 miles (S.S.E.) from Clough, and 6 (S.W.) from Downpatrick; containing 1,773 inhabitants. This parish is situated on the bay of Dundrum, by which it is bounded on the south; and comprises, according to the Ordnance survey, 1,999^1/$_4$ statute acres, the whole of which, with the exception of a few acres of sand hills along the shore, is land of good quality and in a state of profitable cultivation. The system of agriculture is improved, and the crops of wheat, barley, oats, flax, and potatoes are abundant, the lands being much enriched by the facility of obtaining sea sand and weed for manure. Tyrella House, the handsome residence of A.H. Montgomery, Esq., is beautifully situated in a richly planted demesne of 300 acres, commanding extensive views over the bay, with the noble range of the Mourne mountains in the background, and containing within its limits the site and cemetery of the ancient parish church. Off the coast is a rocky shoal extending one mile from the shore, at the extremity of which is a rock called the Cow and Calf, seldom covered by the sea. It is a rectory, in the diocese of Down, forming part of the union and corps of the deanery of Down: the tithes amount to £164.15.9. In the R.C. divisions it is the head of a union or district, comprising also the parish of Ballykinlar and part of Loughin island; there are chapels at Ballykinlar and Drumaroda. About 150 children are taught in a school under the New Board of Education; and there are two private schools, in which are about 70 children, and a Sunday school. In the demesne of Tyrella House, and near the site of the old church, a cave was discovered in 1832, artificially constructed of uncemented stones and covered with flagstones, above which the earth is thickly heaped; it is 43 yards in length, 2^1/$_2$ feet wide, and about 5 feet high, dividing into three chambers, 60, 45, and 24 feet in length respectively, the last extending its width to six feet.

WARINGSTOWN, a post-town, in the parish of DONAGHCLONEY, barony of LOWER IVEAGH, county of DOWN, and province of ULSTER, 2^3/$_4$ miles (S.W.) from

Lurgan, on the road to Gilford; containing upwards of 1,000 inhabitants. The ancient name of this place was Clanconnel, which was changed into that by which it is at present known by Wm. Waring, who settled here in 1667 on lands purchased by him from the dragoons of Cromwell's army, who had received a grant of forfeited lands in this quarter. The new proprietor immediately built a large and elegant mansion, which is still the family seat. In the war of 1688 he was driven out by the Irish army, who kept possession of the house as a military station till the arrival of Duke Schomberg, who remained here for two days on his march to the Boyne. Mr. Waring, who had escaped to the Isle of Man, was outlawed by the parliament of Jas. II. Samuel Waring, a descendant of the same spirited individual to whom the place owes its existence and its name, was the founder of its manufacturing prosperity in the reign of Queen Anne. Having acquired a knowledge of the processes for making diaper during his travels in Holland and Belgium, he introduced them into his own country, and the first piece of cloth of this description made in Ireland was the produce of his estate. He also, when abroad, procured drawings of wheels and reels in Holland, and with his own hand made the first of the wheels and reels now in general use, before which all the flax made in the country was spun by the rock and spindle. The linen manufacture thus introduced and patronised became the staple of the district and is now carried on to a very great extent in all its branches, there being scarcely a family in the town and neighbourhood which is not more or less employed in some department of it. Petty sessions are held in the town every Monday: it is a constabulary police station, and has a sub-post-office to Banbridge and Lurgan. The town was made the site of the parish church of Donaghcloney by an act of parliament in 1681, and divine service has been celebrated here since that period in the church in this town, which had been previously built by Mr. Waring at his own expense for the use of his family and tenantry. It is a large and handsome edifice in the Elizabethan style, to which a tower and spire were added in 1748: the interior is very elegantly fitted up, but is most remarkable for its roof of carved oak resting on 18 carved corbels of the same material: the pulpit, communion table, railings, and pews are all of oak: in 1832 the church, being found too small for the congregation, was enlarged by the addition of a northern transept, which is finished in its roof and all other parts to correspond with the original building, at which time the pulpit and communion table were richly ornamented with carvings and pierced work of wreaths, festoons, and other similar embellishments, executed by the hand of the Rev. Holt Waring, proprietor of the estate, and by him presented to the parish. The bell of the old parish church of Donaghcloney, after having lain for nearly a century in the river Lagan, was raised, and hung in the tower of Waringstown church: engraved on it in rude characters is the inscription 'I belong to Donaghcloney.' Waringstown House, the mansion of the proprietor, is in the immediate vicinity of the town, surrounded by a demesne richly planted with ancient and flourishing forest trees; the pleasure grounds, gardens, and shrubberies are extensive and kept in the best order. Demesne, the residence of James Browne, Esq., is also near the town. The surrounding land is very fertile and in a high state of cultivation, with numerous houses of the gentry and wealthy manufacturers interspersed. The Waringstown male and female school, in which are 147 pupils, with residences for the master and mistress, were built by subscription and are in connection with the London Hibernian Society. Henry McLeary, who greatly improved the machinery for diaper-weaving and invented a slay for expediting the process, for which he received a premium of £100 from the Linen Board, was a native of this place.

WARRENPOINT, a sea-port, post-town, and district parish, in the barony of UPPER IVEAGH, county of DOWN, and province of ULSTER, 5 miles (S.E. by S.) from Newry, and 55¼ (N.) from Dublin, on the road from Newry to Rostrevor; containing 2428 inhabitants. A castle was built near this place in 1212, by Hugh de Lacy, to protect the ferry across the channel where it narrows, and thence called Narrowwater castle: it was destroyed in the war of 1641, and was rebuilt by the Duke of Ormond in 1663. The site of the present town was originally a rabbit warren, whence it has received its name. In 1780 it consisted only of two houses, with a few huts for the occasional residence of the fishermen during the oyster season: it now comprises several respectable streets diverging from a square on the sea side, and containing 462 houses, many of them large and well built. This rapid increase has been principally owing to the extraordinary beauty of its situation, commanding very fine views of the bay of Carlingford, and to its convenience as a bathing-town, for which purpose it has been for several years a fashionable place of resort for visiters from all parts. Petty sessions are held on alternate Mondays; it is a constabulary police station, and has a dispensary. Fairs are held on the last Friday of every month. Its maritime situation has also rendered it a place of considerable commercial activity. Large vessels trading to Newry are obliged to lie here, where there is deep water, good anchorage, and perfect shelter, as the further passage up the channel is intricate and dangerous from the obstruction of rocks, one of which, called Grannaway rock, is particularly marked out by a perch erected on it. Plans are under consideration for improving this part of the navigation. The shipping trade has been still further accommodated by the erection of a quay at which vessels of large burden can load and discharge their cargoes. Two steamers sail weekly hence to Liverpool; one to Glasgow and one to Dublin; by which very large quantities of agricultural produce, cattle, poultry, eggs, provisions, and oysters are exported, and British and foreign produce received in return. In the town is a very large distillery, and near it a windmill constructed according to the most approved principles, to which a steam-engine is attached for working the machinery in calm weather; in addition to its

Warrenpoint. Part of the O.S. map of Co. Down, sheet 54, published 1835 (reproduced at 140%).

practical value, this building forms a striking feature in the landscape when viewed from some distance.

The parish comprises, according to the Ordnance survey, 1,178^1/$_2$ statute acres, all of which, with the exception of 68^1/$_4$ acres under water, are of good quality and well cultivated. Not far from the town is Narrow-water Castle, the residence of Roger Hall, Esq., a very fine edifice in the Elizabethan style, built of hewn granite raised from a quarry on the estate: near the town also is Drumaul Lodge, the residence of Jas. Robinson, Esq.; and the neighbouring shores are studded with seats, villas, and cottages, chiefly erected by the gentry of the surrounding counties as bathing-lodges during summer, all enjoying varied prospects of the lough and its surrounding mountains, which combine in a singular manner the picturesque with the sublime. The living is a perpetual cure, in the diocese of Dromore, and in the gift of the Chancellor of the diocese, as incumbent of Clonallon. The income of the curate amounts to £73.2, arising from an annual salary of £50 paid by the chancellor and £23.2 from Primate Boulter's augmentation fund. The church, situated in the town, and about a mile distant from the mother church, is a small building in the early English style: it was erected in 1825 by Roger Hall, Esq., at an expense of £830.15.4^1/$_2$. British, being a gift from the late Board of First Fruits. In the R.C. divisions the parish forms part of the union or district of Clonallon: a large and elegant chapel in the town is now in progress of erection. There are also places of worship for Presbyterians in connection with the Synod of Ulster and the Remonstrant Synod, the latter of the third class; also for Wesleynn and Primitive Methodists. A well-constructed school-house for boys and girls, with residences for the master and mistress attached to it, was built by R. Hall, Esq., and endowed by him with an annual income of £30; he also has built and supports a school at Narrowwater and an infants' school was built and is supported by Mrs. Hall. In these schools about 300 children are instructed. The extensive ruins of Nuns' island are near the ferry at Narrowwater; they are by some supposed to be the remains of a religious establishment, and by others the ruins of de Lacy's castle.

WITTER, or GRANGE-OUTER, a parish, in the barony of ARDES, county of DOWN, and province of ULSTER, 2 miles (S.E.) from Portaferry; containing 1,116 inhabitants, This parish is situated on the eastern coast, forming a peninsula round which is the entrance to Strangford Lough, and comprises, according to the Ordnance survey, 2,529^3/$_4$ statute acres, of which the greater portion is good land in an improved state of cultivation. On the north side of the entrance of Lough Strangford is Ballyquintin Point, in lat. 54° 19′ 30″ (N.), and lon. 5° 28′ 20″ (W.), from which the coast extends (N.E.) 4 miles to Carney Point, and within this distance of coast are two creeks, which afford occasional shelter to fishing craft. About half a mile to the east of Tara Hill, on which is a moat or earthen fort, is Tara bay, which is spacious and sheltered from all winds except the north-east, but it is dry at low water; and about half a mile farther is Quintin bay, affording good anchorage in four fathoms in offshore winds, and having a tolerably well-sheltered cove. At Tara there is a coast-guard station belonging to the Donaghadee district. It is a vicarage, in the diocese of Down, forming part of the union of Inch; the rectory is impropriate in John Echlin, Esq. In the R.C. divisions the parish forms part of the unions of Upper and Lower Ardes. At Ballygilgat is a R.C. chapel for the parishes of Slane, Ardkeen, and Ballytrustin, and the liberty of Castle-buoy, called the parish of Lower Ardes. On the shore of Quintin bay are the ruins of a very strong castle, built by De Courcy in 1184.

Warrenpoint. Drawn by Andrew Nicholl and engraved by F.C. Bruce. From The Dublin Penny Journal, *vol.3, 1834.*

Acknowledgements

Grateful acknowledgement is due to the following for the use of illustrations in their possession: the Linen Hall Library for the views on pages vi and 75; the map library of the school of geography at Q.U.B. for the O.S. maps; Dean John Dinnen for the view of the Hillsborough wedding scene.

For their valuable assistance thanks must be expressed to Mr John Killen, Mrs Norah Essie, Mr Roger Dixon, Mrs Margaret McNulty, Ms Maura Pringle, Mr Tony Merrick, Mrs Angelique Bell and Mr Patrick McWilliams.